THE ROGUE ARTIST's
SURVIVAL GUIDE
WRITTEN BY RAFI

THE ROGUE ARTIST SURVIVAL GUIDE

The Rogue Artist's Survival Guide
Copyright © 2019 by Rafi Perez

All rights reserved by Rafi And Klee Studios. This book or any portion thereof may not be reproduced or used in any manner whatsoever without the express written permission of the publisher.
First Printing: December 2019
ISBN: 978-1-7343949-0-0
Rafi And Klee Studios
Rafi And Klee
PO BOX 1882
Pensacola FL, 32502
www.rafiandklee.com

THANK YOU!

THIS BOOK IS DEDICATED TO MY BEAUTIFUL WIFE KLEE, MY AMAZING CHILDREN AND THE HUNDREDS OF PEOPLE OUT THERE WHO HELPED MAKE THIS BOOK HAPPEN. THANK YOU.

TABLE OF CONTENTS

Welcome To The club Rogue Artist

WHY I WROTE THIS BOOK 7
THE UGLY TRUTH ABOUT THIS BOOK 10
WHAT DOES IT MEAN TO GO ROGUE? 13
THE CREATIVE CALL OF THE WILD 15
THERE IS NO ROADMAP............................. 21
WHERE DO I EVEN START?......................... 29
SAY YES UNTIL YOU CAN SAY NO................ 41
5 THINGS TO REMEMBER AS A CREATIVE..... 43
YOU WERE BORN A CREATIVE GENIUS......... 47
WE ARE CHARACTERS IN A MOVIE............... 52
Dumb Labels For Artists................................. 57
NEAT LITTLE BOXES AND MYTHS................. 63
EXCUSES, EXCUSES, EXCUSES.................... 69
EMBRACE YOUR INNER WEIRD CREATIVE.... 75
IMAGINATION IS NOT AN EXCLUSIVE CLUB... 79
THE CREATIVE JOURNEY AND LUCK............. 89
LEVELING UP... 94
REDESIGN YOUR AVATAR........................... 101
FACING YOUR CREATIVE FEARS.................. 105
FAILURE IS A WORK IN PROGRESS.............. 106
MAKE ALL THE MISTAKES 111
LIONS AND TIGERS AND BEARS.................. 115
Worrying Makes You Dumb............................ 121

TABLE OF CONTENTS

HOW TO FACE UNCERTAINTY HEAD ON........ 125

YOU HAVE EVERYTHING YOU NEED INSIDE .. 129

CAPTAIN COMPARISON............................... 133

WRITE YOUR OWN SCRIPT 135

The Stickman... 139

LET THE CRITICS BE CRITICS 145

PROBLEM-SOLVING VS FINGER POINTING ... 157

NOT SO GOOD, THE BAD, AND THE UGLY... 159

How To Deal With Conflicts............................ 163

GETTING REJECTED..................................... 167

MAKE A PERFECT MESS............................... 170

Setting Up Your Art Studio............................. 172

DAILY HABITS OF A MADMAN 179

SOCIAL MEDIA... 203

BE A UNICORN 207

GET RID OF PESKY DISTRACTIONS 213

SELF SIGNIFICANCE AND SAYING NO 216

BEING AUTHENTIC IS YOUR BAG 223

WHAT ARE YOU CHASING 233

THE GATEKEEPERS 239

THE ART STOCK MARKET 242

LET'S TALK ABOUT MONEY....................... 249

X MARKS THE SPOT................................... 258

HOW TO GET NOTICED 261

I WROTE THIS BOOK FOR Me MYSELF AND I

* THIS BOOK IS ABOUT "THE ROGUE ARTIST" MINDSET. IT IS BASED ON THOUSANDS OF NOTES I HAVE COLLECTED DURING MY CAREER AS A FULL TIME ARTIST. IF YOU WANT TO BE... ANYTHING... ...IT STARTS IN YOUR HEAD.

WHY I WROTE THIS BOOK

Every day I get up and do something creative with my life and that's how I make a living. This daily ritual is a far cry from where I was just a little over a decade ago. Back then, the idea of becoming an artist and actually making a living from my art was just a pipe dream.

Most of my adult life I've had corporate jobs that were not very creative. The most creativity I would express in a month was drawing a stick figure next to the words "HELP" on the dry erase board at a *"bored"* meeting.

I longed to be an artist for most of my life, but had heard there was no money in it, so I settled for something stable. I was told that was the smart move. Many years later, I found out that job security was an elaborate myth. I was laid off, and the company I worked for went bankrupt. I got another job. Eventually I was laid off again, and that company closed soon after. I found myself at a crossroads, either dust off my resume and get another corporate job, or do my own creative thing.

It was a frightening decision, but I decided that enough was enough. It was time to pursue the ever elusive thing called *BEING AN ARTIST*. When I started my art career, I had a big fat bag of nothing. I had no money, no supplies, no support, and no idea how to get started. What I did have, was this crazy new notion that if I just bumbled forward and kept going, I would figure things out.

I bumbled, staggered, blundered, and floundered quite a bit. But I also kept going despite everyone telling me I was making a mistake. Friends and family thought I had lost my mind and made it a point to express their disapproval every chance they got.

After a few years of looking foolish, making mistakes, and facing every roadblock I could think of, I was living the creative dream. The same friends and family that called me stupid, now tell me they always knew I would succeed. People can be funny like that.

It dawned on me recently that I have been self-employed and supporting myself as an artist for about a decade. I still have no clue what I'm doing, but I've gained the confidence to figure it out as I go. I was told for most of my life that it would be impossible to be an artist for a living, yet I accomplished the impossible. I think we all can.

I'm writing this book because I think it needs to exist, just an honest approach to living a creative life, growing it, and sustaining it without all the pretentious rules that are floating around out there. You'll find no pompous mumbo jumbo in this book about real art vs other art. There is no art world jargon or any of the bullshit that people try to peddle to artists. This book is just a simple way of looking at something that shouldn't be so mysterious or confusing.

I guess I'm writing this book for me... a simple reminder that I was needlessly scared for the majority of my life to begin something that would help me grow in ways I couldn't have predicted. This is a book that focuses on the biggest obstacle we artists face... our own mind.

If you want to be an artist or anything creative for a living, you have to create your own conditions. Create stuff and put yourself out there for the world to see and then persist through all the craptastic insecurities you have. That's it. Anyone that tells you differently is trying to sell you something.

> PEOPLE LONG TO LEAVE THEIR MARK ON THE WORLD... BUT MOST WILL BE TOO AFRAID TO GO ALL THE WAY... THINKING OF: THE COSTS, FAILURES, REJECTIONS, FEARS, NEGATIVE SELF TALK, & HUMILIATIONS LEAD TO SELF SABOTAGE & NEVER TRULY TAKING THE FIRST STEP.

I use the word "artist" a lot when I'm talking to people about life, love, and the pursuit of happiness. That's because I think we are all artists, even if you have never picked up a paintbrush or accidentally sipped from a coffee cup full of paint water. If you are a human, then you are creative. Life is a giant blank canvas. Sure, some people may have already scribbled some shit on your canvas, but you can always paint over it and make it your own.

LIFE IS A GREAT BIG **CANVAS**

THAT IS ME PAINTING

THROW ALL THE PAINT ON IT YOU CAN

THE UGLY TRUTH ABOUT THIS BOOK

Let me start this off by saying I am thrilled that you have purchased this book and that we get to hang out for a little while.

I am also very excited about the information that is about to slam through your brain casing. I think this change of perspective is needed if art is going to flourish beyond the crappy established systems that have been in place for generations. I'm talking about the pretentious mainstream art world and all the bullshit that comes with it.

I am going to lay out some facts about this book before you proceed, just to make sure we are the right fit for each other. Number one, this is my first attempt at writing a book, so it may be lousy... Sorry, not sorry.

Second, I am not going to make any empty promises about whether or not this book is going to help you succeed in your creative career or get you to prominent places in life.

You're the one that's gotta do the work.

YOU Gotta Do THE WORK Play...

I haven't got a clue as far as where you are in life, how far you've come in your creative career, where you live, what opportunities you have around you, and what your comfort zones are. I don't know your specific situation or circumstances, so I can't make any promises about anything. It's all in your hands.

I'm also not going to blow smoke up your behind and pretend like everything is going to be easy either, because it's not. There is no secret formula. The information in this book is all stuff you probably already know. I'm going to repeat myself, I'm going to ramble, and I'm going to go on and on about my experience... I know, "Riveting Rafi, thanks for selling us on this book."

I'm not going to pretend like I have my shit together either, because I don't think any of us do. I am highly skeptical of any so called expert who says they've got all their ducks in a neat little row. If they talk about some proven method or say they have secret answers, they can kiss my sketchbook.

Listen, I have made tons of mistakes, run into roadblocks, been in hopeless situations, been super broke, made terrible decisions, and behaved like a noob. I have been wrong more times than I'm willing to admit, and have failed so much in my life that my face should be the logo for the words "*OH CRAP.*"

I can't promise you much, but I can promise you my honest opinion and experience in traversing this crazy thing called a creative career.

This book has my experience of jumping into the most talked down profession in history. I plan to demystify that whole starving artist myth and focus more on the rogue artist's point of view.

The Rogue Artist Mindset is what got me to where I am, where I am going, and remembering to enjoy the ride.

I call myself a rogue artist because I didn't follow the rules.

I created my own rules, broke them, created more, and broke those too. The biggest enemy of creativity is believing there is an actual guide or instruction manual. There are no rules, and your mind can be the biggest obstacle of this whole thing. Your mind is also what makes it possible for you to succeed.

Things in this book will challenge a lot of rules and beliefs about the art world, society, and the way we are supposed to behave. I'll give you my opinion, and you can make up your own mind from there.

Please remember that these are *my* opinions, observations, and thoughts from *my* perspective. If something doesn't fit or work for you, don't take my word for it.

THE ROGUE ARTIST SURVIVAL GUIDE

No one else has the right to tell you how to live your life, what to do, and where to go… including me. That my friends, is *The Rogue Artist's Way*.

WHAT DOES IT MEAN TO GO ROGUE?

If you look up *rogue* in the dictionary, you may be surprised to see that it is not the most flattering description. You may wonder why I used it instead of the word rebel... well, *the rebel artist* was taken and honestly kind of overused, so I went with ROGUE. Here's the definition:

rogue
/rōg/

noun
A dishonest or unprincipled man.
"You are a rogue and an embezzler."
synonyms: *scoundrel, villain, reprobate, rascal, good-for-nothing, wretch.*
An elephant or other large wild animals driven away or living apart from the herd and having savage or destructive tendencies.
"A rogue elephant."
Verb: To remove inferior or defective plants or seedlings from (a crop).

Just to be clear, this book does not contain spicy details on how to become an artistic scoundrel, villain, rascal, wretch, giant elephant, or defective plant remover. For the purposes of this book, we are going to ignore the information above. Because word meanings change all the time, we are only going to focus on what it can mean to be a rogue in this day and age.

When I say rogue, I mean *"A person or thing that behaves in an aberrant or unpredictable way."*

That's right, we are going to upturn the status quo of the art world by behaving in a way that does not comply with how things are supposed to be done. It's all about blazing your own trail and creating your own success without having to pander to the gatekeepers.

This book is for the creative rebel, the nonconformist, or *anyone* who wants to do their own thing... *The Rogue Artist.*

THE ROGUE ARTIST SURVIVAL GUIDE

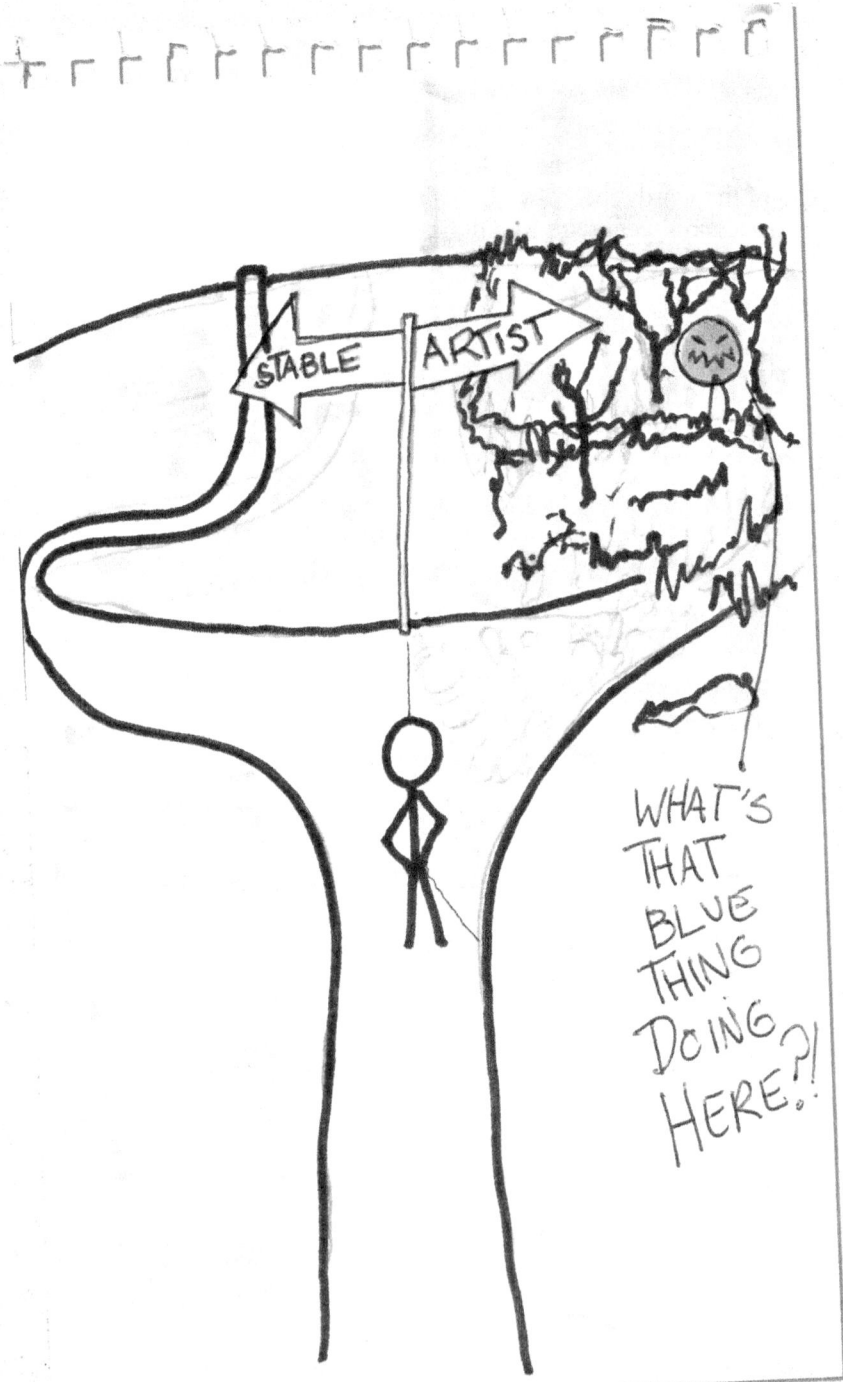

THE CREATIVE CALL OF THE WILD

We sometimes find ourselves at the crossroads between two paths in life. One path might call to your creative side. This path usually leads out into the wilderness, into the unknown, and seems nearly impossible to navigate from where you are standing.

Most times, the other path of life is what you've been living. It is paved with what is familiar and safe. That familiar road is our comfort zone, and although it's called a comfort zone, most times, it's not very comfortable at all.

The problem with pursuing your creative dreams and heading down the unknown path is that it's usually full of reasons to turn around. It may contain a bunch of tree branches, fog, and some creepy blue thing in the darkness.

Most times in life, you just see the two paths... It's usually just this or that, and you feel like you have no other options.

Here's the good news, as a rogue artist, you see many more possibilities. You are more willing to think out of the box, pull out a machete, and have at it.

The definition of **Blaze a trail** is: Find a new path or method; begin a new undertaking. By extension, to be the first to do something, often that which is later emulated or built upon by others. *Note: New trails or routes through forests were often marked by 'blazing' which involved making white marks called 'blazes' on tree trunks, usually by chipping off a piece of bark.*

As a *Rogue Artist*, you see more opportunities than the trails that were laid out before you. You see the whole landscape of possibility and not just the suggested paths. That being said, if there are portions of the well-worn path that suit your needs, you don't avoid them, but you make sure not to get comfortable with the "normal" of it all. When you have your machete, the whole landscape is accessible to travel on, and there is no limit to where you can go.

When I first started thinking about making my art career a reality, I only saw the paths that were laid out before me. My brain was full of false theories about what it meant to become an artist. I was plugged into that belief system and couldn't see beyond it.

My belief system was all the things I had assumed about what it meant to be a "real" artist. Things I had learned, things I had watched in movies, things I read on the internet, and conversations about art. The things I thought I knew about being an artist ended up being my biggest obstacles.

I spent most of my life talking about becoming a full-time artist and gathering information about the best way to go about it. I would take one step towards the creepy blue thing in the trees and freak out. I would get caught up in branches and it was the end of the story. I would quit, lick my wounds, and tell myself I just wasn't ready.

This went on for most of my life, my half-assed attempts would be thwarted by something, someone, or myself, and I would quit for long periods of time.

Eventually, I convinced myself that I was too old to start an art career and settled into my corporate job on the paved road outside of the creative wilderness.

For twelve years, I did not pick up a paintbrush or even allow myself to admit to anyone that I was an artist. In fact, the less I thought about it, the better I thought I would feel. I got used to filling my head with bottom lines, P&L spreadsheets, and employee discipline reports, but honestly, that nagging feeling of disappointment never left me.

The more I tried to bottle the desire to pursue art, the more miserable I became. The call of the creative wild had a hold of me, and my excuses were not cutting it anymore.

I know, right?! It sounds like a theatrical movie plot, full of heartbreak, misery, and betrayal of self.

Looking back at that experience from where I am now, I have to wonder... Why wasn't I just creating art? Why did I put the paintbrush down for 12 years? Who decides who is too old or too young? Why didn't I make time for painting? Why didn't I start my art career while I had the financial security of my job?

The two paths.

In my mind, it was either one path or the other; I was either free or in bondage to my corporate job. I didn't realize back then how much I limited my ability to step out of my comfort zone because I had narrowed my perspective to just those two options. My world was limited by what I *thought* I knew about the world.

I knew how to do corporate jobs. I knew how to do art. I just didn't know how to do both. I definitely didn't know how to go about actually pursuing art as my job. Turns out, I didn't know anything.

Sure, if you follow the standard that most artistic "experts" layout for you, becoming an artist goes a little something like this:

Go To Art School (The right art school, not one deemed crappy)
Spend Years In Obscurity (Starving artist myth)
Or
Get Discovered By A Dealer (Gatekeeper)
Get Picked By A Curator In A Large Group Show (Gatekeeper)
Come Out In Bi-Annuals (Gatekeepers)
Be Allowed To Solo Through The Galleries (Gatekeepers)
Be Traded In Auctions (Gatekeepers)

**You made it! You are an artist!
Until they decide you're not.**

What I had learned about what it took to become an artist was a path full of requirements, gatekeepers, and pretentious ideals. That well worn path is dominated by the go-betweens of the art world. This is what I thought needed to happen to become an artist. Again, turns out *I didn't know anything.* It wasn't until years later that I realized there was no singular path for artists and everything I thought I knew was just an elaborate story.

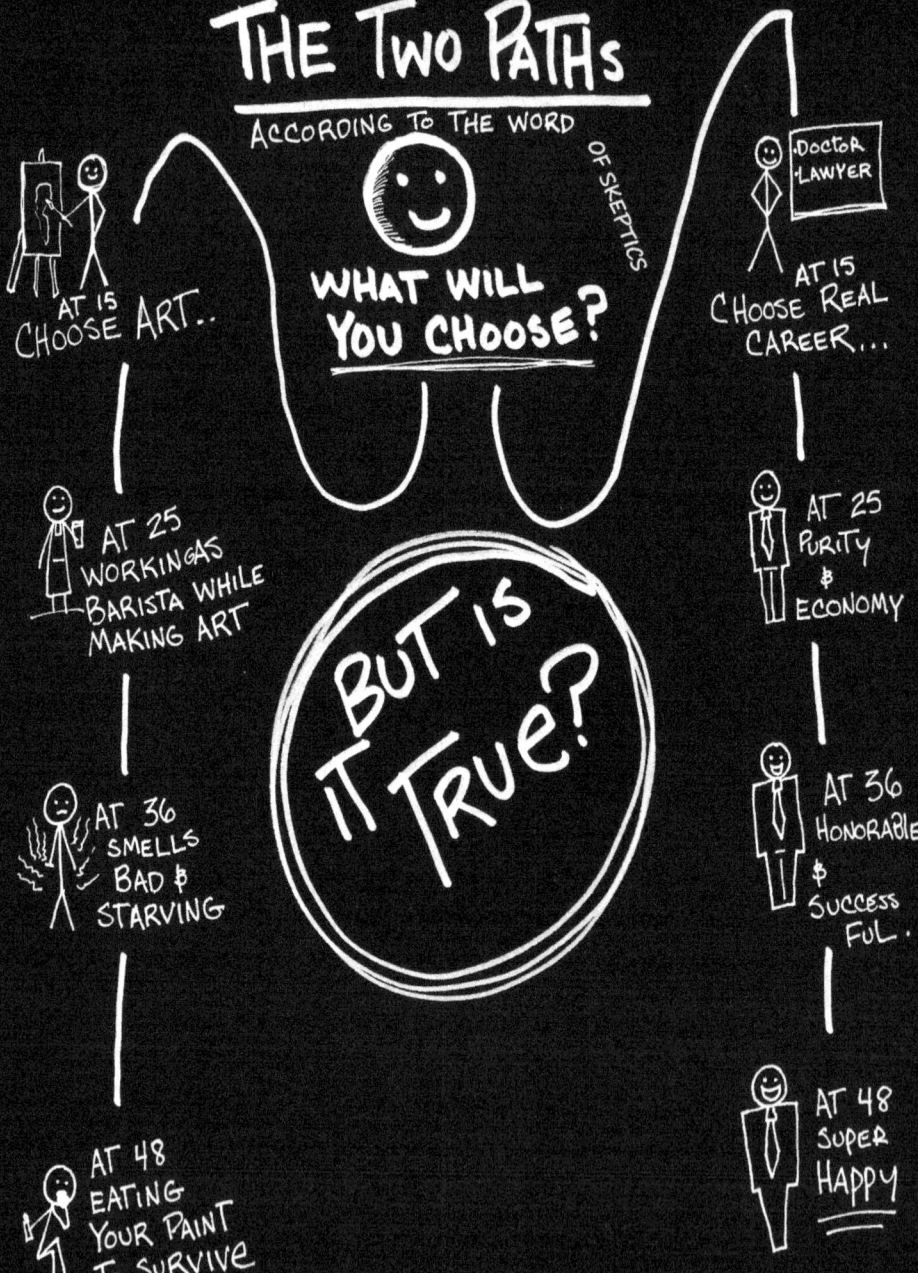

Create your own path. Let go of everything you think you know about what you want to pursue. I guarantee that you don't know as much as you think you know... and honestly, nothing is written in stone, especially when it comes to anything as creative and subjective as an art career.

Following the creative call of the wild is simple. *Create what you can with what you have and put it out there*. Keep creating, keep improving, keep growing, and keep putting it out there. Then be patient. Persist through the bullshit...

... and bring a machete.

It is very simple, but it is definitely not easy. You are going to stumble, get lost, have sleepless nights, and run into all kinds of roadblocks. You're going to wonder if you have what it takes and you're going to second guess your every move.

People may try to discourage you. They'll probably even tell you that you are stupid and not good enough. You are also going to give yourself every excuse in the world to quit. That's when you need to hack away at the doubt and insecurity that you may get caught up in.

There is no path you can follow, and there is no map. There is only opportunity. Instead of seeing a limited number of ways you can go, make the whole landscape yours. It will have its ups and downs and will seem utterly impossible at times, but you got this.

You'll have to trust yourself, even though you feel you are completely unqualified. You'll have to keep moving forward even though you have no idea what is around the next ridge. It's going to be tough, and you are probably going to want to give up every day.

The thing is, you will also grow in ways that you never thought possible. You will learn things as you go that will help you make each day better and better. You will become confident in your decisions, and will show yourself that you are a creative bad-ass. The path is not easy, but it is something that will change your world.

Believe it or not... You are a *Rogue Artist* even if you don't know it yet.

THE ROGUE ARTIST SURVIVAL GUIDE

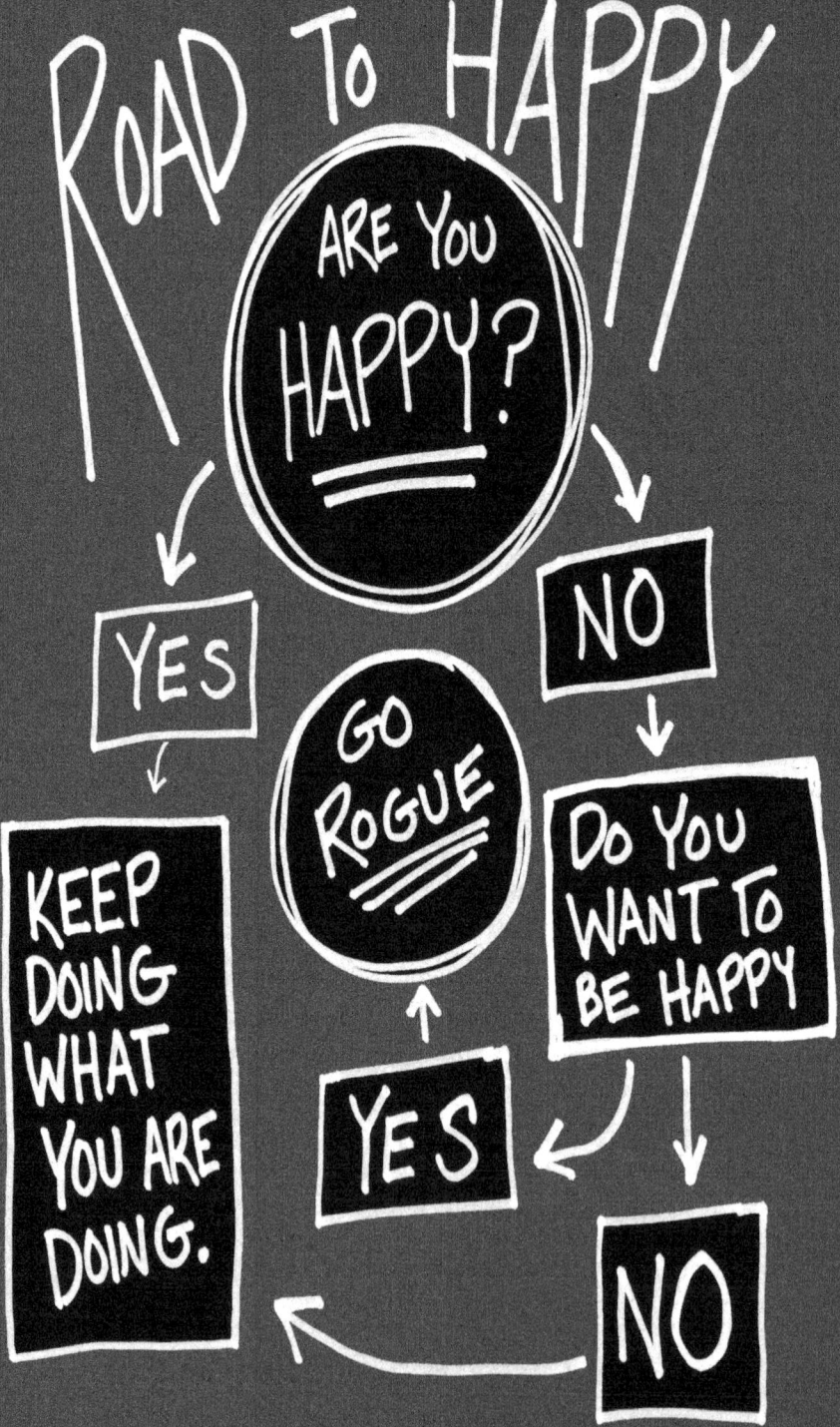

THERE IS NO ROADMAP

When it comes to pursuing a creative life, there really is no roadmap. There is no fairy dust, no proven method, no magic formula, no google map address, and no online course that can tell you where to go.

There is only you, your imagination, and your backbone. The possibilities are endless when you invoke your creative power as an artist to forge your own path and blaze the trail ahead of you.

This is a journey you will need to embark on with the awareness that you are uniquely *you*. Also, YOU are AWESOME.

Listen, I'm not saying you are unique and awesome to try to make you feel better about yourself. Unless you understand that you are the only person that can truly guide you through the plethora of bullshit advice that is floating around in the world, you will feel lost and discouraged.

Despite people promising $100,000 a year if you take their online courses and use their proven methods, when it comes down to it, as a creative, your lasting power lies within your unique perspective.

The fact that you see the world and interact with it unlike anyone else, is a superpower. That's your machete. But if you don't believe in your superpower, you might as well eat a bowl of frosted kryptonite flakes.

Most artist's courses and books offer cookie-cutter advice that is not going to set you apart. They will teach you how to market a product, but it may drain your creativity in the process. When you follow someone else's path, it may ultimately lead somewhere you didn't want to go.

Most courses are helpful, but I'll be honest, desperate artists make easy targets for all kinds of unscrupulous people out there with promises of fame, fortune, and artistic glory. Please be skeptical of anything that seems too good to be true.

Remember, proven methods are not a roadmap, they are simply suggestions and opinions selling themselves as a sure thing. There are no roadmaps in the art world, and as well-meaning as someone may try to be, the fact remains that they haven't walked in your shoes. They have no idea who you are or what you are capable of.

They haven't experienced your fears, discouragement, and disappointments. They can't predict your struggles because we all struggle with our own insecurities and our own set of roadblocks. Knowing more about marketing strategies is not going to help with this.

In business, you create a product, then you target your market, and you advertise to that targeted market. Funneling, mass marketing, creating a product that is in high demand in your area, networking, email marketing, social media marketing, and event partnerships are just a few of the things that these courses introduce to artists.

Usually, they make it seem like it is the ultimate answer to all of your dreams. These art marketing courses can work for some, but I know a lot of artists that were left disappointed by the results. In a desperate quest for answers, I think we can easily get lost in the idea that we are missing something, and that someone else has the full recipe.

As you traverse through the creative wilderness, it is essential to remember that being desperate in a survival situation will get you killed. We make horrible decisions when we are feeling desperate. A lot of artists feel desperate in their fledgling careers. They can feel desperate about money, exposure, validation, and a number of other things. This leads to some bad choices.

Desperation is a choice. It is not in your pocket and you can't find it outside of you. It is the way you choose to feel as a response to your circumstances. The opposite of desperation is to feel empowered. I find that my decisions are much more beneficial to my art career and my life when I put myself in an empowered mindset. We simply make shit choices when we are desperate.

I get it, it's not easy. We are continuously looking around for solutions to our problems, but I've seen artists lose their optimism when those "proven methods" don't work out for them. The truth is, you are going to face unique obstacles, and the moment you take that first step into a creative life, everything you fear will become a reality.

All of those excuses to *avoid* going for it, all those possible rejections, criticisms, judgments, struggles, and so on, will pop out of the woods and greet you. It's like a bad horror movie.

Try not to get ahead of yourself and react to the obstacles. Instead, choose how you will respond to threats effectively when they happen. Basically, you are creating your own unique roadmap to artistic badassery. Take that machete and hack down your fear step by step, inch by inch, and circumstance by circumstance.

Believe it or not, you are going to do everything you can to self-sabotage. You will scare yourself into quitting so you can run out of the woods with your hands flailing helplessly in the air. We all do that because it is safer to remain small and invisible than to be bold and put yourself out there.

It is scary. Rejections, criticisms, and failures are lurking behind the trees ready to jump out at any moment. Most times when we are afraid of something, we learn to avoid it. We avoid anything that is uncomfortable, including the things we don't want to *think* about.

Ignoring the fear or obstacle only prepares you to run into it with no plan and no way of responding. Facing it, even in your thoughts, lets you decide how to deal with it.

Most of your obstacles will come from your own noggin. Burying your fear is like trying to walk with your head on backwards, it is unnecessarily burdensome and looks stupid. Think about getting your head on right and make it easier for yourself. If you don't, you are going to have a rough go.

The following timeline contains our (my wife Klee and I) first year of experiences when we started our art careers. Remember, these are our experiences and not a roadmap or anything. The biggest obstacles were not the things we did, but how we felt about what we were doing.

THE ROGUE ARTIST SURVIVAL GUIDE

This is meant to show that everyone gets started somewhere. Things are not going to go according to plan, your journey through the woods is not a straight line, and some opportunities might be disguised as setbacks.

- Nov 2010 - Put sketches out at Flea Market and Klee jewelry.
- May 2011 - Start showing art and jewelry every Sat and Sun.
- Sept 2011 - Klee making some sales, I've been creating paintings.
- Nov 2011 - Dropped iPhone in a pool, no money to replace.
- Dec 2011 - 30 Videos In 30 Days on YouTube. (Failed)
- Jan 2012 - Computer virus, no more videos.
- Jan 2012 - Owe Flea Market over $500.
- Feb 2012 - Sold my first painting.
- Feb 2012 - Sold more art paid off half of what I owe.
- Feb 2012 - Sold more art paid off all of what I owe.
- Mar 2012 - Sold no art... owe booth rent (look for more options).
- Mar 2012 - Opened Etsy store online.
- Mar 2012 - Things still slow, look for more opportunities.
- Apr 2012 - Check out Gallery Night, talk to artists about shows.
- Apr 2012 - Move studio from a suitcase in the garage to the house.
- Apr 2012 - Show at Art Party.
- Apr 2012 - 150 likes on Facebook!
- May 2012 - Sold some pieces today at yard-n-art sale.
- May 2012 - Nothing happening online. Crickets...
- May 2012 - Little fat girl smacked my paintings, called them inappropriate and ugly.
- May 2012 - Copper jewelry by Rafi (failed).
- May 2012 - Got my first commission.
- May 2012 - Sold my first piece for over $400.
- May 2012 - Showed my art at Gallery Night good sales!
- June 2012 - Tornado touched down at the market. Make repairs.
- June 2012 - Auctioned off a piece for a wildlife sanctuary.
- June 2012 - Showed at Palafox Market - Better opportunity.
- June 2012 - Display art at Mezza De Luna, downtown.
- June 2012 - Look for other businesses to show art at.
- June 2012 - Festival - Art On The Bayfront - Good sales.
- July 2012 - Market and Flea Market every weekend.
- Aug 2012 - Put pieces up at local businesses.
- Aug 2012 - Ft. Walton Beach Art Walk every second Friday.
- Sept 2012 - Show 3 days at Seafood Fest - Good sales.
- Oct 2012 - Speak in front of the Art Association. Got paid.
- Oct 2012 - Came out in the local newspaper.
- Oct 2012 - River Art Walk Festival - Good sales.
- Nov 2012 - Invite to Crystal Studios. (eventually a big mistake).
- Nov 2012 - Featured In PO1OTIAL Magazine.
- Nov 2012 - Let Loose and Paint With Rafi Class...Fun.
- Nov 2012 - Local business show art.
- Nov 2012 - Local business show art.
- Dec 2012 - Open Studio Visits - Great sales.

THE ROGUE ARTIST SURVIVAL GUIDE

From these humble beginnings, as of 2019, I have been featured in a documentary, come out in newspapers, magazines, and have won awards for my art. I have been voted *Best Of The Coast*, and have sold thousands of paintings, sculptures, installations, and murals. We have a nice sized following on the internet and loyal collectors all over the world. It's been 9 years, and we are still just getting started.

As you can see, it wasn't a straight ride from point A to point B. You may have to meander about, climb up and down, go around obstacles, cross rivers, get your bearings, and be willing to change direction and backtrack a little. Most importantly, you need to look around and come up with your own opportunities. Stop waiting for permission.

No one could have laid out my plan for me. No one could have predicted or told me what to expect. Most times, when you hear success stories you think it was overnight, but success takes time.

There is no such thing as an overnight success. We all get started somewhere, and it is usually very humbling. It's more of a 10 to 20-year success. All you can really do is get started, try new things, and keep going despite the obstacles.

As you can see from our timeline, we tried new opportunities as they presented themselves. Facing the fear was the only way to really put ourselves out there, and that became the goal. Obviously, money is great, but selling wasn't the goal. Aiming your sites on money as the measure of success is short term thinking and dangerous. There are a lot of insecurities wrapped up in the green stuff and it can complicate things. Besides, the more people that know you exist, the more sales you will eventually make. So my measurement of success was meeting new people who didn't know about my art. You have to be prepared to play the long game and give yourself time to deal with your insecurities, fears, and doubts.

To get my stuff out there, I had to be willing to do some crappy shows. I had to get started somewhere, and a lot of the big-name shows were way out of my budget. I was also not going to wait around to be accepted by a gallery, I had to take my destiny into my own hands. This meant that I had a lot of failures and a lot of financial struggles.

I find it essential to put your focus on your success, but don't ignore the failures because they are just as crucial to the growth of your career, if not more. I love the fact that things were financially hard and not working out when I started. I had every excuse in the world to give up, but I kept going. I didn't quit. I know that can be difficult, and I don't recommend that kind of struggle for everyone, but it really put a fire under my ass to find solutions.

You know best how to deal with your own situations and circumstances. You have to make choices that work for you. The only thing I suggest is not giving up, no matter what. Keep going.

Change direction if you have to, but don't give up.

Putting yourself out there means heartache, roadblocks, trials, mistakes, failures, hard times, and rejections. That is what happens when you express who you are in public. It is also freeing.

The bad is the pain. The good is the freedom to become your own kind of human and live life on your terms.

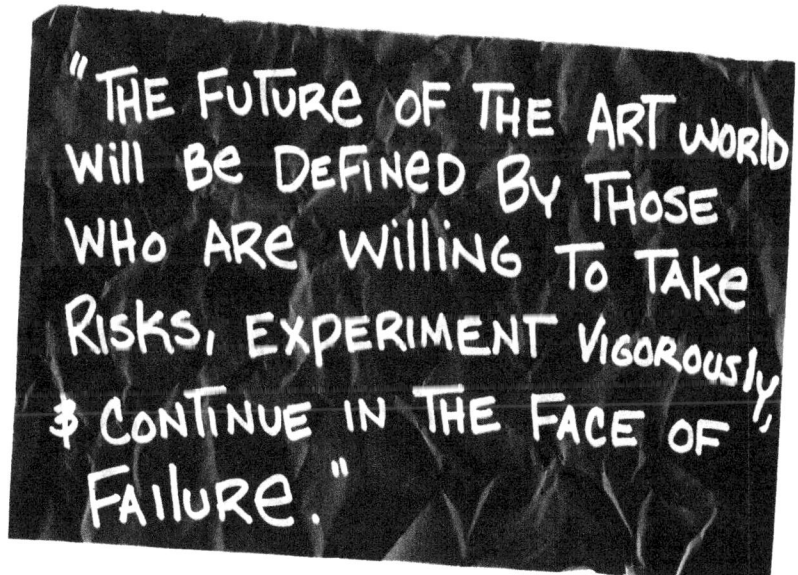

WHERE DO I EVEN TRY TO ST(aRT)?

> "If you're going to try, go all the way. Otherwise, don't even start. This could mean losing girlfriends, wives, relatives and maybe even your mind."
>
> — Charles Bukowski, Factotum

WHERE DO I EVEN START?

I can't even begin to tell you how many times I've asked myself that question throughout my life. As a kid, it seemed to me that becoming an artist, musician, actor, poet, writer, or all-around creative person was simple.

You create stuff, people see it, you keep going when times are tough, and BOOM you are an artist or whatever.

Somewhere along my journey into more wrinkles and the odd hair growing in unusual places, things became more complicated. I think as adults, we tend to overcomplicate the world. We actually convince ourselves that things are supposed to be difficult to be worthwhile. Let's face it, chasing your dreams *SHOULD* be hard and complex. If it wasn't hard, everyone and their mama would be doing it. Right?

So as a kid, was I just *naive? Stupid? Childish? Uninformed? Weird?*

Sure. I was probably all of those things.

Were the ramblings of that kid just total bullshit?

No... I don't think so.

I think, as children, we lack the added drama of complexities and anxieties that come with growing up. When you are a kid, the world is simple, less convoluted, and the message is clear... *just get started, stupid.*

> "Everything should be made as simple as possible, but not simpler."
> Albert Einstein

As adults, we tend to have extra concerns about the sides of things. We talk about the business side, the personal side, the emotional side, the financial side, the occasional side hustle, inside, outside, side to side, the electric s*(l)*ide... you get what I'm saying.

Most times when something is scary, we think about the worst-case scenario and run for the hills without ever actually getting started. Some of us scare ourselves out of thinking about *thinking* about getting started.

No wonder more people don't follow their dreams.

Things seem to become way more complicated in our skulls once we've convinced ourselves that we have to be responsible adults. Most times, we only realize we reached adulthood when someone points out that we are the same age our parents were when we were kids. That's usually when you realize your parents probably didn't have all the answers because you sure as hell don't.

Don't get me wrong, I love being an adult. I can go anywhere I want, I can eat breakfast at night, I can enjoy cupped lightning (coffee), and I don't have to worry about getting grounded by my parents. I don't have to do what people tell me, and I can be my own person.

This doesn't mean I'm an ass-hat or that I disregard other people and their feelings, but it does mean I'm not ruled by the status quo. I can continuously question the validity of everything I am told to believe and think for myself.

The problem is that as adults, we rarely question what we think we know. We just buy into our own crap.

The fact of the matter is that if you are alive on this planet, you probably have learned one way or another, how you *should* do things. How you *should* live your life. How you *should* go to school. How you *should* get a good job. How you *should* behave. How you *should* do this or that.

The **shoulds** of the art world are many, but few ever question how valid they are. For the most part we just buy into them, get confused, and flop around like a fish out of water.

There are a lot of **shoulds** that you probably have floating around in that serious adult brain-jar of yours. How many times have you questioned the things you think you know?

Chances are if you are thinking of becoming a creative, somewhere in your brain, something is telling you that you should be careful, you will starve, and should pursue something stable.

This is why, for most of my life, my attempt at starting a creative career was a series of bold efforts to stick my toe in the water. Half-hearted endeavors to make an art career a reality by making one bold move.

Like contacting a gallery, showing my art at one show, and then dropping off the face of the Earth because I didn't hear positive feedback.

One rejection, and it was over.

I tried... for the sake of being able to say that I tried, but I never really committed because why *should* I commit to something impossible?

You *should* create a body of work before you put your stuff out there.
You *should* rent studio space.
You *should* target your market.
You *should* get into a gallery first.
You *should* build your resume.
You *should* put yourself out there.
You *should* go to art school.
You *should* have your own style.
You *should* join an art association.
You *should* network.
You *should* have business cards.

No Way... Not me... I'm going all the way! UNSTOPPABLE.

So many rules. So many *shoulds*. I didn't know where to start. Everything just felt so daunting and confusing. The truth is, I would try something, get overwhelmed, and quit. Over and over, that was my pattern.

Everywhere I looked, there was a different opinion on how to get started or what it even meant to be an artist. There were a lot of contradictions, and nothing seemed clear. I was hoping someone would give me the easy answer, not realizing that there were no answers.

I don't think I understood what it meant to go all the way. I didn't comprehend what it was to really commit to something like this. I thought I was committing by trying it out, by doing the research, but really all I was doing was setting myself up to fail. I bought into all the **shoulds** because I wanted an easy answer, I wanted to be told what to do.

There are so many creative people out in the world that have unusual gifts that we will never see. Musicians, artists, writers, sculptors, designers, and all-around creatives who try to follow the rules and stifle their creativity for the sake of stability. They want to be given permission to share their creativity. They want to be told how to do it and what the rules are.

I have found that to become a creative and share our creations with the world, we may have to break some of these stupid rules.

We have to stop asking for permission.

If you are not satisfied with life, you can't continue doing the same things and expect it all to change on its own. At some point, you may have to challenge the status quo and forge a new path.

I had spent so much time and energy trying to find someone to tell me what to do, that I didn't *just do*. I half-heartedly tried things, but I never committed to my own ideas. I didn't know that I could make my own path. Blaze my own trail. *Go all the way*.

Going all the way means that you are willing to make a lifestyle change and embrace who you are, despite objections from the peanut gallery.

Going all the way means that you understand that things are going to be difficult, and you are willing to face them head-on.

Going all the way means that you will keep going even when the rest of the world doesn't believe in you, including family and friends.

Going all the way means that you understand that rejection is just part of the journey, and you will be rejected a lot.

Going all the way means that no matter what, you will always pick yourself up and keep moving forward. *(Thank you, Rocky Balboa).*

Going all the way means you understand that it is impossible to fail unless you give up. The moment you give up, it's over.

Going all the way means that when people say you should do something, that it is merely a suggestion. It is an opinion and not a fact.

Going all the way means that you will trust yourself to make the right decisions because even if you make mistakes, you learned something.

A great quote that motivates me to face the reality that comes with blazing my own creative trail and being a creative bad-ass is the following:

"If you're going to try, go all the way. Otherwise, don't even start. This could mean losing girlfriends, wives, relatives, and maybe even your mind. It could mean not eating for three or four days. It could mean freezing on a park bench. It could mean jail. It could mean derision. It could mean mockery--isolation." - Charles Bukowski, Factotum

I'm sure you were expecting unicorn farts and happy rainbows, but the truth is much grimmer than that. I'm not going to lie, it is immensely difficult to do your own thing and face the consequences of putting yourself out there.

Whether it's art, painting, crafting, pottery, music, writing, jewelry, building stuff, graphic design, inventing, or whatever else you love, the creating part is fun… the rest of it, not so much.

That being said, putting yourself out there is not a total nightmare. I have enjoyed every step of the way. It is NOT easy, but it has been a thrill to see what I am capable of accomplishing when I choose not to give up so willingly.

THE ROGUE ARTIST SURVIVAL GUIDE

It's the financial worries, staying motivated, not getting discouraged, facing rejection, or worse, not being noticed at all. Those things can turn your self-esteem and sense of empowerment into a poof of sad confetti.

So WHERE did I get started?

Where I was, with what I had, and with what was available to me.

Create stuff and put it out there for the world to see... and be persistent through the bullshit. I had it right as a kid:

"You create stuff, people see it, you keep going when times are tough, and **BOOM**, you are an artist or whatever." - *Little Rafi*

Keep creating stuff, keep practicing, keep learning, keep sharing it, keep finding new ways to share it, and keep putting yourself out there. There really is no secret sauce to creating a career from your creativity, it really is that simple.

You gotta start somewhere, so why not just get started now?

The standard advice for creatives is to start putting together a body of work. They'll say you should have a collection of work before you put yourself out there. In my experience, this is stupid advice.

First off, you are going to spend years in obscurity anyway while you are building up a following. Why would you wait to build an audience?

Instead of spending years building up a body of work, and then more years building a following, just combine the two... just a thought. Take a close look at the *shoulds* and question them, they may be holding you back.

When I got started creating an art career, I had no money, no job, I was in a new town, I had no friends, and didn't know the first thing about running an art business.

I had some old paint that had mostly dried and some old brushes. I had no canvas to paint on, so I went out and found discarded wood panels from the side of the road. *Glamorous* is not a word I would use to describe my humble beginnings.

I'm not going to lie, it was hard, and I spent a lot of time wondering if I could pull it off. The little bit of money I made went back into art supplies and paying off our mounting debt.

We didn't have galleries and art collectors knocking down our door. We were virtually invisible on social media; no one knew who we were or what we did. Despite what some people think, neither myself nor my wife are trust-fund babies, so there was no back up plan.

The traditional route of selling my art was not an option, but instead of giving up, I looked around for other opportunities. I made up my own rules and sent tradition packing.

At the time, Klee was creating jewelry, and I was working on paintings. I knew that if we could just get our work out in front of people, we would be able to get the ball rolling. The only option that seemed plausible and immediate in our area was the flea market.

Once we decided to commit (which was terrifying to me because I had never really shown my art like that), we put a plan together to set ourselves apart and stand out.

We wanted to have a unique impact on anyone who saw us at the flea market, something that would set us apart from the other stalls. The traditional system in the art world dictates that you have to figure out a way to fit in while simultaneously setting yourself apart. I decided that I would just stand out and not worry about fitting in.

I created all kinds of signs, wooden displays, shelves, and walls. They were vibrant, fun, and unique which is not the typical plain white look of the art gallery environment. We found Christmas lights and made our area look warm, inviting, and fun. Our space reflected our personalities.

With all that, it was still difficult. There were so many opportunities to quit, but we persisted through the bullshit and made the most of the experience. We allowed ourselves to have fun and be goofy.

Eventually, things started to come together as the months passed by slowly. The more we put ourselves out there in a playful way, the more opportunities began to present themselves.

Soon we started doing other events that people would tell us about. We did local markets, art walks, gallery nights, live paintings, and any other activities that looked interesting.

As our reputation grew, we started to get approached by more abundant and more significant opportunities.

Eventually, we were making enough money to be comfortable and started to focus a little more online. We started to very slowly grow our following by sharing who we were and what we were about.

Everything was new, everything was exciting, and everything was absolutely terrifying. We made a lot of mistakes and had a lot of challenges, but we were in it, full steam ahead. Quitting was not an option.

We were approached by a lot of people who had different opinions on what we **SHOULD** do. We listened, discarded the ones that didn't agree with us, and tried the ones that sounded like fun.

That's how we started. I didn't find it in any book. We just made it up as we went and kept going when things seemed impossible.

Almost a decade after those humble beginnings, we have thriving art careers. We have accomplished so much in such a short amount of time, simply because we were willing to go all the way… and the adventure is not over, I feel like we are just getting started.

Honestly, the most challenging part of this whole thing is what is going on inside your head.

- Rejection.
- Feeling discouraged by people not believing in you.
- Fear of lack of finances.
- Feeling a lack of talent.
- Feeling like a victim to gatekeepers.
- Feeling like you don't know enough.
- Feeling invisible.
- Feeling like you don't matter.
- Insecurity.
- Feeling unqualified.
- And a whole bunch of other great excuses to quit.

It's easy to become paralyzed by the feeling that you don't know enough. I was consumed at times by feelings of lack, or that I was a fraud. I still question whether I'm considered a real artist, which is ridiculous. Those feelings of insecurity will always be there to one extent or another, no matter how long you've been doing this. The trick is understanding that they are not real, it's just your insecurity saying some wack shit.

I think for people who quit, eventually those feelings can become so overwhelming that they force the dream aside. Opting to put it back in the 'someday' category that is always moving further away is a choice you may regret.

That's All Fine And Dandy, But Should I Quit My Job?

Throughout my life, my dream of becoming an artist had moved to the outskirts of Siberia and stopped emailing me until I entirely just gave up on it. For more years than I am comfortable admitting, I allowed myself no creative outlet. I denied a considerable part of myself to have stability. That kind of living is not sustainable, even with the fat paychecks, certificates of recognition printed at Kinko's, and adoring coworkers at my job.

That being said, I think it's important to note that I don't believe you need to quit your job to pursue a creative career. I think you can do both. I had no job when I started, but honestly, that was a life decision I made based on other factors.

At the end of the day, what really matters is allowing yourself to express who you are fully, every part of you. Whether you go into your creative life with a job or no job isn't the point.

We live in a world where it's the norm to pick one thing or another. You are asked to choose sides, and you are labeled either this or that. Why not just see the world how you want to see the world?

Why not make choices that are more divergent than picking between this or that? Why not choose option 3, or 4, or 42?

Why limit the possibilities that exist for you? Label yourself whatever you want... a fire breathing, corporate management rocking, salsa dancing artist if you choose. Don't limit yourself to just choosing one.

You can choose to see the world according to what other people believe is possible for you. You can follow the rules and do what they say you *should* do. You can conform, or you can choose your own possibilities because you decide to make it so.

"SHOULD" IS MERELY A SUGGESTION!

ARTIST RULES TO LIVE BY

1. **ENDLESSLY EXPLORE** WAYS TO EXPRESS YOURSELF.
2. **BLAZE YOUR OWN TRAIL.**
3. **THE JOURNEY IS THE REWARD.**
4. DEDICATE YOURSELF TO EXCELLENCE IN **EVERYTHING YOU CREATE.**
5. **FEED YOUR FANS.**
6. TRY TO BREAK THE RULES AS OFTEN AS POSSIBLE.
7. **JUST DO IT!**
8. **DON'T BE SHY.**
9. CREATE AS MUCH AS POSSIBLE.
10. **EVOLVE.**

Art By RAF

SAY YES UNTIL YOU CAN SAY NO

Recently I watched a documentary in which the artist's advice was that you should say *yes* until you can say no. Admittedly at first, I thought this was the stupidest advice I'd ever heard.

After thinking about it for a little while, I came to the conclusion that this is both some of the best and worst advice you will ever hear. Adopting this way of thinking can have a huge impact on your creative career... or even your life.

Saying *yes* to projects and challenges can help you push out of your comfort zones. I've had people ask me when would be a good time to start taking commissions, and my answer is ***now***. There is no time like the present to say yes.

What I mean by yes until you can say no, is that you will not push out of your comfort zone until you try new things. Your own insecurities may cause you to say no. You may say you don't think it is time, or that you are not ready.

How do you know unless you've actually tried it? A lot of my growth has come because I was willing to try new things despite feeling like I wasn't ready. *I had never done them before*, of course I wasn't going to feel prepared.

There are people out there who are unwilling to try new foods and will exclaim, "I don't like it!" without ever having tried it.

What's interesting about that is: It's been found that when you try new foods, it creates new neural pathways in your brain along with increased brain health. It also allows for more divergent thinking, which is excellent for us creatives.

If new foods can do that, imagine what new experiences will do.

SAY YES TO NEW ADVENTURES.

Personally, I have changed perspectives, introduced new tactics into my art, and my career has grown simply by trying new things. I feel more confident about my decisions because I experienced something new that I had previously determined was out of my wheelhouse. All because I said *yes* to a challenging project.

I also know what I am willing to say no to, based on *ACTUAL* experience. Say *yes* for the lesson until you can say *no*. Say no because it's something that you've tried, and you know that it's not your bag.

That being said, there are certain things that you know are off-limits.

At a solo show, I was approached by a man who liked my splatter technique. He wanted an image of a woman putting a gun to her head with brains splattering out the other side.

I knew immediately that was not something that I wanted to pour my energy into. On the other hand, I was approached by a charming woman who wanted me to create a beach scene.

For years I had stubbornly proclaimed that "I don't do beach scenes!" It was my bold protest to the local beach culture. When I first got started, local artists in the area told me that I would not succeed unless I did beach scenes. I refused on principle.

When she asked me, I remember being offended. I thought, "How dare she ask me for a beach scene! Doesn't she know?" I paused. I realized I had never even attempted to do any kind of beach scene that I *enjoyed*. How did I *actually* know I don't like doing that subject matter unless I tried it? I ended up saying *yes* with the stipulation that I was going to create something unique and more me than the typical beach painting.

I ended up creating something unique that I had never created before. The buyer loved it. I now have a unique series that I would never have discovered had I said no. Try new things and have fun. If something rubs you the wrong way, then say no, but don't allow yourself to walk away from an opportunity to grow simply because deep down, you're afraid to go there.

5 THINGS TO REMEMBER AS A CREATIVE

When I was in school, the question "Can I make a living with my art?" wasn't something that was up for debate... you couldn't.

If you were planning on being an artist, you either got discovered, or you starved. I would fantasize about a Bohemian lifestyle where I would paint massive cheeseburgers and sell them just so I could eat one.

Honestly, it's one of the biggest misconceptions of the art world: You've got celebrity artists who could smear feces on a photograph of a smurf and sell it for a million dollars. Then you have people who are dedicated, talented, yet tragically unappreciated until the day they die. It doesn't seem to make any sense and is too confusing to navigate, but it's actually quite simple.

There are so many interpretations of what the art world is, that honestly, I don't think anybody knows what they are talking about when they say "*Art Market*."

There are a lot of **shoulds** floating around based on an illusory portrayal of what the art market is. Honestly, it's a bunch of pompous opinion about what is or isn't art, or what qualifies as the *serious* art market. It's pretty ridiculous when you stop and take notice.

That's why I think you can create your own art market and not rely on anyone else's opinion of what an art market should be. When you do this, operate outside of the system, you can then navigate the whole system quite easily from your unique outside perspective.

A lot of wannabe artists feel that the art world is a make or break place. You either make it or you crash and burn into obscurity, but honestly, that's all bullshit. The advice I would tell myself when I was a young starry-eyed wannabe artist would be these five things.

- **Artists self-promote.** I showcase on social media, as well as my own website. I started at the flea market, have done festivals, shows, fairs, and anything else I could do to get myself and my art out in front of people. You have to let people know that you exist, and let them see your work.
- **Be confident about your work yet be flexible.** Create what you love, but always be willing to grow and expand your abilities. I love experimenting and pushing the boundaries of my own limitations. Keep growing, don't get stagnant in your creating.
- **Socialize with people and let them know who you are and what you do.** I like to practice an elevator pitch. That is something short and concise that describes who you are and what you do in a couple of sentences. Such as "Hi, I'm Rafi. I create emotionally charged fine art pieces meant to inspire, for people who are looking to fill their walls with empowering awesomeness."
- **Invest in your business and pay your taxes.** As an artist, you are the business owner of a brand that is *you*. Make sure you invest in yourself, education, books, buying new materials, equipment, and other fun things to create with. See yourself as an artist, especially when no one else will. Just don't be all serious and shit, because that's dumb, and remember to have fun. Also, check out local business licenses, pay your taxes, and hire a bookkeeper when you start making money with your art.
- **You cannot fail.** Basically, you are running a business and everything that comes with that. Your success is dependent upon how dedicated you are to making it work. Sure, things will go wrong, some weeks might be a little tight, or VERY TIGHT, but what are you doing about it?

If you're whining and blaming anything or anyone when things are not working out, then you probably won't last very long. If you are creating solutions and learning from mistakes, then you will succeed. It's impossible to fail unless you give up.

THE ROGUE ARTIST SURVIVAL GUIDE

CREATIVE GENIUS AT WORK

Yes, You!

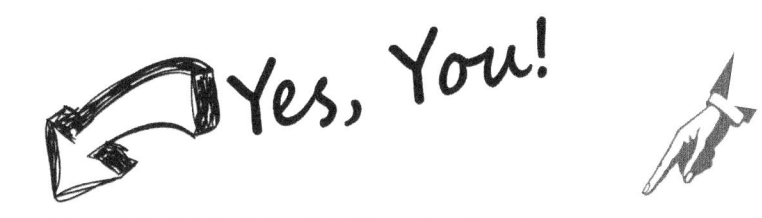

YOU WERE BORN A CREATIVE GENIUS... REALLY

When I was born, no one knew the creativity that was waiting to burst out from my drooling tiny lump of a body. The truth was set free the day I discovered markers and scribbled my art on every surface of my house.

Honestly, if you're not feeling creative, the simple fact is that you unlearned creativity by following rules and being well behaved. Sorry.

I'm not saying you have to be an anarchist, but my grade school teacher telling me that I couldn't draw on or in my folders and notebooks was an attempt at controlling my creative output. In my mind, I was like, "You don't own these, they're mine. I can do what I want with them."

If I hadn't had that mentality, I don't think I would have gotten so much practice drawing and sketching while my teacher droned on about stuff I wouldn't remember or use in life.

The educational system started as a great thing. To educate all classes, because back then, only rich kids were taught. Unfortunately, this was all occurring during the industrial revolution when the factory system was being developed.

Eventually, standardized testing and large factory-style schools became a thing. Some believe that the "factory model" of school was *"Designed to create docile subjects and factory workers."* This is because the model includes top-down management, outcomes designed to meet societal needs, age-based classrooms, efficiency, focus on producing results, and standardized progress reports.

Whether or not the school system is turning us into conforming factory robots is beyond the scope of this book. My focus is primarily on the role of creativity and innovation in a system that is standardized and uniform.

What happens to a creative when they are subject to a non-creative environment of rules and regiment?

In 1968, Dr. George Land tested the creativity of 1,600 children. He re-tested the same children at 10 years of age, and again at 15. The results were astounding to say the least.

Test results amongst 5-year-olds: 98 percent creative
Test results amongst 10-year-olds: 30 percent creative
Test results amongst 15-year-olds: 12 percent creative
The same test is given to 280,000 adults: 2 percent creative

"What we have concluded," Land wrote, "is that non-creative behavior is learned."

The enemy of creativity and innovation is conformity. Fitting in, being normal, and meeting expectations can really be a drag for your creative self. Luckily, compliance can be unlearned.

Some excellent ways to unlearn conformity are experimenting, exploring, questioning assumptions, using imagination, going outside comfort zones, starting a project you are not sure you can do, and doing vs. thinking about doing.

Life can be much broader once you discover one simple fact: Everything around you was created by people that were no smarter than you are. They just embraced the possibility of the impossible, which can only be done by seeing the world outside of any system that dictates conformity and social norms.

Everyone wants to be taken seriously and seen as necessary. Conformity ranks you in a system of checks and balances for the illusion of status and importance.

In my opinion, a real artist doesn't need anyone to take them seriously. When I get asked, "How did you become so creative?" I usually respond with, "I ate a lot of paste as a kid."

So how *do* we reignite our creativity if it was trained out of us?

Separate The Halves. Convergent And Divergent Brain Goo.

Convergent thinking is usually associated with problem-solving. It is the calculated, analytical side involving the bringing together of different ideas to determine a single best solution to a problem.

Convergent Thinking Traits:
- Analytic
- Finding probability theory
- Critical
- Objective
- A single right answer
- Verbal
- Linear
- Focuses on detail

Divergent thinking is usually associated with creativity and innovation. This is the brainstorming about the unusual, non-traditional, forward-thinking, and the whole concept related to out-of-the-box ideas.

Divergent Thinking Traits:
- Lateral, Associates the whole
- Finding possibilities
- Free of criticism
- Subjective
- Many right answers

When people talk about creativity, they are often referencing divergent thinking. However, you also need convergent thinking for the magic to happen. That's where most ideas become a reality.

Take that out of the box grand-scale idea and set a plan in motion by applying realistic goals. Break it into chunks that are achievable within the scope of your current circumstances. Start with the stuff you can take action on now, instead of waiting until you have what you think you need.

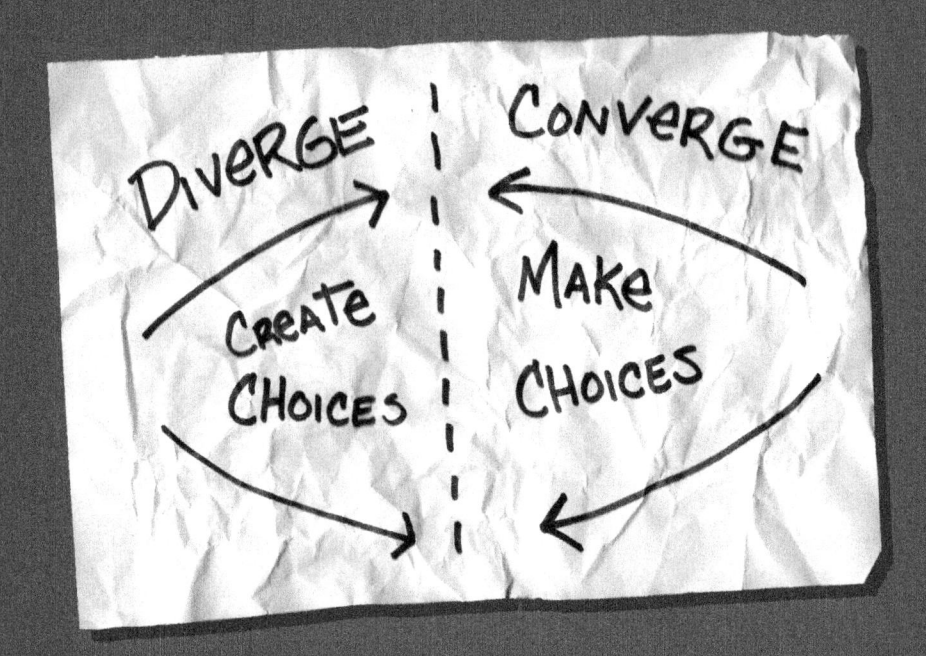

THE ROGUE ARTIST SURVIVAL GUIDE

DIVERGE → ← CONVERGE

Create Choices | Make Choices

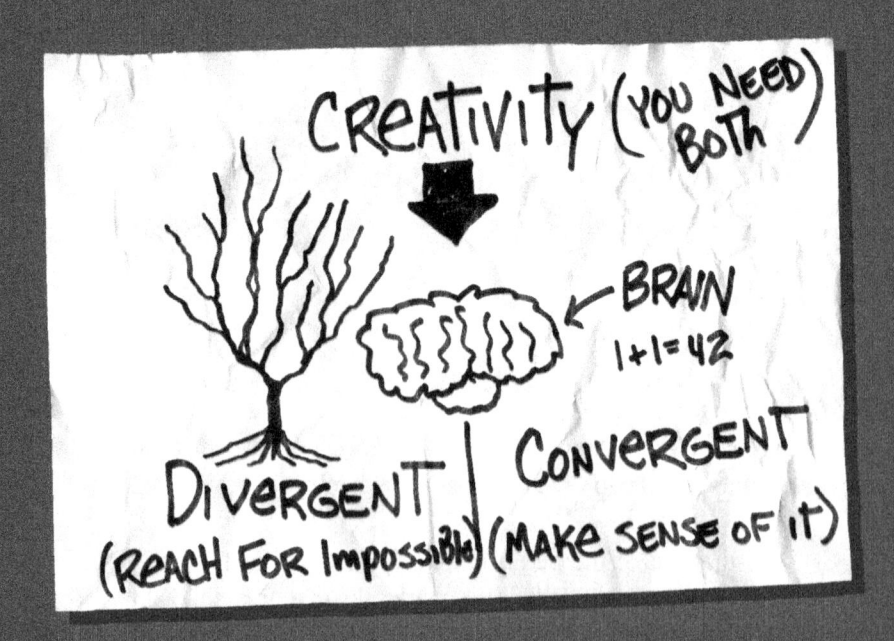

CREATIVITY (YOU NEED BOTH)

DIVERGENT (REACH FOR IMPOSSIBLE) | CONVERGENT (MAKE SENSE OF IT)

BRAIN
1+1=42

The research found that most people use both parts of their thinking at the same time. Unfortunately, this is "no bueno." What was discovered is during the education process, we are taught to use both opposite sides of our brain in the most unproductive way possible.

When divergent and convergent thinking is simultaneously combined, it results in the decline of creative and innovative thinking.

In other words, we get the "creative genius" dumbed out of us.

To retrain yourself to be a creative genius, think like a child. Allow yourself to open up to the limitless possibilities and imagine unrestricted ways of seeing the idea.

For example, if you had never seen a plastic water bottle before and didn't know what it was "***supposed***" to be used for, your "knowledge" wouldn't get in the way of coming up with a multitude of uses.

Such as:
- A container. (not as divergent)
- A prism and reflector of light. (slightly divergent)
- A flotation device. (slightly divergent)
- Cording. (divergent)
- As a bug trap. (divergent)
- As a paint pen. (divergent)
- As a supply organizer. (slightly divergent)
- As a spray paint container. (divergent)
- As a sprinkler head. (divergent)
- As a dog toy. (slightly divergent)
- As a planter. (slightly divergent)
- As a hummingbird feeder. (slightly divergent)
- As a piggy bank. (slightly divergent)
- As art flowers. (divergent)

THE ROGUE ARTIST SURVIVAL GUIDE

The further away from the routine use of a plastic water bottle, which is a container for water, the more different and innovative the idea. People that think out-of-the-box like this, disassociate from the labels of things. They look at the world differently and tend to see more opportunities.

For the creative geniuses, convergent thinking then steps in and gives you the step by step on how to make it happen. You may have to cut the water bottle in a certain way, add glue, or other materials in order to make your innovative idea come to life.

Step 1 (Divergent Thinking) Come up with fresh, unusual, unique, extremely different, or completely new ideas; be weird, courageous, daring, adventurous – take risks, or experiment with new things to stand apart. Reach for the stars. Look at random items and come up with as many different uses for them as you can.

Step 2 (Convergent Thinking) Come up with the best solution to make it happen now. Concentrate on finding out the best method. This is where deadlines, goals, and task lists happen. Break it down into doable.

People have the tendency to value one side of our thinking over the other, but when you train your mind to use both sides of the gray matter in your head, separately but equally, something creatively spectacular happens.

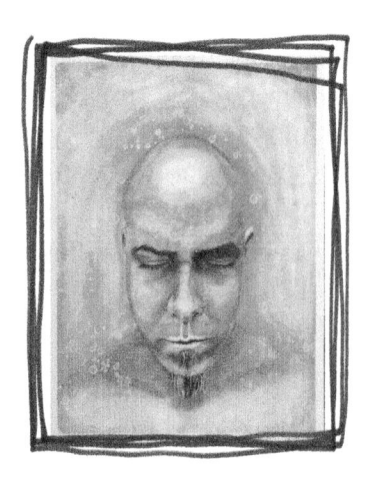

WE ARE CHARACTERS IN A MOVIE

If you've watched the movie "The Matrix," you probably remember the scene where the title character Neo was given a choice to take the red pill or the blue pill.

"You take the blue pill, and the story ends. You wake up in your bed and believe whatever you want to believe," Morpheus says. *"You take the red pill, and you stay in Wonderland, and I show you how deep the rabbit hole goes."*

A lot of the stuff we believe about the art world is a myth. In fact, I would venture to say that most of the things we think about art etiquette and being an artist are fabricated bullshit. That fabrication is the blue pill and the red pill is you questioning it.

Putting yourself out there with your creativity is like plunging full speed down the rabbit hole. It's terrifying, but the opposite is playing it safe, and no one who plays it safe ever really disconnects from the machine.

Just in case you are one of the five people in the world who has not watched The Matrix, I'll explain the reference. In the movie, we find out that the world is actually a computer simulation. People think they are experiencing actual life, yet they are just a bunch of batteries plugged into a supercomputer network. The network creates the illusion of the world they are living in. According to the story, we are all asleep and living within the illusion. Eventually, people unplug from it, find out the truth, and kung-fu fight for freedom. It's pretty epic.

As much as I'd love to say that living a creative life involves exciting kung-fu battles and stopping bullets with your mind, it's really not that thrilling.

THE ROGUE ARTIST SURVIVAL GUIDE

To-Do List

- ☑ Create Art
- ☑ Watch Paint Dry
- ☑ Create More Art
- ☑ Stare at Blank Canvas
- ☑ Keep Creating
- ☐ Drink Water
- ☐ ~~Take a Shower~~ Create More Art

Sometimes the most excitement I get is sitting in front of a canvas, wondering how long it's been since I last showered.

Despite my hygiene, there are several notions of what an artist's life looks like. There are a lot of ideas based on labels, misconceptions, history, stories, thoughts, and perceptions. The problem with these illusions is that, as creative humans, we really cannot be labeled so simply.

Labels make things easy for some folks. Give it a name, generalize, make it easy to swallow, there is a need to label just about everything.

That's why there are such ridiculous labels as "real artist" and "fake artist." This distinction is an illusion I've heard artists use to make themselves feel better in all the confusion.

If you create art, then you are an artist, plain and simple. Who gives a flying fart about why tweedle-dee is justifying himself as an artist, by saying tweedle-dum is not? It doesn't make it true. It's just his dumb opinion. For the most part, any view that puts someone down is based on some deep-seated insecurity.

Now, said long enough, over the years, by more and more people, any obscure opinion starts to look like a fact. That is the Matrix that we live in. It's still not true, but we are less likely to challenge it because more and more people are repeating it.

When you stop and question a word like "artist", which means: A person who practices any of the various creative arts, such as a sculptor, novelist, poet, musician, or filmmaker, the answer is pretty broad. Especially when you add: A person skilled at a particular task or occupation.

Who really has the authority to say what is a *REAL ARTIST* or not?

No one.

THE ROGUE ARTIST SURVIVAL GUIDE

Think about it, someone who has no interest in creating a painting would not create a bunch of paintings, suffer through rejection, and just for the heck of it call themselves an artist unless they had it in them.

I had a roommate who admitted to me that he could not understand how musicians worked. When he looked at an instrument, all he saw was wires, wood, and brass. He had no interest in creating music and found the whole process confusing. He is, however, an artist when it comes to computer programming.

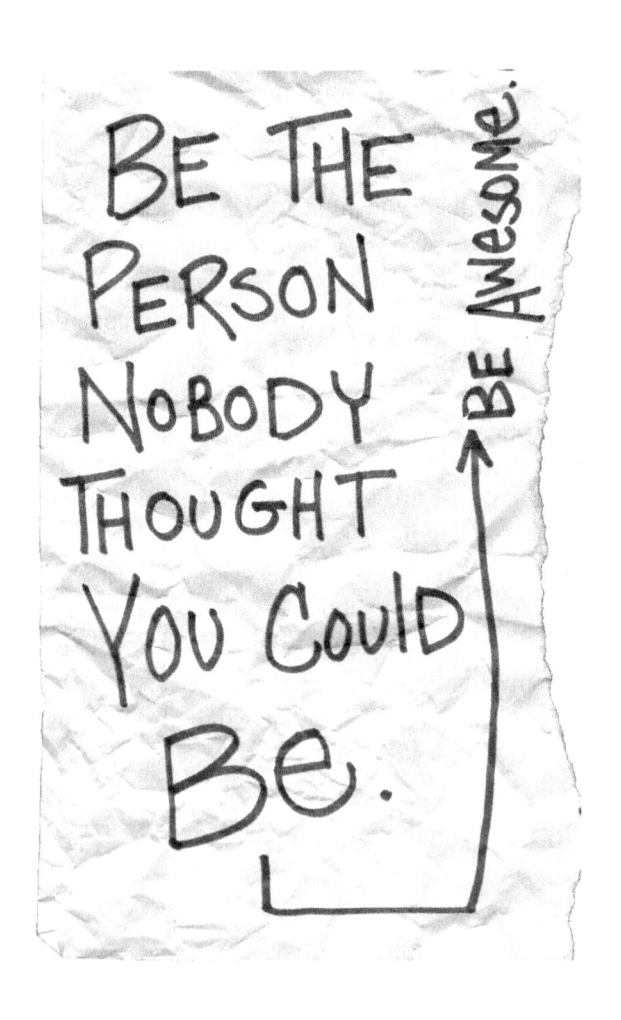

BE THE PERSON NOBODY THOUGHT YOU COULD BE.

BE AWESOME.

Everyone has a different take on what it means to be an artist, and honestly, that's their business. If you want to call yourself an artist, then call yourself an artist. It's like calling yourself human... who can honestly say you are not?

Experts, And Other Dumb Labels For Artists

People call themselves an expert in something because they memorized all the labels, know the history, and have all the stories down.

That may make them an expert on the history of a subject, but everything is in a constant state of change. If everything is evolving and changing and they are stuck on quoting how it was back in the day, then they are not keeping up.

Even the rules of language and grammar change over the generations based on new cultural norms. Someone who speaks medieval English would be called a moron by today's standards. We would also sound like morons if we got dropped into the 1800's with our modern speak.

The point is that most of what we know about living a creative life, or the art world, or anything really, is based on stupid ideas that became popular at one point or another throughout history.

Some of the labels that people have for artists are quite specific and laughable. Yet, this is the way that a lot of folks interpret what they think when they see an artist. Some of us even have these labels for ourselves or others. See if you relate to any of these.

The Eccentric Artist: A quirky, eccentric genius who poops rainbows into everything they create. All of their creations are applauded as groundbreaking or completely useless... but intriguing.

The Sad Cynical Artist: This one is trendy in Hollywood movies. Sad and cynical wretches who all but bleed pain into their art. They are usually addicted to some type of destructive substance. These artists are generally starving and misunderstood.

THE ROGUE ARTIST SURVIVAL GUIDE

The Starving Artist: (submitted by Artist David Macauley) The artist who believes that to be a "true" artist, you have to be dirt poor. If you are making money, or God forbid: making a living, you are a sell-out, commercialist, pandering to the "Man."

The Political Artist: Fights the system. The activist who stands up for something by creating shocking ways to put down the other thing that they are standing against. They are usually quite reclusive and outspoken at the same time.

The Hipster Artist: The professional freelancer that walks around with coffee in one hand and a portfolio in the other… they are usually wearing hipster glasses, skinny jeans, and are generally found in a cafe working on a computer.

The Hippie Artist: Similar to the Political Artist, but all about love and peace. Most people try to label me as this kind of artist because I talk about empowerment. They also assume I wear Birkenstocks and smell like patchouli… which I don't.

Fundamentalist Artist: (submitted by Artist Norella Bouchard) This artist is someone who has created a world in their mind where their type or execution of art is the only way. They are very one-sided. An example would be a painter who ONLY uses oils, and who believes if you do not use only oils, then you are not "an artist".

The Wannabe Sexy Artist: These are the artists that usually have huge followings on social media. They present pictures of themselves painting with their shirt open, rocking side boob, or just plain naked. There is usually some sort of sexy fantasy that gets evoked involving six-pack abs covered in paint, passionate lovemaking as art supplies get thrown about… which all of us artists know, is not going to happen. That shit is expensive, and you don't want to get it in certain areas.

The Amateur Artist: This is the artist no one seems to want to be. This artist knows nothing but enthusiastically pursues their passion. Secretly we walk around feeling a sense of impostor syndrome and are terrified to be revealed as an amateur. I personally love being labeled as an amateur. When I first got started in my career as an artist, there was a freedom that came with not knowing anything. I took risks, experimented, tested the waters, and tried everything under the sun.

> A world turned into a stereotype, a society converted into a regiment, a life translated into a routine, make it difficult for either art or artists to survive. Crush individuality in society and you crush art as well. Nourish the conditions of a free life and you nourish the arts, too.
>
> — *Franklin D. Roosevelt* —

THE ROGUE ARTIST SURVIVAL GUIDE

I felt like this for a long time. In fact, I worked in a basement and everyone had theories about my mental state.

The Isolated Introverted Artist: (submitted by Artist Jo Pearson) You always see their work (it's dark and foreboding), but no one ever sees them. Are they making it all while housed in an institution of some sort (prison or a mental health facility)? A basement? Or perhaps it's all just an illusion made up to sell the work, no one knows for sure, but there are lots of theories.

Psychotic Artist: (submitted by Artist Kelley Dominguez) The one who is mentally disturbed and paints with his teeth while wearing a straight jacket only finding inspiration from the glimpse of a tree in his holding cell window?... maybe cuts off an ear.

The Arrogant Artist: (submitted by Artist Christopher Doll) This is an artist who has had some success, and thinks his or her shit doesn't stink. They demean those beneath their skills and mock anyone who doesn't "get" their art. Aloof, but addicted to social admiration, The Arrogant Artist will always turn the conversation back to them.

The Professional Artist: Boring. Pfft. An artist who does it for a living blah blah blah.

Obviously, you may feel you relate to one of these or none. Just keep in mind that these are stereotypes; none of these labels really have much to do with what kind of artist you are, or whether you are an artist at all.

These are just labels and stereotypes that have developed over the years to try to peg the elusive thing we call creative. Some people believe these are models of behavior that you should personify if you want to be taken seriously as an artist, which I think is hilarious.

As you can see, my favorite label is to be an amateur. Not because of the name, but because of what the label implies. To get started, share your work as an amateur.

To keep going, keep learning like an amateur, keep growing like an amateur, keep experimenting like an amateur. I started my career by sharing what I love and allowing like-minded people to find me. I have successfully kept growing my career because I understand that I will always be a student, I will always be an amateur at the next step in my journey.

I've played the role of many of the artist stereotypes in my own life, and it was always an attempt to be something that I wasn't. I would do this so other people would see me as an artist. Even being a professional artist was a label that I wore like a badge.

Believe it or not, seeing myself as a professional artist at one point made things much too serious for me. It actually limited my creativity to my reputation and what I was known for. Things became much more bogged down by what I *thought* I knew. I stopped having fun.

When you consider yourself a professional, it is way too easy to start taking yourself too seriously. I began to make choices based on protecting my reputation and maintaining my status as a professional. As embarrassing as it is to admit, I became more concerned with how people saw me and was less willing to take risks.

Listen, you don't have to be anything other than yourself to be called an artist. Let people have their stereotypes, labels, judgments, critiques, and disputes about what is art and what isn't. Meanwhile, you keep creating and being Awesome.

THE ROGUE ARTIST SURVIVAL GUIDE

DO YOU FIT IN?

WHY WOULD YOU WANT TO?

NEAT LITTLE BOXES AND MYTHS

Regardless of how open-minded we are when we are young, we end up using labels to differentiate ourselves from one another, sometimes using stereotypes as a basis of comparison. This persists through adulthood, even though most of the time the label has no actual basis in fact.

How we might see ourselves and what we think we are capable of may have more to do with a label than actual truth.

These ideas are handed down the generations, from parents, grandparents, and other influences. Because we learn them as kids, we rarely question their validity. We hear these off-hand comments and come to conclusions we believe to be factual without question.

"Oh yeah...she's crazy. It's OK, she's an artist." This makes it seem like all artists are crazy. Maybe she was deranged, perhaps not, but it is highly unlikely the association applies to *ALL* artists.

"Cousin Gerald said his life would have been easier had he gone to school for business and not art." Maybe. But how would he know? What if he went to school for business and wished he had just become an artist? Does he mean using his business degree for his art career? What if the grass is always greener on the other side for Gerald?

Despite those questions, this statement can easily become fact about how being an artist is a dumb idea.

We put people into these neat little boxes with a label that offers one adjective. We usually don't question it all, yet we know in reality people are way more annoyingly complicated than that.

I wear a red bandanna, I have a beard, and I drive a jeep. Some people will immediately jump to the conclusion that I'm a jeep guy that goes off-roading or some shit like that. Without the vehicle in that combination of traits, some may assume I'm about to sail the seven seas and yell "YAAARG!" at random times as I hoist up sails and stuff.

THE ROGUE ARTIST SURVIVAL GUIDE

ARTIST

I AM ME → Rogue Artist Creative

NOT A ~~HIPPIE~~ ~~PIRATE~~

Pick WHAT EVER YOU WANT TO CALL YOURSELF

I was once at a pretty high-end art show, and a woman walked into our space and started asking Klee questions about one of my paintings. I had gone to fetch us some Piña Coladas and casually walked up with our drinks. As I approached, I could tell Klee was uncomfortable.

I caught them in mid-conversation. Klee quickly handed her off to me, grabbed her drink, and walked away. This should have been a red flag, but I engaged with the woman anyhow.

I proceeded to explain how that piece of art symbolizes my transition from working in the corporate world to being an artist. A passionate symbol of when the blinders came off for me to become…

"A pirate," she said.

I paused.

"Yes, a pirate." then I walked away.

People are going to think of all kinds of things about you. Some of the things they think are going to be absolutely ridiculous. People are going to have their perception about you no matter how you present yourself. Neat little labels and elegant little boxes. There are all kinds of ideas about what an artist is and isn't supposed to be.

Whether it is crazy, eccentric, lazy, good for nothing, creative, reclusive, or a pirate, it is merely their perspective. A police officer once told me, "It must be nice to not have a real job." That off-handed comment had more to do with how he felt about his life than mine. Don't take it personally, and understand that you don't easily fit in any box.

For some people, being an artist means you have to be weird. I've had people ask me, "What if I'm too normal to be an artist?"

First off, there is *no such thing* as normal; we are all weird and have our individual quirks. Most artists indeed tend to wear these quirks on their sleeves. Society already thinks they are crazy… so why not? But we are ALL weird, artist or not.

As *Rogue Artists*, we get to challenge the illusions, labels, perspectives, and status quos of the world. We question the things people believe to be true. We examine the things we believe to be true, mainly because some of those beliefs might be holding us back.

For example:

If you become an artist, you will starve.

As far as I know, there have never been any artists who have actually starved to death because they were an artist. Sure, things are going to be tough, and you are going to have crappy days. Honestly, sometimes it's going to feel like the end of the world is looming.

That being said, you are not going to starve anymore than any other person starting a business... so maybe a little at first.

Deciding to become an artist is the same thing as being an entrepreneur. As an artist you are launching and running a creative business. Of course, being an entrepreneur doesn't have the stigma of being an artist and all the neat little labels that come with the title.

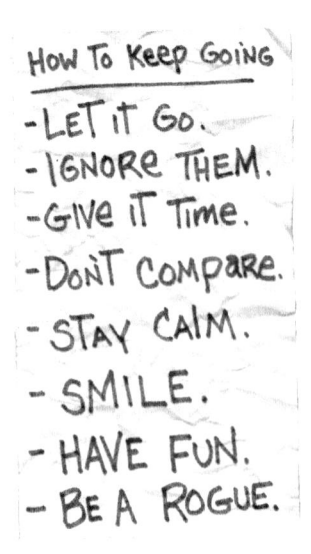

How To Keep Going
- LET IT GO.
- IGNORE THEM.
- GIVE IT TIME.
- DON'T COMPARE.
- STAY CALM.
- SMILE.
- HAVE FUN.
- BE A ROGUE.

For generations, it was thought that to be an artist you had to *get discovered*. That is simply not true; to become an artist you have to create your opportunities and push forward, the same as an entrepreneur.

Unfortunately when it comes to being an artist, we are bombarded with sweeping generalizations and myths. These are based on whatever label or stereotype a person may have in their head. The following tales are part of the neat little boxes that can be discouraging and confusing to artists.

- *Don't become a sellout. You will starve if you are not a sellout.*
- *There is no money in art. Paintings sell for millions.*
- *You should do something stable with your life.*
- *You have to be a good salesperson. Artists are not good at sales.*
- *You have to be naturally talented to get noticed.*
- *You're too old/young to become an artist.*
- *The art market is small and exclusive.*
- *You have to get into a gallery.*
- *(Whatever art you are creating) is dying.*
- *The stuff you like to create just doesn't sell.*
- *You are too ordinary, artists are emotionally unstable.*
- *Being an artist means you don't have a real job.*
- *Artists are not good at business.*
- *Artists are not good at marketing.*
- *Your prices are too high/low.*
- *Unless you went to art school, you are not a real artist.*
- *You should only show your art when it is perfect.*
- *You are not an artist unless you know how to draw.*
- *Without a bio, resume, and statement, you're not an artist.*
- *You are too ugly to be successful as an artist.*
- *You are too fat, aren't you supposed to be starving?*
- *No one will ever take you seriously in the art world.*

Any one of these myths can discourage you from going all the way in pursuing an art career, and chances are you believe more than one of these gems. These have been tossed back and forth so many times over the generations that they almost sound legit when people say them.

Listen, there is a lot of great advice out there, but there are also a lot of people making bunk-ass comments and giving crappy advice as well. Some of this bad advice has been going on forever... and ever.

Just because some successful expert, full-time artist, teacher, critic, gallery owner, art agent, or your mom (who knows everything) says you should do something, doesn't make it accurate. Take it with a grain of salt.

Don't ever allow an authority figure to make choices for you in your life. There are all kinds of predictions that people will make based on what they think they know. They take that prediction and place you into that box, but they have no idea what you are capable of.

Keep in mind that most of these boxes are based on things that have been repeated over and over in life. Portrayals in movies, ideas our parents had, books, teachers, the news, comments in passing, or one bad experience is all it takes to program the myth into our wee little brains.

We live in a neat little box of opinions based on life experiences that are not our own. Although we can indeed learn and grow from those experiences, ultimately we need to decide what is correct and best for our own lives.

We are the only expert that matters when it comes to our own lives and the kind of careers we want. Think for yourself and don't buy into the hand me down "script" that is so common to accept. You can challenge these myths by starting with examining your own neat little boxes.

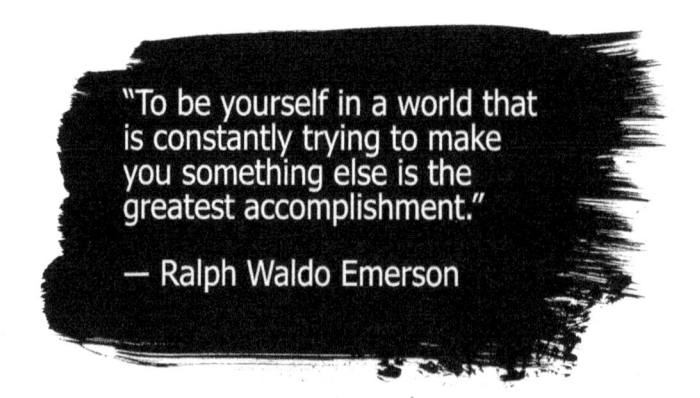

> "To be yourself in a world that is constantly trying to make you something else is the greatest accomplishment."
>
> — Ralph Waldo Emerson

EXCUSES, EXCUSES, EXCUSES

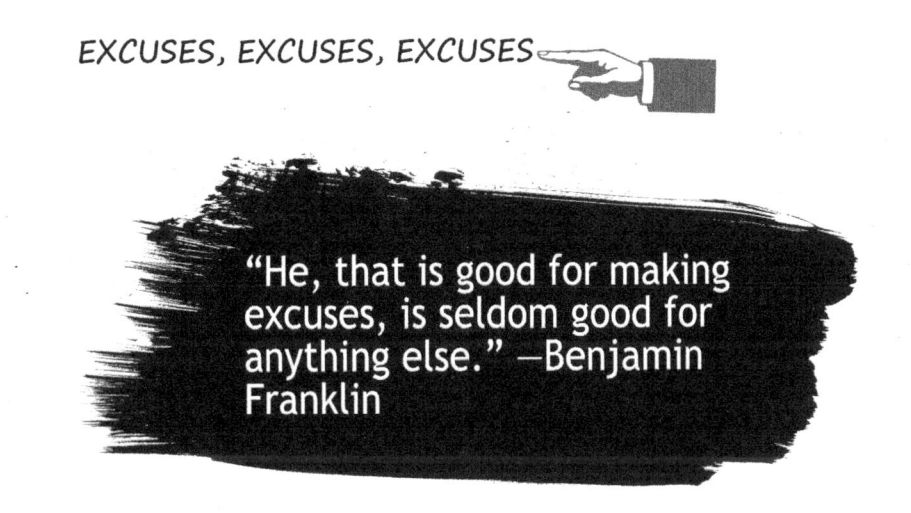

> "He, that is good for making excuses, is seldom good for anything else." —Benjamin Franklin

Back in the day, making excuses was like breathing air for me. I had some great ones, in fact, they were so good that I didn't realize I was even making excuses.

I had ten go-to excuses that I could rely on to completely devastate my chances of doing anything extraordinary.

Excuse #1: There's just not enough time...

I still use this one every once in a while. Usually, at the core of this excuse is the fear that I'm not good enough to do the thing that I'm claiming I don't have the time to do. There's usually a lot of stalling involved.

The moment I feel overwhelmed by lack of time, I can talk myself out of anything. Sometimes it may be something that I genuinely don't want to do, and in that situation I would rather cancel the project than keep it rattling around in my brain jar.

When it is something I really want to do, but my claim to non-fame is that I don't have enough time, ever... then I think twice about that excuse and take some action.

THE ROGUE ARTIST SURVIVAL GUIDE

Excuses Are Confusing

IS IT AN EXCUSE?
- Yes → TAKE ACTION ON YOU?
  - Yes → DOES IT LIFT?
    - Yes → FOCUSED ON SOLUTION?
      - Yes → DOES IT MAKE YOU FEEL COURAGE?
        - Yes → IT'S TRUTH
      - No → IT'S BULL-SHIRT!
- No → BLAME SOMEONE
  - Yes → IT'S BULL-SHIRT!
  - No → DOES IT LIMIT?
    - Yes → IT'S BULL-SHIRT!
    - No → FOCUSED ON PROBLEM?
      - Yes → IT'S BULL-SHIRT!
      - No → DOES IT MAKE YOU FEEL LIKE IT IS IMPOSSIBLE?

ARE YOU HAPPY
- Yes → IT'S TRUTH
- No → IT'S BULL-SHIRT!

70 The Rogue Artist Survival Guide

When I look back at my behavior in moments of overwhelm, I actually become less productive, which causes there to be less time, and even more overwhelm. So, just make time and take action. Stop thinking about it. Excuses can get confusing if you buy into them.

Excuse #2: There's just not enough money...

I find that no matter how much money I have in the bank, whether it is thousands or a negative balance, these words will blurt out of my mouth like a bad habit.

To be honest, I have a weird relationship with money that I have been working on throughout the last few years. I think it is vital that we look at our relationship with money because it is either one of two things: a good relationship or a bad one.

In other words, if you feel like a victim of green pieces of paper, then it's a bad one. Most of my baggage when it comes to money was partly from a weak money mentality in my household when I was growing up. Like most relationships, it is something you can improve once you look a little deeper into yourself. I talk more about money a little later in the book.

Excuse #3: I don't have an education...

This was my number one excuse when it came to pursuing art as a career... well, it was one of many number one excuses. Numerous multi-millionaires and billionaires have nothing more than a high school education. Some don't even have that.

Yet, I spent a lot of time in my life wasting my precious brainpower believing this gibberish. I'm not knocking education, there's value in it. If you want to pursue an education, pursue it. If you're going to be an excellent brain surgeon, definitely go to school. If you're going to sharpen your creative skills by taking classes, by all means...

...but don't let an education, or lack thereof, define what you can accomplish with your talents.

DEFINE YOUR OWN DESTINY

Excuse #4: I'm just too old or too young...

I'm old enough to have used both of these excuses. Right now, it's too old. I'm not a spring chicken, but I'm not ancient either. Societies around the world seem to all have a different take on what it means to be too old or too young. Doesn't make it true, just makes it a popular opinion.

It's easy for me to think I'm too old to be in a band, I'm too old to do YouTube, I'm too old to make a significant impact on the new generation of humans, and I'm too old to make a difference in art. These excuses love to pop up whenever I'm on a roll.

While you may not see me on American Idol anytime soon (they have a no-geezer age limit of 28 which I find outdated and discriminatory, but whatever...) I am most certainly young enough to excel at whatever I gosh-darned well please. As long as I'm breathing, I got plenty of time.

Excuse #5: I don't know how...

This is an excuse I rarely use anymore because I am very stubborn at figuring stuff out. I am a stubborn figurer-outer. This means I make mistake after mistake after mistake until I get it. I simply don't like not knowing how to do something or being afraid to try. This has, so far, worked out in my favor.

Excuse #6: I just can't change...

This used to be true for me. I was pretty set in my ways and the words *"That's just who I am!"* would spout out of my mouth as an excuse to justify some stupid thing I did. It wasn't until I started thinking long term that things changed for me. Determining whether I want to still be dealing with the same crap in ten or twenty years, made me think about ways of changing it.

When you think about the cycle of stubborn habits repeating time and time again over twenty years, you get a fire under your butt to start that change immediately.

Excuse #7: I'm afraid to fail...

I'm pretty sure we get taught this stupidity in school... "Do everything you can to succeed, failure is the mark of laziness or lack of skill."

I'm sure that might seem like sound logic to those who have never tried to do something that hasn't been done before, but it's not. If you want to blaze your own trail, you are going to have to fail several times to reach anything resembling success. Embrace failure, learn from it, and plan ahead, so you know how to use the failure to do it better the next time.

Excuse #8: It's just not the right time...

Yeah, if these little words pop out of your mouth, then you should just swat them down mid-air like a fly before they reach anyone's ear holes.

I met a wonderful woman who was in her 90's that fused the following words into my brain *"If not now, when?"* She embodied that mantra every day and it was a joy to be around her. I get it, sometimes it's just not the right time to take action. However, more often than not, this is just a lame excuse.

Excuse #9: I am not ready...

Sometimes you will hear this coming from someone who is standing at the edge of a pool, about to jump in, and they say, "I'm not ready!" when actually they are merely paralyzed by fear.

There they are, like an idiot, standing in their swimsuit, the water is good, just jump... how much more ready can you get?

There's nothing wrong with planning for the future or taking the time to lay out a clear plan of action. However, if planning is all you do, this could indicate that there might be fears preventing you from moving forward. Understand this, and you will overcome your need for over-planning... in due time.

Excuse #10: I'm just not inspired...

This is a big one, yet I find that most of the time when these words come out of my mouth, it has more to do with stagnant inertia than inspiration. Sometimes you are just being lame. I know that's harsh, but it's true.

Sometimes I'm not inspired because I'm too busy feeling sorry for myself and clogging up my brain circuits with all of the above excuses. Whatever the cause, when this excuse crops up, I know it's time to take a leaf blower to whatever doom cloud is lurking overhead, and start fresh.

Sometimes we get so absorbed in making excuses about how things didn't turn out the way we had expected, that we forget to focus on making the best of every situation — no matter what the outcome.

So go out and make excuses for how awesome you are. Make excuses for how you have more than enough time, how it is the right time for you, and how failure is no big deal. You can say and do anything you want, just pay closer attention to the words that come out of the hole in the front of your face.

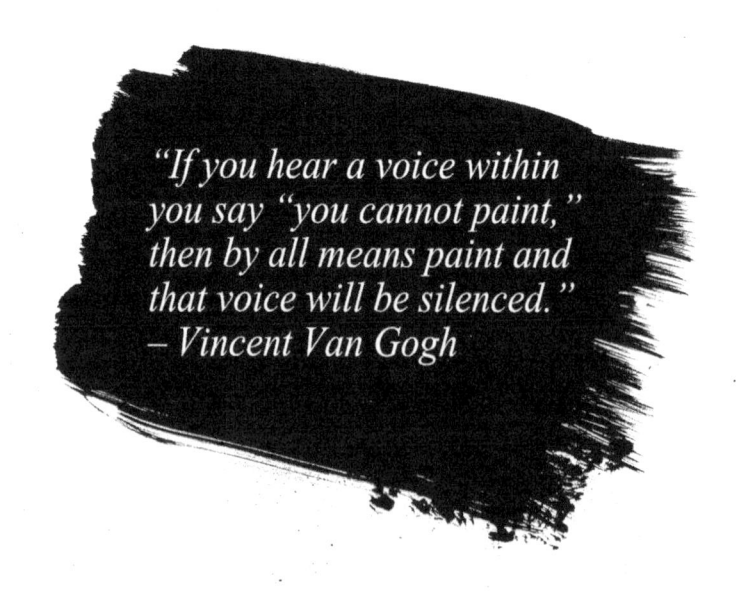

> *"If you hear a voice within you say "you cannot paint," then by all means paint and that voice will be silenced."*
> *– Vincent Van Gogh*

#ARTLIFE

EMBRACE YOUR INNER WEIRD CREATIVE

I grew up with a fear of being seen as different, weird, or crazy. My mom had a rough childhood, and because of it, it was vital for us to be seen as "normal." Being weird was a bad word. Later on, I realized that it was just a *word* that means different things to different people.

The fact is, we are *ALL* weirdos in our own way. Spending too much time trying to figure out what it means to be normal can really feed into your excuses. Klee is my hero when it comes to embracing your own brand of weird.

I mean, be YOUR OWN KIND OF WEIRD. I don't mean that you should *act* weird. I'm saying you should be your unique concoction of weird. Be the kinda weird that only you can be. There are five reasons I think being weird is the best way for people to perceive you, especially when you are an artist.

Reason Number One – Make The Mundane Interesting.

You can dress up for a Harry Potter book release. Not a book signing by the way, not an opening for anything grand... Just a bookstore in an obscure suburb. That's what I call "*Klee* weird."

What makes this awesome is how you can turn something mundane, like waiting in line, into an epic adventure. I remember having to wait in a line that was going to take a few hours to get through. I played a game of name that tune with the people around me.

I began by saying, "Excuse me, I've got this song in my head, and I can't remember where it's from, can you help me out?" Then I sang. Let's be real, being an artist is not a thrilling adventure. It can actually be quite dull at times, so come up with creative ways to turn the mundane into an adventure. Allow yourself to not care about what the neighbors might think.

Reason Number Dos – You Get To Be You

You don't have to worry so much about reputation or what people think of you when they think you are weird. I mean, c'mon you're weird, you don't have a reputation.

This is the part I love most about being a weirdo. You basically get to be yourself, every day, every moment, and not try to follow some facade of normal that doesn't actually exist.

As a creative, I think there is a power in being who you are, especially when you give yourself the freedom to express yourself however you deem appropriate.

Reason Number Three – You Get To Live In Excitement

You can get super excited about things that no one else thinks are exciting. I have to say, Klee is quite possibly the most awesome and nerdy woman I have ever met in my entire life. She gets SO excited about things that no one else even thinks twice about.

She designs beautiful jewelry for a living and gets super excited about the stones, their history, how they were formed, how they were mined, cut, polished, and on and on. She gets really thrilled and doesn't even care if no one else shares in her excitement… That's awesome.

Reason Numero Quatro – You Get To Go Against The Norm

No matter what is going on, even if the weather is terrible, you stubbed your toe, and everyone around you is in a bad mood, you can be blissfully weird. This means that no matter what is going on in your life, you get to smile and laugh as if every day is the best day ever. You get to interrupt patterns of behavior by hanging upside down from a tree to get a different perspective, or walking backward and rewinding the moment that just happened so you can experience it again or differently.

LET'S All BE WEIRDOS :)

Reason Number Five – The More The Merrier

When you give yourself a license to embrace your weird side and put it out there in a genuine way, you attract other weirdos to you that are your kind of weird. What a great way to live life, surrounded by others who are weird enough to be themselves, happy, easily excited, and seem to make everything fun.

Once you start questioning the artist myths, stereotypes, and excuses in the art world, some people are going to perceive you as weird. The status quo and conformity is normal, even in a landscape as diverse as the creative path. Sometimes anything that is outside of that neat little box is considered weird.

I've seen many artists fall back in line into the struggle because they were afraid to be seen as weird. They were too worried that people would think they were crazy.

"What will the neighbors think?" was a considerable concern for Klee's grandmother. A lot of people from older generations were worried about status within their social structures, and passed on those worries to their children.

Embracing your weird is voicing who you are and what you believe. Trust me, this creative journey is going to have its twists and turns, and if you aren't prepared to be you, it's going to be a hard road.

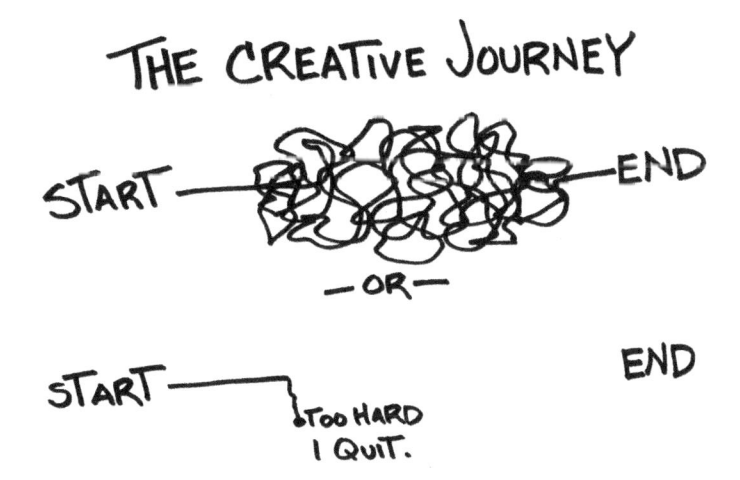

THE CREATIVE JOURNEY

START —〰〰〰— END

— OR —

START ——┐
         └ TOO HARD
           I QUIT.   END

THE ROGUE ARTIST SURVIVAL GUIDE

IMAGINATION IS NOT AN EXCLUSIVE CLUB

As a creative person, chances are you have a lot more practice guiding your imagination than someone who doesn't rely on it for their craft. Yet, despite what some people think, everyone has a powerful imagination, and everyone is regularly using it.

Imagination is the ability to form a mental image or concept of something that is not actually being perceived through the five senses at that moment. It is the fantastic ability of the mind to build a mental scene.

Objects, events, smells, tastes, feelings, structures, circumstances, situations that have never existed, things that are not presently happening, or things that have occurred in the past will take place in a vivid instant.

Everyone is aware of a certain degree of imagination ability. Some people believe that imagination is weaker in some than it is in others. I personally don't see any compelling evidence for that. I think we all have a powerful and vivid imagination. The question is, are we aware of how we use it?

Whether you believe it or not, you experience the whole world inside your head. Everything that happens to you every day gets processed through a complex neural network that is continually adapting and changing based on the experiences that you have.

Those experiences don't necessarily have to happen in the real world either. In fact, most of those experiences happen in between your ears.

When most people think about their imagination, they believe it is a series of images and film reels that pass through the mind, like a movie.

They can picture something in their mind but overlook the other experiences such as smell, taste, feeling, touch, sounds, and other physical factors within their imagination.

It's more like immersive virtual reality than a movie.

The experiences you have in your imagination are just as powerful and vivid as being there in person. In fact, research has shown that practicing something in your mind actually causes similar physical responses and changes to practicing for real.

The thing about the world of our imagination is that it is a vivid world of absolute inclusion. Everything that you can experience in real life and beyond can occur in your imagination. Everything you observe or think about will take place in your imagination, including the things you don't want to think about.

For example:
Don't think about an elephant.
Don't think of an elephant standing on its hind legs.
Don't hear the elephant trumpet.
Don't hear the circus goers applaud.
Don't hear circus music.
Don't smell the popcorn or feel the bucket in your hands.

Were you at the circus just now? Were you able to not think about it? Did you smell popcorn for an instant? That is a taste of how your imagination actually works, and it is working like that ALL the time.

The imagination is not exclusive to just when you choose to use it, and it is not unique to creative people. It is a powerful virtual reality engine that is constantly going full throttle in all of us.

- When you are worried about showing your art for the first time, you are using your imagination.
- When you are stressed that you may not make enough this month for bills, you are using your imagination.
- When you are terrified to give a speech in front of people, you are using your imagination.

Actually, in these examples, your imagination is using you, and you may not even be aware of it.

The Darkside Of Imagination.

The virtual reality engine of our imagination is continuously in motion, and not understanding this is a problem. If you are picturing worst-case scenarios, things falling apart, dangers around every corner, severe outcomes, and feeling like a victim to your life, then chances are you don't have a grip on your imagination. As a creative pursuing something as abstract as an art career, an imagination running amok can lead to problems.

A positive mindset is a powerful thing, but I think there is considerable misunderstanding about how it works. Usually, most of the stuff that I have read guides people to imagine positive outcomes to the situation they are stressed about.

For example, if you are showing art for the first time at an art festival and you are worried that it will go badly: Positive mindset people will say to picture it going really well for you.

Or you are giving a speech in front of a large group of people, and you are worried that you'll bomb: Positive mindset people will say to picture the perfect words coming out of your mouth, along with applause from the crowd.

The problem here is that it doesn't address the valid concerns that your mind is posing. Instead, you are guided to throw a band-aid over your concerns and only focus on a positive outcome. The concerns are still there, and you just buried them for later.

The real problem comes up when the thing you were worried about shows up in your life, and you are entirely unequipped to deal with it.

I get it, we don't want to face the things we are afraid of. We don't want to think about rejection, failing, bombing, embarrassing moments, losing, betrayal, or anything else that sends us into a tiffy. Unfortunately, ignoring it doesn't make it go away.

Those negative thoughts and imagined scenarios are going to pop into your mind. If you are continually running away from them, it's like having wild horses chasing close behind you, ready to trample you at any moment.

You can set your fears and insecurities on a shelf, but the wild horses will eventually burst out and trample you unless you face them head-on.

It is important to get a grip on the reins of your imagination. By taking control of that wild beast and taming it, you are tapping into a creative power that is in a class of its own.

I love the analogy of the wild horses, mighty beasts that have been living wild and completely un-wrangled. Dangerous and unpredictable they are, yet capable of being a powerful ally.

Our imagination, if unchecked, is unpredictable and wild. Here are some concepts you can use to harness the full power of your imagination.

Your Imagination Is Constant.

The first thing to understand is that your imagination is continuously running around in your head, kicking up dust and making a ruckus. Sometimes you are guiding it consciously, imagining some art project or thing where you are aware that you are using your imagination. When you are done, there is no off switch; you may have just gotten used to tuning it out, but it's still running.

Believe It Or Not, The Bad Is The Good.

When you imagine a worst-case scenario, do you immediately just swat it away from your mind? Do you feel like a victim of your own thoughts?

Are you telling me that you have access to the most powerful virtual reality engine on the planet, and you are using it to think flowery thoughts and run away from the things you are afraid of?

Every time your mind poses one of those scary questions, it is an opportunity to face your fears, figure out a solution, and practice how you will respond, empowering yourself to meet any and all situations and circumstances.

What if you *do* bomb at your speech? So what? How will you handle it?

What if you gave the crappiest presentation in the world? Oh well. I can either laugh about it or cry in my cornflakes. How do I want to respond?

Facing the worst-case scenarios and finding a way to feel empowered with the results is such a great use of the imagination. You get to start over, replay it, say it better, check and see how you feel.

I think, as an artist, this is powerful. Most of our fears and obstacles to living a creative life are wrapped up in our own insecurities. Imagine for a moment that you can face your fears in your mind and find a way to feel empowered enough to face them in real life.

I mean that you get to choose how you feel, you get to decide how you are going to respond. Your sense of self is not dependent on anyone else's opinion, how they react to you, or winning an argument.

When you are truly empowered, no one else needs to change their mind, they don't need to prove anything, they don't owe you, and there is nothing they need to do for you to feel better.

Feeling like a victim requires you to blame someone else or something for how your life is going. Whenever you do that, you are handing away any control or power you might have had. Feeling empowered means that you take that power back, grab the reins of your own life, and choose how you respond.

RESPOND RATHER THAN REACT.

Allow your mind to focus on a fear you may have. Like the fear of being rejected at the next juried art show.

What if you get rejected?
So what?
How will you handle it?
What will it mean to you?
Can you walk away from the experience feeling strong and confident?

Most importantly, have fun and try not to take it so seriously. Listen, you are going to feel terror when facing an imagined situation, but you can start over, change the outcome, and walk away from it feeling powerful.

Treat it like a virtual reality game and understand that sometimes your body is going to respond physically to what you imagine. Those negative thoughts are going to pop into your head, so you might as well use them to empower yourself.

In your imagination, you can travel anywhere at the speed of light, you can fly, climb the highest mountain, ride on the back of a dragon. You can do anything, there are no limits to what you can imagine.

I remember being absolutely terrified to show my work at my first show, which was quickly coming up the next day.

I would panic slightly when I thought about it and would talk myself down by reminding myself that everything was going to be OK. This worked to calm me, but it wasn't getting rid of the fear.

I asked myself, "What is the worst that could happen?"

"People will hate your art, you are going to fail." I responded.

"Ok, and what happens then?" I asked, trying to remain calm.

"I feel horrible. I'll feel like a fake." I responded.

I looked closely at my response to the imagined comment. Someone said something terrible, and I responded by feeling bad and taking it personally.

I realized at that very moment that I had spent two weeks practicing this scenario in the back of my mind. I had put in hundreds of hours imagining this negative outcome.

I had been playing this virtual reality reel in my brain and didn't think to change the story. When you avoid facing fear in your mind by brushing it off and ignoring it, you leave it right where it is. You find no resolution, no sense of empowerment, and it just gains momentum the more it plays out in your brain.

I think it is incredible that our brain will set us up with the things we Fear. Every instance is an opportunity to choose how you will respond to the obstacle if and when it shows up.

You have a powerful imagination, and it is continuously active. Be aware of that, and make sure you get a grip and use your imagination versus your imagination using you.

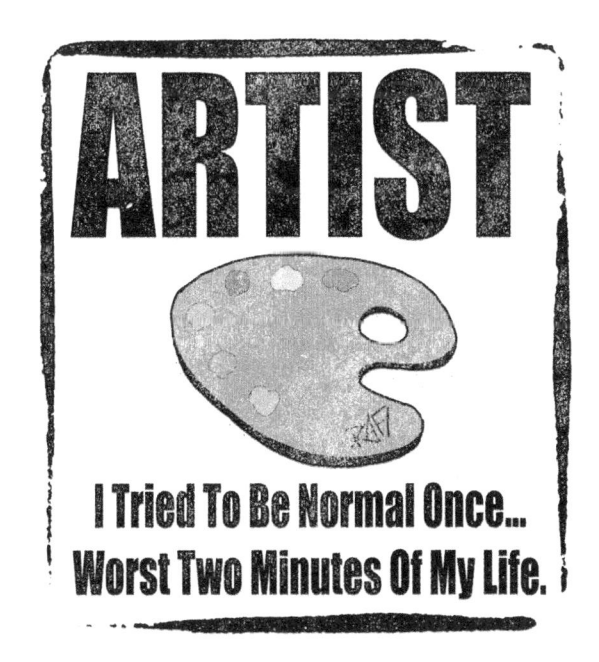

ARTIST

I Tried To Be Normal Once... Worst Two Minutes Of My Life.

THE ROGUE ARTIST SURVIVAL GUIDE

LOGIC MAY GET YOU FROM A TO Z

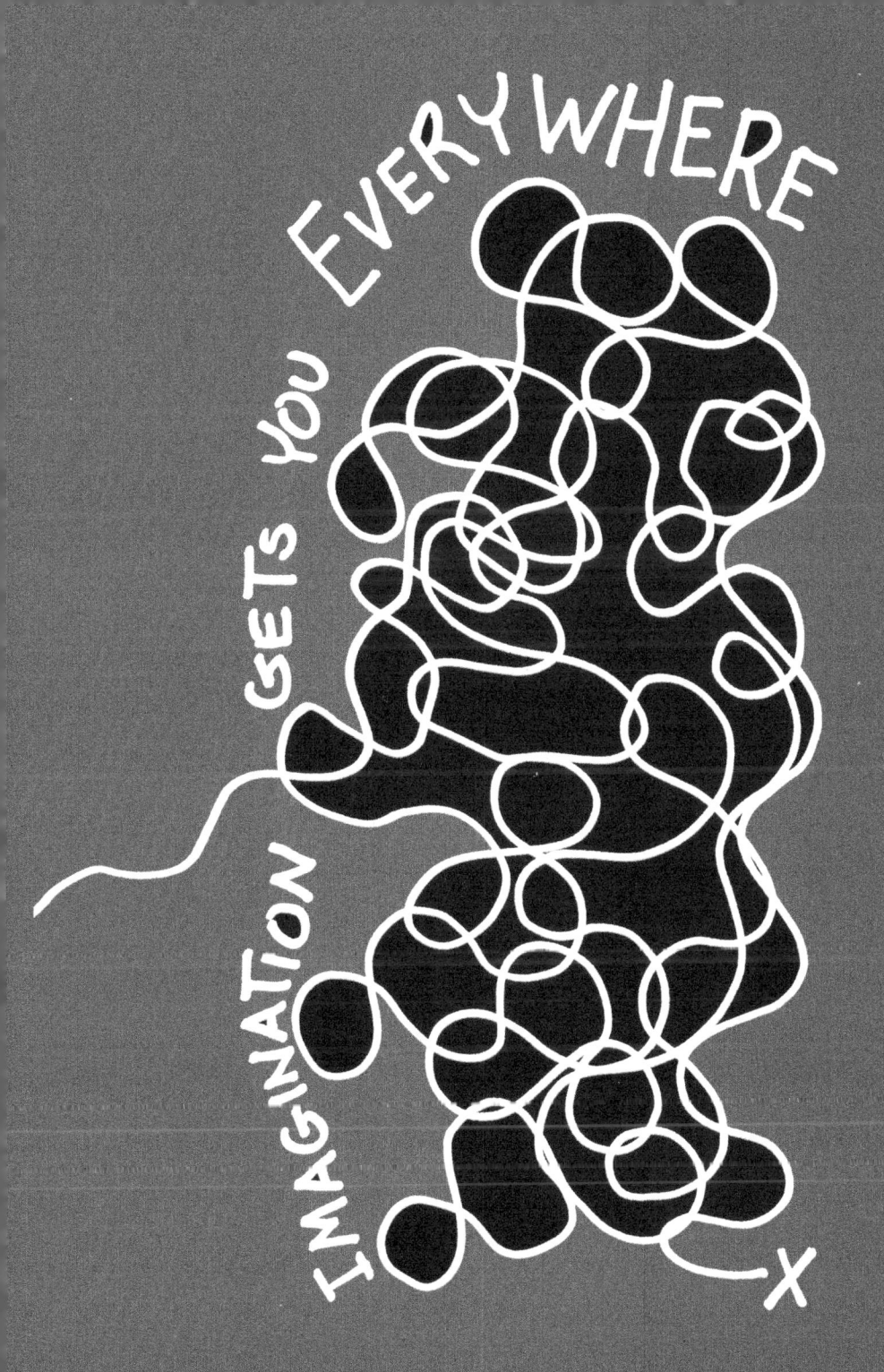

IMAGINATION GETS YOU EVERYWHERE
x

THE ROGUE ARTIST SURVIVAL GUIDE

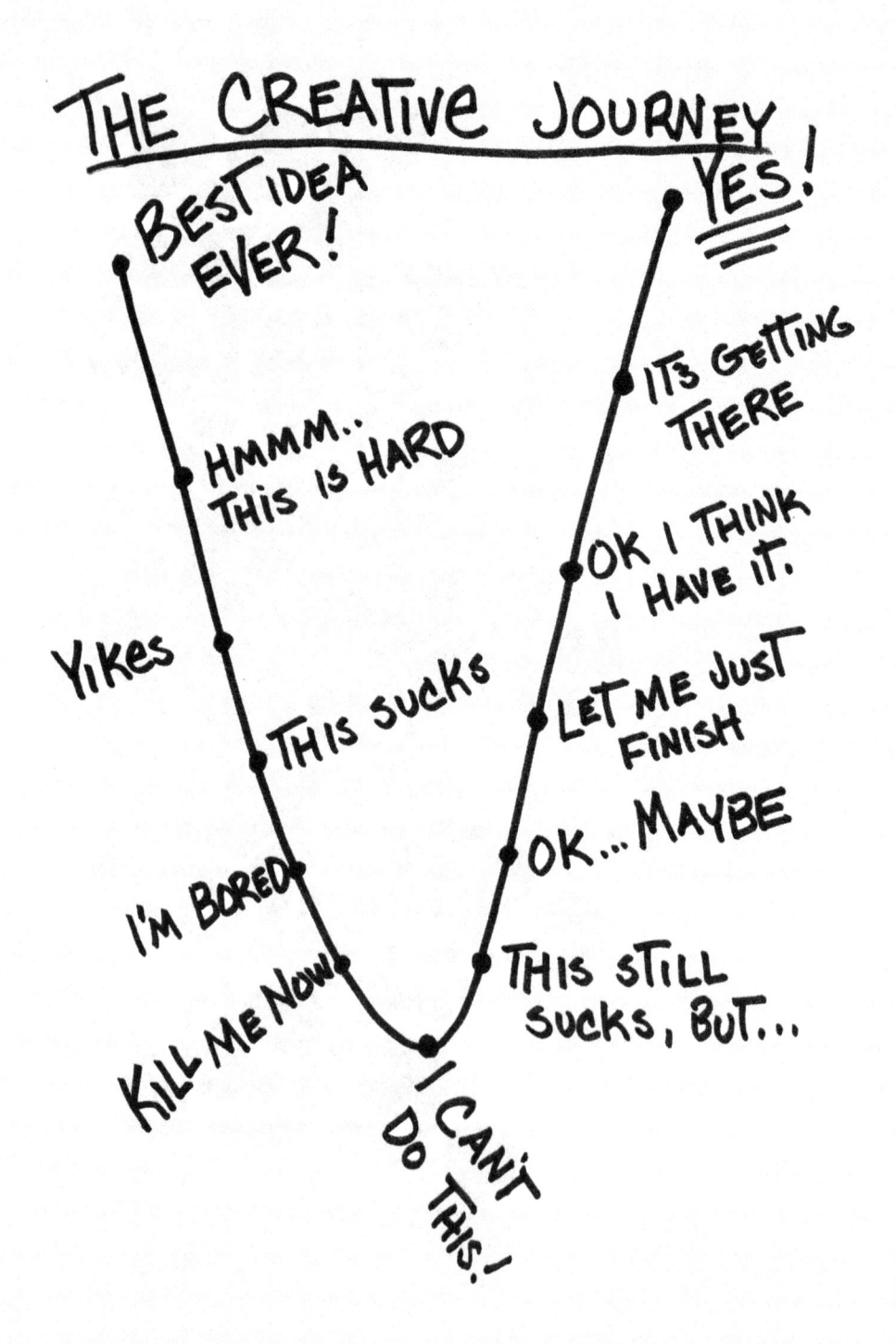

The Creative Journey

- Best Idea Ever!
- Hmmm... This is Hard
- Yikes
- This Sucks
- I'm Bored
- Kill Me Now
- I Can't Do This!
- This Still Sucks, But...
- OK... Maybe
- Let Me Just Finish
- OK I Think I Have It.
- It's Getting There
- Yes!

The Creative Journey And Luck

Some people look at my life and say that I am lucky. I create art for a living, have a successful studio business, am married to my best friend, and have a large following of fans and art collectors from all around the world. I really love the work that I do, and I spend a lot of time feeling ridiculously fortunate to be in that position.

As much as some people like to say that I'm lucky, luck had nothing to do with it. Although sometimes timing, circumstance, serendipity, and privilege play a part, your deliberate action determines the course of your life.

People don't get to do what they want for a living, get awards, come out in newspapers, or get the things they want in life simply because they are lucky. I feel like it is insulting to tell someone they are lucky when they achieve something awesome in life. Luck rarely has anything to do with what actually goes on behind the scenes.

I personally get inspired by stories of long rejection runs, for example the story of Haim Saban, who spent 8 years pitching Power Rangers. Whenever Saban presented the Power Rangers pilot, network execs would ask, "Why do you embarrass yourself with this?" Eventually, someone picked it up and the Power Rangers has been a tremendous success for 30 plus years.

- J.K. Rowling was rejected by about 12 different publishers.
- After just one performance, Elvis Presley was fired by Jimmy Denny, and told, "You ain't going nowhere, son. You ought to go back to driving a truck."
- Stephen King's first novel, Carrie, was rejected 30 times before it was published.
- Steven Spielberg was rejected by the University of Southern California School of Theater, Film, and Television, THREE TIMES.

Rejection has everything to do with opinion and nothing to do with fact. Power Rangers was rejected by networks because it looked cheap and there was nothing else like it out there to compare it to. They could not SEE beyond the scope of what they knew and based their rejection on popular opinion. Rejection is simply an opinion based on a particular person's perspective. Rejection is all part of the game, so get used to it and keep going.

THE ROGUE ARTIST SURVIVAL GUIDE

Most times, the success that you see is just the tip of the iceberg. What you see accomplished is only a tiny proportion of what that "lucky" person TRIED to accomplish.

If by "luck", you mean putting yourself out there — all the time — into situations where you are probably going to be rejected, fail, or make a fool of yourself, then yes... you are on the right track.

A lot of people ask me how I got to where I am in life. As if there is some secret formula or answer to getting lucky. Usually, I tell them, "The hard way." I honestly don't feel like it is supposed to be easy, I think the suck is all part of the journey and what makes it so beautiful.

To illustrate what I mean, here's a list of just some of the things I have been rejected for over the last 10 years. See if you can find the inspiration behind the rejection or failure.

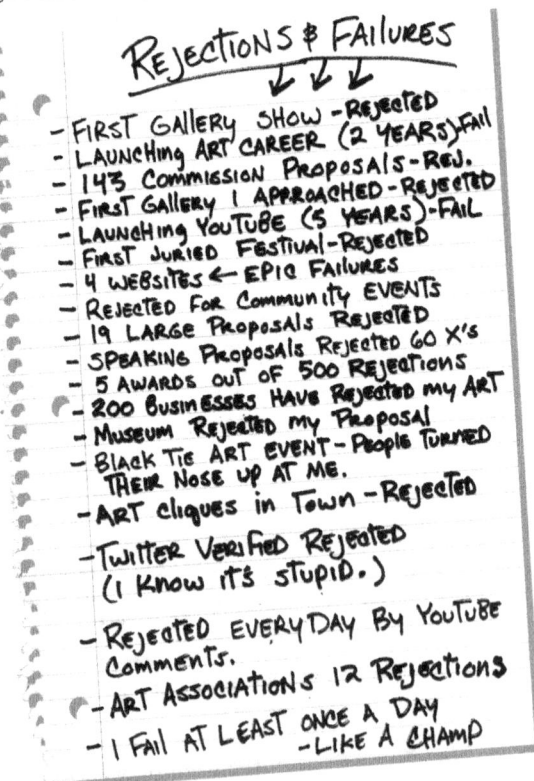

> **REJECTIONS & FAILURES**
> - FIRST GALLERY SHOW - REJECTED
> - LAUNCHING ART CAREER (2 YEARS) FAIL
> - 143 COMMISSION PROPOSALS - REJ.
> - FIRST GALLERY I APPROACHED - REJECTED
> - LAUNCHING YouTUBE (5 YEARS) - FAIL
> - FIRST JURIED FESTIVAL - REJECTED
> - 4 WEBSITES ← EPIC FAILURES
> - REJECTED FOR COMMUNITY EVENTS
> - 19 LARGE PROPOSALS REJECTED
> - SPEAKING PROPOSALS REJECTED 60 X's
> - 5 AWARDS OUT OF 500 REJECTIONS
> - 200 BUSINESSES HAVE REJECTED MY ART
> - MUSEUM REJECTED MY PROPOSAL
> - BLACK TIE ART EVENT - PEOPLE TURNED THEIR NOSE UP AT ME.
> - ART CLIQUES IN TOWN - REJECTED
> - TWITTER VERIFIED REJECTED (I KNOW IT'S STUPID.)
> - REJECTED EVERY DAY BY YouTUBE COMMENTS.
> - ART ASSOCIATIONS 12 REJECTIONS
> - I FAIL AT LEAST ONCE A DAY - LIKE A CHAMP

Each one of these was a blow, and that's not even the full list, we'd be here ALL day.

Being rejected or failing is shit. It's hard not to take it personally, and to keep going when it feels like a consistent barrage of 'nope' and 'EPIC FAILS'. The only way to do the *awesome stuff* is to put yourself out there, to put yourself in a place where you might get rejected constantly, and To be in a place where you might fail big.

Everything doesn't always come up roses, and I am not told yes every time I want to do something. That is ridiculous. It is also ridiculous to quit just because you failed, or get your feelings hurt because you were rejected. That's why I keep going — ALL the time. I apply for things, I try things, I put myself out there. I make a huge effort to go for almost everything that piques my interest and pushes at my comfort zones.

I've been at this for 10 years and can tell you that it takes time to get to a place where you will have people call you "lucky". It can mean years upon years of rejections and failures that don't ever end. Sometimes it will feel overwhelming, and you'll have to become your biggest cheerleader to get through. That is how you get there, you just have to do it and quit stalling to avoid failure and rejection.

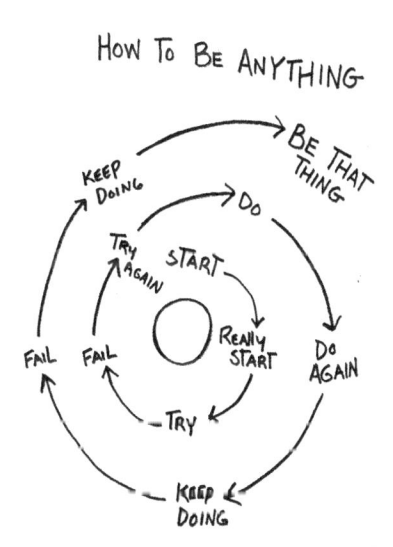

How To Be Anything

Success means that you failed and were rejected more than anyone else. Growth means that you will always be facing rejection and failure throughout your career. If you are not, then you are not growing.

ART... BECAUSE THERAPY IS EXPENSIVE

Creating Your Own World.

I remember being in class and being told to get my head out of the clouds and pay attention. This was usually followed by me pretending to pay attention and figuring out ways to daydream without anyone noticing.

Of course, I also thought I was a bad kid, or there was something seriously wrong with my ability to focus. I imagine if it happened today, I would have been labeled with some kind of attention deficit disorder and given drugs or something to fix me.

Honestly, I was just bored. Not all the time, some of my teachers were fantastic at capturing my imagination and taking me on a fun learning adventure where I soaked in every detail of the experience.

Other teachers were bland, and it was much more fun to venture into my mind than to listen to them yammer on about the boring textbook. Either way, I inadvertently spent a lot of time developing the skill of purposefully creating pictures in my mind and playing out complex scenarios that involved slaying dragons and saving a damsel in distress.

I think everyone can create pictures and complex scenarios in their minds. Whether or not they are practiced at doing it on purpose, is another question. I know people who walk around for days frustrated and angry because they create an entire story in their mind that is entirely false. What's worse, is they believe it actually happened.

I think this is really powerful. I mean, think about the last time you flipped your lid because you thought something was going on that wasn't actually going on. You felt all the emotions, all the anger, sadness, and momentum as if it had actually happened right in front of you.

Now imagine if you could use that power of emotion on purpose.

Instead of letting your thoughts run away with you, you can decide to think about whatever you want to believe. I mean, they're your thoughts, you actually decide to entertain them or not. I guess it just takes a little practice and consistency. Creating a new habit of thinking and connection in the brain doesn't actually take long, but consistency is key.

Just imagine how awesome it would be to put your head in the clouds and let your imagination soar and take you wherever you want to go. I know that if you do this enough times, eventually your life catches up, and a new story is told all around.

You spend a lot of time in your head anyway, might as well think about stuff that makes you feel fantastic. Honestly, it doesn't matter if it's right in front of you or in your head, it all feels the same.

We've got no one telling us to get our head out of the clouds anymore, and if someone does, well... that's what the finger next to your ring finger is for.

LEVELING UP

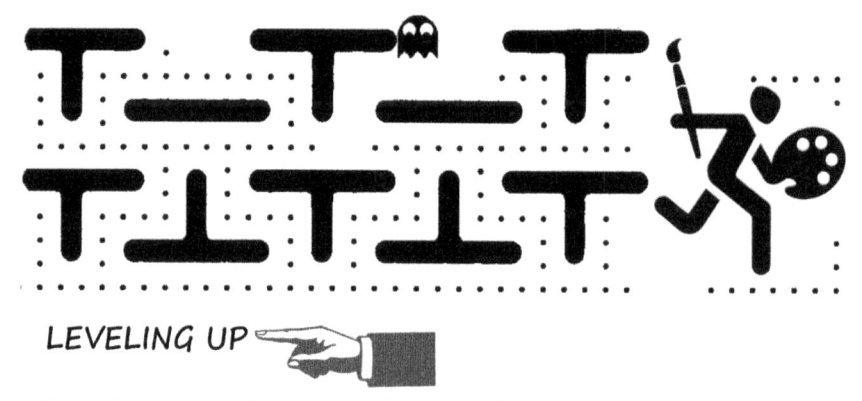

Just about every human on the planet has played one video game or another. In a typical video game, you begin at the most manageable level, and your character is given three lives. This means that you can make mistakes and die at least three times in the game before you need to start a new game.

Doing anything extraordinary in life is all about pushing yourself to level up. It's like video game levels of the creative world. Think of these extra lives in video games as real-world opportunities to bounce back from failure.

In essence, you are given training wheels. You know you can confidently test the waters and make mistakes because you have a chance to come back and try again. The more experience you have at that level, the easier it gets. Usually, you die a whole bunch of times before you gain the expertise you need.

You may pick up some tips and tricks from the internet or friends that are playing the same game. Those may help to get you further along, but ultimately you are in control of your destiny.

Even if your friend is sitting next to you and telling you where to go, it doesn't guarantee that you are not going to fall into an open sewer and plummet to your virtual death.

You learn by doing it and taking the risk yourself.

After hours of play and dying multiple times, eventually, you have so much experience at a level that you can pass it with your eyes closed.

Once you quickly pass a level and it no longer poses any challenges, something interesting happens, it becomes boring. You know what to expect and just go through the motions of completing the level as quickly as you can so you can get to the next challenging level.

The creative life is similar to the levels in a video game. The more we continue on this path, the more challenges we run into every time we choose to level up.

I started my art career by putting my art out at a flea market. Eventually I was doing well, people knew where to find me, and I got comfortable. Things became predictable and pretty safe. It was time to level up.

Despite the flea market being my only source of income, I decided to Leave. I started doing festivals and another market closer to home. Another couple of years went by, and things became predictable and safe. It was time to level up.

Again, I decided to step out of my comfort zone and tackle the worldwide online market, which I felt I knew nothing about. It has been a rollercoaster ride so far and completely unpredictable, but it is slowly getting to where I want it to be.

Whenever I made a change in my career, people would ask, "Why leave what you built?" and "Things are stable, why not just keep doing what works?"

As an artist, I tend to people watch a lot. I also have a fascination with body language and micro-expressions that I use in my figurative art. In all cases where I made a change, I asked myself one question.

"Do I want to do this for the next 20 years?"

With the flea market, I didn't want to establish myself as a flea market artist. There was a cap to my possibilities, and although I had created something quite beautiful, I didn't want to be there in 20 years.

Looking at some of the vendors, most were just going through the motions week to week. A lot of them just didn't look happy.

With the festival circuit and local events, we started to really make an impact on the community with our art.

A lot of show-goers became collectors because they saw us at just about every art event there was in the area. We were doing very well, but eventually things became comfortable. It wasn't easy, setting up for events and festivals is grueling work, but we knew what to expect.

Klee and I had been doing the markets and festivals every weekend for seven years. On an unusually hot day at the market, I was miserable. I looked around and saw people that didn't want to be there, but they relied on the market for an income. I realized I wasn't there for the thrill of sharing my art anymore. I was there just to make money.

"Do I want to do this for the next 20 years?"

What was next? What would be leveling up from where I was?

The next hurdle for me was my fear of going online. I knew how to make money at festivals, markets, and in person. Heck, you can drop me in any town, and I am confident that I can make money with my art. The internet was an entirely different unknown creature. It was time to level up, and I did. I left the familiar and headed into the unknown.

My career has been a series of taking risks and leveling up whenever I start getting too comfortable. It is wholly unpredictable and lacks the security most people crave, but it is what works for me. I enjoy the challenges.

I'm not saying you should quit everything and bumble through it the way I do, trust me, I know I'm extreme.

JUST DO IT ALREADY!

Klee doesn't jump in with both feet, she takes her time to transition, reducing her commitment little by little, slowly. This method works for her, although it takes a bit longer. Whether you slowly transition or tumble in head first, it will always require risks when you choose to level up.

We don't fear the ramifications in a video game because they are not real. Also, if we fail, we can simply start the game all over. This doesn't mean we are careless with our efforts, but we don't fear the consequences.

I think we would all benefit from looking at life a little more like a video game. We tend to be so serious about the outcomes of everything, that we forget the fun in the challenges of doing the thing itself.

Most games are played simply because you want to prove to yourself that you can beat it. No matter how many times you fail, you are willing to start all over from the beginning and go again. You get excited to face the game with the little bit of extra knowledge you learned in the last failure.

Leveling up in your creative career means you are heading into the next unknown; be prepared to make every mistake. Also, if you are anything like me, be ready to make every excuse to return to what was comfortable.

I know some of you are thinking that I've lost my mind. You may think there is a vast difference between reality and a game. I agree. I'm not saying you should jump over giant spikes, battle mega-creatures, or take unnecessary risks.

What I am saying is that most of the things you are afraid of are just as real as being in a video game. The only difference is that you take them way more seriously than you would if it was a game.

The creative mind is a virtual reality video game powered by the most influential tool you have in your arsenal as an artist, your imagination.

You are the main character, the hero, and ahead of you is a level that you have never faced. In this level, there are all kinds of seen and unseen obstacles and monsters that you have created in your mind.

OVERWHELMING Thoughts

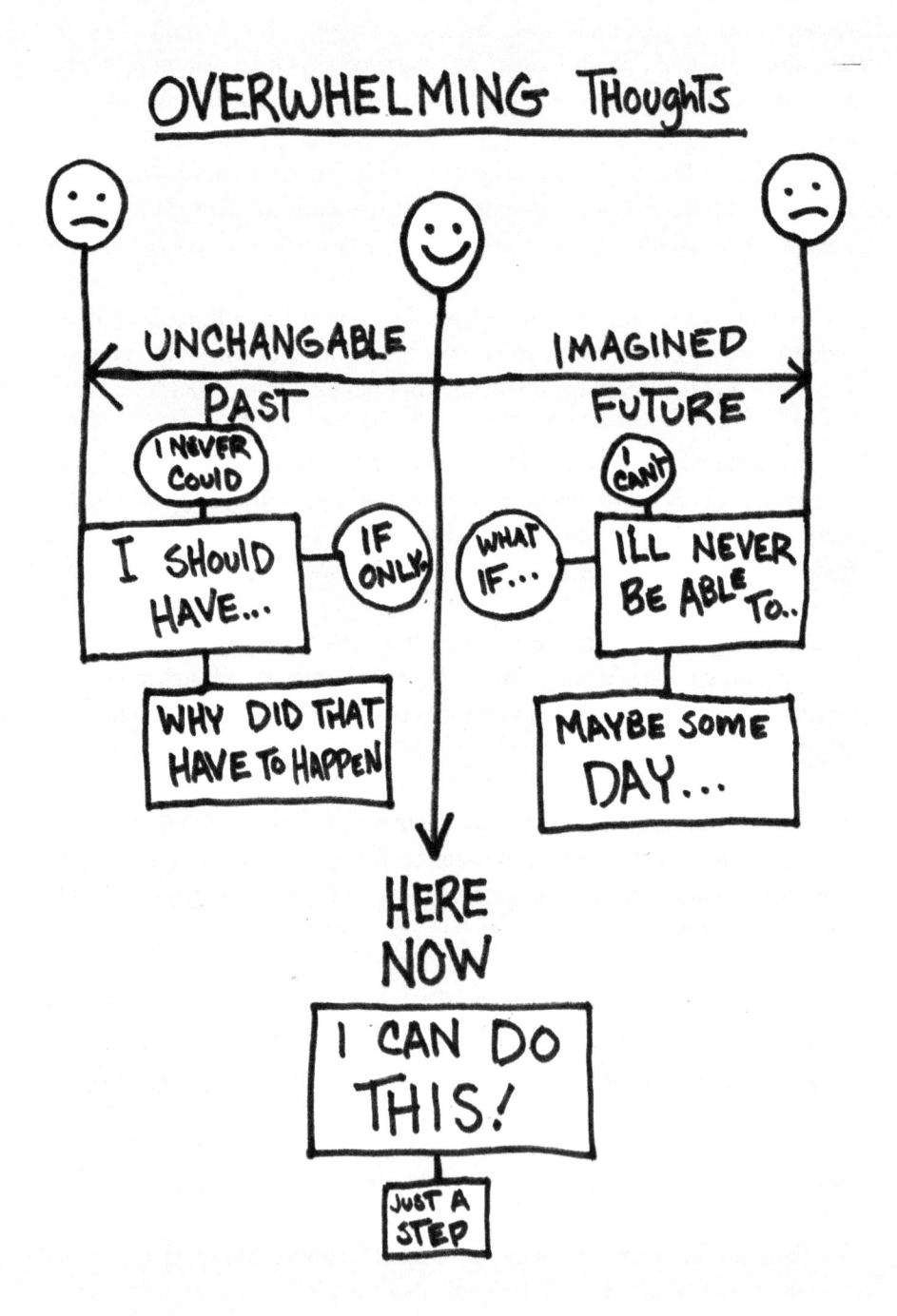

UNCHANGABLE PAST ← | → **IMAGINED FUTURE**

- I NEVER COULD
- I SHOULD HAVE...
- IF ONLY
- WHY DID THAT HAVE TO HAPPEN

- I CAN'T
- WHAT IF...
- I'LL NEVER BE ABLE TO..
- MAYBE SOME DAY...

↓

HERE NOW

I CAN DO THIS!

JUST A STEP

As the fantastic creative creatures that we are, we can conjure and vividly imagine a wide variety of brilliant excuses to limit ourselves to where we are and where we think we belong.

We can easily use excuses to rationalize our actions in any given situation or circumstance and not even realize that it is an excuse.

I like to call them *stories*.

Like any epic video game writer, we tend to tell our epic story, pose our limitations, and explain away why it is not the right time to pursue something.

We tell these stories with such effortlessness that we don't even see them as the anticatalyst to our lives. A lot of these stories have been floating around for so long that they make sense, and we don't see how lame they actually are.

"I didn't pursue an art career because my art teacher said I would never succeed."

There you are, your little video game avatar standing at the starting line bobbing in place.

On the screen before you is a virtual image of your art teacher shooting daggers from his eyes and blowing "You're not as talented as you think!" energy waves out of his butt.

That was me, true story. I just bounced in place for years, while the obstacles just kept adding up in front of me. Teachers, parents, friends, and discouraging comments only fueled my fear.

What a boring game.

The stories we tell, and excuses we use, are the main hurdles that any creative will find as they blaze their own trail through the creative wilderness.

THE ROGUE ARTIST SURVIVAL GUIDE

CHOOSE YOUR AVATAR

REDESIGN YOUR AVATAR

The best thing I ever did was take the image of my little bouncing video game avatar and turn him into a *bad-ass*. A while ago, I realized that my self-image (in my imagination) was not a very empowering one. In fact, there were a lot of situations where my self-image looked and felt like a victim.

When I looked back at that situation with my art teacher telling me that I would never succeed, my self-image was angry, yet downtrodden and hopeless. I looked like someone who had the wind knocked out of his sails.

What occurred to me, was that every time I thought about that moment, or talked about that experience, I was feeling emotions provoked by the self-image attached to that memory. I felt sorry for myself, I was a victim to this teacher who ruined my chances of an art scholarship, and affirmed that I would never make it as an artist.

Looking at that version of me and feeling sorry for him was utterly dis-empowering. I realized that no matter what has happened in my past, if I carried it with me, it would have an impact on my life now.

I had to rewrite that story and empower that sad little version of me from my memory into a *bad-ass* artist. Luckily there is a hack for that.

We think that our mind is like a video recording device that records moments in time. We believe our memories are actual flawless renditions of events that happened. Fortunately, they are not. Most of our memories are fabrications based on small tidbits of memory, suggestions, and feelings.

It's more like a game of telephone where you tell someone something, then they tell someone else, and after ten or so retellings, it is a different story than the original.

"Memories are malleable and tend to change slightly each time we revisit them, in the same way that spoken stories do." says Catherine Loveday, an expert in autobiographical memory at the University of Westminster. "A memory is essentially the activation of neural networks in the brain, which are consistently modified and altered." she says. "Therefore, at each recollection, new elements can easily be integrated while existing elements can be altered or lost."

Our memories are influenced by our perceptions, state of mind, knowledge, and even the person we are talking to when recalling events. This is also why the company you keep is so important.

I decided to change the story in a way where I didn't feel sorry for the younger version of me. I told the most empowering story I could tell, without taking away the learning experience.

The new story went, "One day in anger at my defiance, my teacher said I would never succeed as an artist. I took it personally and decided to quit my class. I blamed him for quitting for years. I used that experience as an excuse not to pursue my art. Ultimately I realized the choice was mine, despite what anyone says. I've got no one to blame. It's my choice."

This was way more empowering than the story I had been telling, which was "I wanted to do art for a living, but my art teacher ruined my chances." Something interesting happened. The more I told this story to myself and others, the more empowered I felt about the memory.

The more you tell an empowering story, and feel empowered while saying it, the more potent that memory becomes. The fact is that I told that original story so many times to so many people that I can't even be sure that it played out as terrible as I remembered. All I know is that it made me feel like a victim now.

In retelling the story from a different perspective, not only do I not feel like a victim anymore, but I am better prepared to face similar obstacles in the future.

We Make Up Stories

When ever we tell any story about something that happened to us, we feel all the emotions & are experiencing the moment again & again. With every experience, the memory changes slightly. The more you complain about something that happened the less "real" it is.

THE ROGUE ARTIST SURVIVAL GUIDE

DON'T BLAME ME
I WAS BORN
AWESOME

FACING YOUR CREATIVE FEARS

Fear gets a bad rap these days. It seems like everyone talks about conquering your fears, pushing through your fear, burying your fear, and getting rid of fear. I think fear is a good thing. It's the thing that causes you to be hyper-aware when you are standing next to a 1000 ft drop.

Unfortunately, fear is also what keeps us safely wrapped up in our comfort zones. It can prevent us from venturing out into the unknown and experiencing more possibilities. When it comes to my art career, every day is an unknown, there is no security blanket, and my next big failure is right around the corner.

Not every fear is created equal. Some fears are staring you in the face, and you have nowhere to run. Some fears take place entirely in the mind and are a figment of your imagination. Either way, you have to face them.

If at this very moment you are thinking of a deadline, or some art event that isn't happening right now, then it's imagined. We are poorly trained in dealing with imagined fear and problems. Chances are, when you are standing in front of the actual problem, you'll handle it much better than you think.

A moderate amount of fear is good, but being overwhelmed by anxiety can be paralyzing. If you can't actually do the thing that scares you just yet, then practice facing the fear in your mind with the intention of taking action. You can practice talking about your art in the mirror. You can also practice people rejecting your art and how you will handle it.

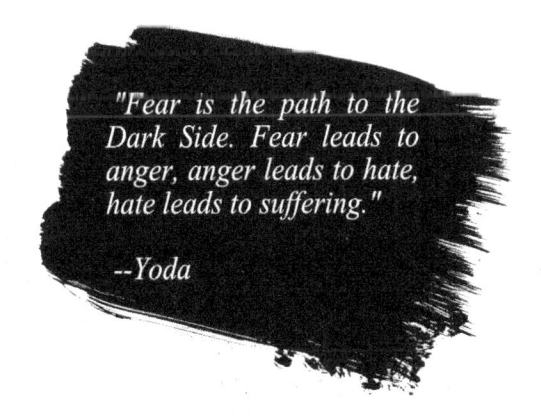

> "Fear is the path to the Dark Side. Fear leads to anger, anger leads to hate, hate leads to suffering."
>
> --Yoda

Get your friends to help you if you think it will be fun. The more fun you have with facing your fears in your imagination, the less power the fear will hold over your choices.

Imagine difficult situations before they occur. Imagine the result of giving into your fear. Really feel the cost of being ruled by fear, then feel the benefits of showing yourself that you are capable of facing the fear. Carefully weigh the two and see the difference.

Just be confident in your ability to figure out your way.

FAILURE IS A WORK IN PROGRESS

Avoiding failure is one of the most powerful motivations behind the intricate stories we come up with, that keep us from what we want. It's an interesting dynamic; we avoid doing things because we are afraid we will fail and in turn, feel like a failure anyway because we avoided trying in the first place.

In the video game reference, failure is like giving up one of your extra lives. In the real world, we fear failure because it comes to us with the promise that it is *one and done*. Yet, we can fail multiple times and still pick ourselves up and keep going.

I had a girlfriend that came with me to a ranch to go horseback riding, where I learned a powerful lesson about failure.

Admittedly, as much as I wanted to romantically ride off into the sunset when I was a kid, horses and I are not friends. I know, it's totally Me; horses are massive creatures that are very powerful, and they scare the crap out of me. Heck, we use horses as a measurement of power, that shows you how powerful and terrifying they are.

We were riding our horses around the ranch on a beautiful autumn day. I tried to look as macho and confident as I could muster on horseback. Someone had once told me that horses could sense fear, and I was hoping my *macho-ness* would mask the yellow-bellied emotional state.

Side Note: In European culture, the color yellow is linked to being cowardly or timid. The idioms yellow-bellied or just yellow are also used for fainthearted people or for people who aren't brave.

I was *yellow* that day.

My girlfriend suddenly started to gallop her horse around the track, and my horse decided it would follow eagerly.

Faster and faster, I pulled back on the reins and yelled at the horse to stop. I was terrified of falling off the horse.

Just then, her horse took a sharp turn, and my girlfriend went flying into a plastic barrel, bounced in the air, and landed hard in a sand dune.

I got off of my horse as quickly as I could and went to her.

She was leaning back on her arms, giggling to herself. I thought for a moment that she must have damaged her brain in the fall.

Then she got up, dusted herself off and got right back up on the horse. She waved me over to my horse.

I glanced over reluctantly at my steed... for the rest of the day, she had a blast, and I walked around the stables swatting horse flies.

My fear of failing at riding a horse put images of death in my mind and actually paralyzed me from enjoying myself. My girlfriend on the other hand, failed epically, picked herself up, dusted herself off, and got back in the saddle.

Whether or not you ride horses, play sports, create art, write music, or do anything in life, you are going to fail epically. I'll be honest with you, if you are pursuing a creative career, failure is unavoidable. It is inevitable when you are trying something new. When you take any risks, chances are you will fail multiple times. The problem is that we believe that failure is the end of the story.

Failure just means that things did not go according to plan, because things rarely go according to plan. This is when you need to pick yourself up and dust yourself off. This is where being flexible, adjusting, and getting back on track makes all the difference. It is impossible to truly fail unless you give up altogether. You can change direction, you can choose a different path forward, you can backtrack a little, you can adjust, just as long as you keep going.

We will talk, threaten, or scare ourselves out of committing to a project or a new idea simply because it is full of uncertainty, and success is not guaranteed.

You are going to fail, and I'm not saying that you might fail, or there's a possibility that you will fail; I am stating that if you take a risk, you are going to fail. You are going to fail hard, you're going to fail big, and you are going to fail a lot.

> A SINGER SINGS HORRIBLY IN PRIVATE WHEN PRACTICING TRYING TO HIT A NOTE... FAILING OVER & OVER UNTIL THEY HIT IT. FIND YOUR VOICE.

I have failed in my art career at so many things that I can't even count them for you. I have made mistakes, bad calls, right calls, bad decisions, bad choices, educated guesses, and they have all led to epic failures at one point or another.

You failed. So what?

Just remember, instead of giving up, adjust, change your tactics, switch it up, start something new, try again. Keep going, stand up, brush yourself off, evaluate the situation, and determine a new direction for yourself.

I don't mean that you keep stubbornly doing that same thing, the same exact way, and expect a different result. That's just insanity. Evaluate, change your tactic, adjust, and find a way to keep stepping forward. Make due with what you have, where you are. Sometimes that means being flexible enough to head in a completely different direction.

If you fail and keep going, then it is not a failure… It is merely a work in progress.

Everything I need to know about creativity I learned by making misTakes.

MAKE ALL THE MISTAKES

Be prepared to make mistakes. They are going to happen when you put yourself out there, or take any kind of risk. Chances are, you are going to make some huge mistakes. It's all part of any hero's creative story.

We are going to make mistakes, we are going to fail, we are going to make an ass of ourselves.

We may trust the wrong person.
We may make bad decisions.
We are going to make poor choices.
We are going to ruin a creation.
We are going to overthink things.
We are going to miss opportunities.
We are going to make a million mistakes, and that is perfect.

Making a mistake seems like the end of the world, but it's not. It means that you are putting yourself out there. You can't learn anything new without messing up and trying to make sense of it after.

How do you bounce back from it? How do you keep going? How do you respond to your mistakes?

I personally would want advice from someone who made mistakes along the way, because their knowledge is experiential and more profound. If the shit hits the fan, they are likely to have the know-how and flexibility to change direction and guide me.

Making mistakes is beneficial and critical to your growth in anything you want to do. It is what you do after the mistake that matters.

Many people put so much focus on avoiding error that they drive themselves crazy. They run in circles trying to predict outcomes to everything they do, in order to avoid getting it wrong. They wait for things to be perfect before taking action, only to find that perfection never comes.

> TO ~~ERR~~ ERR IS HUMAN.
> TO ART IS DIVINE.

I have a hard time recalling mistakes because I hardly see them as mistakes anymore. An error implies that it went all wrong, and you get nothing out of it but setbacks. Yet, everything that I have done in my career, whether it turned out awesome or sucked royally, has been a benefit to me.

One of the biggest mistakes I made in my career was putting myself in a situation where I felt like an employee to a gallery I joined. The experience lasted about a year, and I could call the whole endeavor a waste of time, but it wasn't.

In fact, I learned something compelling about myself: I am not willing to compromise who I am to follow the status quo or someone else's agenda. I learned that no matter what other people define as success, ultimately it is up to me to decide what I want out of life and what it means to be successful.

That makes the whole experience worth it… whether it was a mistake or not is just a moot point. Our knee jerk response to making a mistake is to feel bad, to feel like we did something wrong, or to feel like an idiot. I think that when we take a close look at how we react to making mistakes, we can challenge the fear.

We are going to make mistakes, they are unavoidable and necessary for growth, but how we respond to them makes all the difference.

The more mistakes you make, the more it means that you're pushing yourself into the unknown. Allow yourself to make as many mistakes as you possibly can, because then, and only then, will you know that you were heading down a path that you were blazing for yourself.

Focus on what you can do now. What kinds of things can you tweak to make them work for you? Be willing to make all the mistakes as you figure out how to be a Rogue Artist.

> Challenge is nothing more than a seed of opportunity.

Art By RAF

THE ROGUE ARTIST SURVIVAL GUIDE

WHAT IF...

- A GOOD THING?
- A BAD THING?

DOES IT MAKE YOU FEEL ~~STRONG~~ HAPPY & EMPOWERED?

YES → CAN YOU FOCUS ON GOOD WHILE FACING A POSSIBLE BAD OUTCOME?

NO → WHAT WILL YOU DO IF IT HAPPENS THAT WILL MAKE YOU FEEL STRONG?

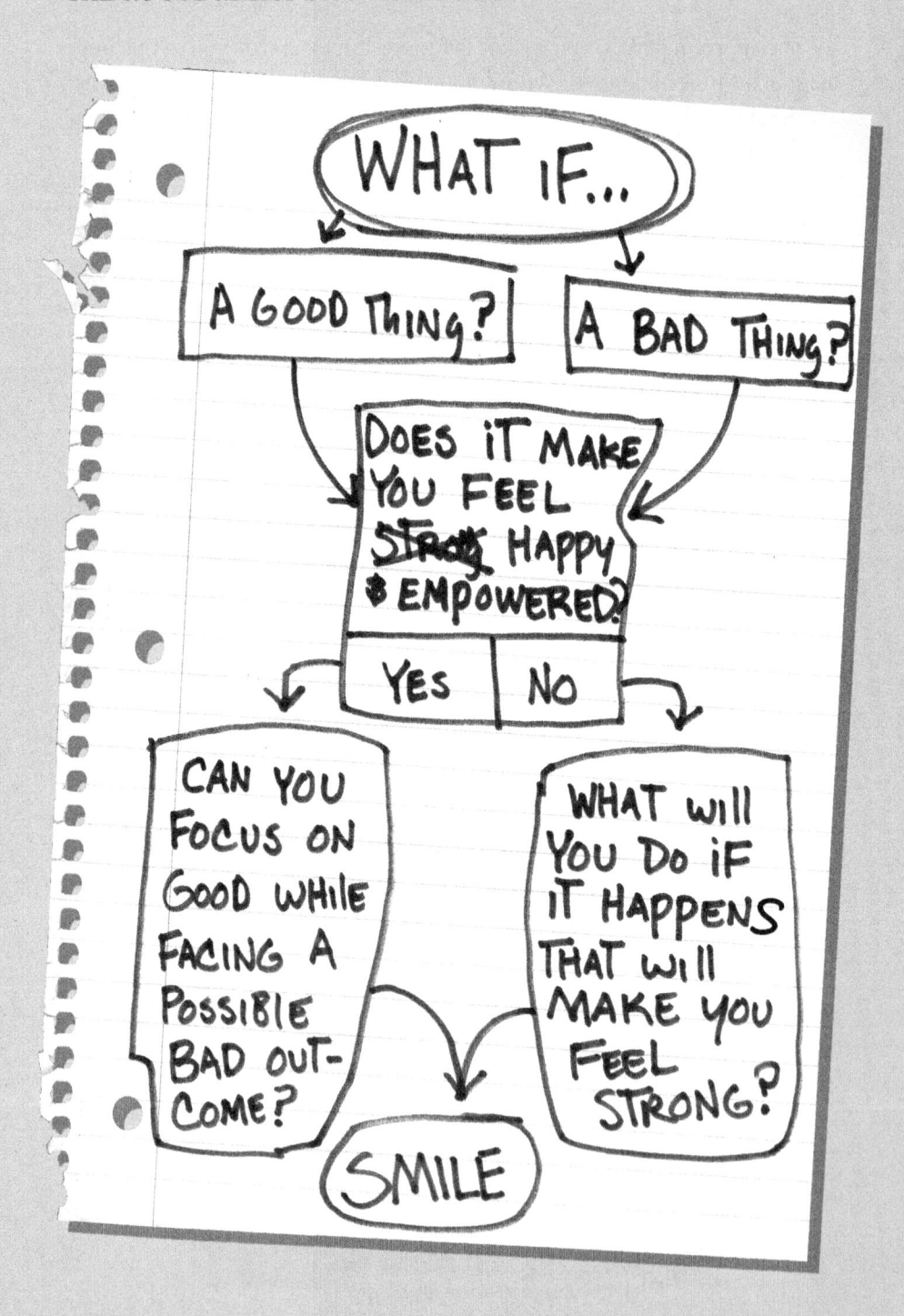

→ SMILE

LIONS AND TIGERS AND BEARS... OH MY

Uncertainty about the future is one of the main reasons we all cling to some semblance of security. It's easy to fear risk in something you've never done before, but sometimes people try to blanket themselves in safety that in of itself, is uncertain.

We've heard it thousands of times: There is no security in art, it's too risky. Don't be stupid, get a stable career.

We then spend our lives taking classes, getting jobs, and filling up our resume to achieve some stability. We chase stability and security for survival.

I worked in the corporate world for twelve years. In that time, I have worked for two companies that eventually went bankrupt. I was laid off and have been fired for not being sleazy enough to take clients to a strip club to close a sale.

When you work for someone else, there is the illusion of security, but there is nothing stable about it. You have someone telling you what to do, when to do it, and how to do it. Some of us find security in that. We know we will be told what to do, and we get paid for it. It's simple, reliable, and secure. At least until it is not.

As a self-employed creative, all the choices are in your hands, and no one is telling you what to do. That can be terrifying for some people. Since you don't have the experience to start an art career, you just flail around second-guessing every choice you make. You have no idea what the outcome is going to be, it all just seems like a risk.

Well, life is full of risks.

I had to train myself to be comfortable with uncertainty because most of my life, I was taught to avoid it. I spent a lifetime of people telling me what to do and what to think. Parents, teachers, bosses, and society were just a few of the influences that molded my way of thinking. If it wasn't part of the well-worn path, it wasn't considered safe.

This fear of uncertainty led to all the *"What if"* questions that I asked but never really answered with anything other than heartache and disappointment.

"What if things go horribly wrong, and I make an ass of myself?"
"What if I get rejected at the gallery?"
"What if I make no money?"
"What if I have to come crawling back?"
"What if I'm just not good enough?"
"What if..."

These are terrifying questions.

Because our ancestors spent most of their waking hours running away from lions and other deadly animals with large teeth, fangs, claws, and a taste for human flesh, we have a biological system in place to help us deal with dangerous situations.

The problem is that getting rejected at a gallery is not really a dangerous situation. Unfortunately, your body doesn't know that.

The same system that is perfectly designed to protect you from imminent danger is horrible at predicting outcomes.

Because we are not hunting animals and gathering berries to survive, we have associated the same dangers that come from lack of resources to money. We've balled up every fear associated with living into the almighty dollar.

Usually, the *what if* questions are dominated by the topic of money. Shelter, utilities, communication, food, warmth, clothing, transportation, and everything other than the air you breathe has been monetized. So instead of thinking "I need to gather our food." you think "I need money for food."

Everything we need to survive is in the green stuff. Our brain interprets that as an imminent threat that is always looming in the air.

The thing is, that our fight or flight system wasn't designed to stay in a constant state of stress, which is what you get when you fear uncertainty.

In the wild, an animal out in the savanna minding its own business, sees some bushes move and suddenly a lion shows up. Fight or flight kicks in. Suddenly it experiences an acceleration of heart and lung action, digestion slows down or stops, and it experiences an effect on the sphincter… in other words, the animal's butt puckers up.

In fight or flight we also experience reduced blood flow, dry mouth, dilation of pupils, and a whole cocktail of other symptoms.

All of these uncomfortable symptoms are because a superpower takes over. For the animal who noticed the lion, it will be able to haul ass out of there or battle with the best of them.

We all will experience this when we are in fight or flight, and for a good reason. If something is attacking you, the combination of all of these will make you quite formidable and bad ass.

Unfortunately, if you are in your living room worried about getting rejected, then it is less beneficial and becomes an anxiety attack. We humans are the only animals on the planet that can stay in a constant state of fight or flight. I think it has something to do with our powerful imaginations.

The thing that sucks is that it is not sustainable. Being in fight or flight for long periods can wreak havoc on the body and your emotional state.

In the wild, an animal will pop out of fight or flight once the threat is over and go back to grazing, or whatever animals do.

We humans imagine the threat over and over in our minds, which can keep us in varying degrees of that anxious state.

Changing your perspective on how you respond to uncertainty is vital to your state of happiness and your creativity.

I think the most important thing we can do is wrap our minds around the idea that security is an illusion, yet no matter what comes our way, we can always figure something out.

If you are alive and breathing right now, chances are you have already faced:

- *Rejection.*
- *Criticism.*
- *Failure.*
- *Money issues.*
- *Emotional issues.*
- *Betrayal, abuse.*
- *Mistakes.*
- *Accidents.*
- *Loneliness.*
- *Ridicule.*
- *A plethora of other things that live in the realm of uncertainty.*

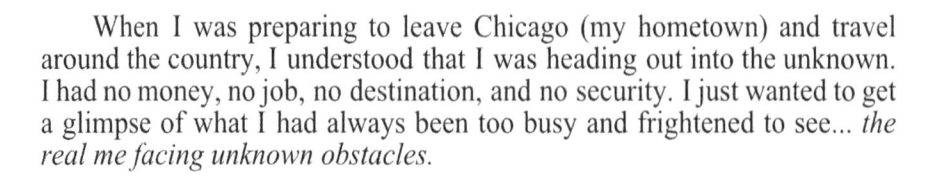

When I was preparing to leave Chicago (my hometown) and travel around the country, I understood that I was heading out into the unknown. I had no money, no job, no destination, and no security. I just wanted to get a glimpse of what I had always been too busy and frightened to see... *the real me facing unknown obstacles.*

I had spent my entire life up until then, feeling trapped in fear of uncertainty. Most, if not all of the decisions I made in guiding my life, were based on making sure I stayed safe and stable... what job I had, how much money I made, where I lived, where I hung out, and what my plans were for the future. Everything was designed to stay safe and predictable.

I had spent most of my life pretty unhappy, like I was living in someone else's skin and watching my life on a bad sitcom. Juggling problems and money to keep everything I had built from going to ruin had become a daily affair. I put aside my creativity because it wasn't safe and risk taking didn't fit into the model I had built.

Then I lost *everything*. Everything I feared actually happened, and despite the depression, remorse, and sadness, I was still there, and I had nothing left to lose.

I decided to try a new approach to life. I was going to do something different.

I want to point out before I continue, that my story is an extreme one. I am in no way suggesting that it is necessary to drop everything to move forward through uncertainty. I also think it is essential to be safe and not put yourself in any harm. Ultimately, you decide what is best for you and your life, but make sure you are doing it for the right reasons.

I met Klee around the time I was preparing to leave. Saying that it was love at first sight, doesn't even come close to expressing the immediate connection I had to her. She knew that I would be heading out on my adventure soon and made the decision to go with me.

Although I was delighted to have her join me on my journey, I had to make sure she understood the choice she was making.

"I can't promise you any stability or comfort. This trip is going to be really hard and push at every insecurity you have. You have to make sure that you are going for you... not for me." I said. "I have no idea where the money will come from, whether we will break down somewhere, or where we will sleep. The only plan I have is to face obstacles as they come."

I continued, "I plan to show myself that I am capable of facing my fears and overcoming anything. I have no backup plan. I only have three rules, I will not ask for a handout, I will not beg for money, and I will face every adversity with optimism and a smile. This trip is to teach me to enjoy life as it comes, warts and all."

She looked straight into my eyes and said, "I'll be taking this trip for myself, you're just a bonus. It is my decision."

I think that the most important lesson I learned that day was that if you are facing uncertainty, you have to choose to do so for yourself.

ART
RHYMES WITH FART.

JUST SAYIN'

If you ever find yourself having difficulty facing fear, uncertainty, or anything else habitual, try throwing a pattern interrupt at it. Something that is so out of sorts and weird that it throws you out of your downward spiral and onto a new track. Just something that distracts you, like the statement above did.

Worrying Makes You Dumb.

People will often tell me that the world is going to hell in a hand-basket, and that things have gotten worse over the years. Honestly, I don't buy that. The world has always been a bit turbulent, and political tribalism has always been a thing.

Just a couple hundred years ago, you would have been called a witch and burnt at the stake for bathing every day.

Overall, I think things are actually getting better.

People have always been afraid of the uncertainty that comes with the future. Whether it is your creative career, your relationship, your general sense of well-being, peace of mind, or the way you look at the world, you can look at the future with hope or fear.

You don't know what tomorrow brings, and the less information you have to go on, the more irrational and erratic your decisions can become. As artists, we are going to be navigating a minefield of uncertainty, and if you don't know how to handle uncertainty, you are going to make a lot of stupid decisions.

People seem to be under the impression that when you worry about the future, it means that you are being careful and rational. The truth is, that's not really how our brain works.

The limbic system responds to uncertainty with a knee-jerk fear reaction, and fear inhibits good decision-making and sends you right into fight or flight. When people are afraid, they make poor decisions.

That's right, when you are afraid of future circumstances, are desperate, or overwhelmed, you make bad choices.

This is why before I pursue a project, try to make money, or make any choice, I make sure I'm of sound heart and mind. Any ideas that I have had while feeling desperate for money, have always ended in disaster.

THE ROGUE ARTIST SURVIVAL GUIDE

Listen, I get it, we want to be in control. After all, people who feel like they're at the mercy of their surroundings seem to get stuck feeling like victims in life and don't move very far. I'm not suggesting you toss the reins aside and be at the mercy of your surroundings, I think you are much more powerful than that.

You can overcome any obstacle, but you have to be confident in yourself and your ability to roll with the punches.

Klee and I traveled for two years, and we experienced a fantastic adventure full of trials, tribulations, amazing moments, challenges, and life-changing opportunities. At no point did I fool myself into thinking that I was in control of the world around me. I wasn't at the mercy of my surroundings, I was in control of the way I chose to respond to any given situation. We ran into difficulties, and each one was an individual challenge to persist through the crap with optimism. I was focused on the solution and not the problem with every challenge.

On the road away from safety, I realized that the difference between life and death hung in the balance in every moment we experienced. We survived by making sure we embraced uncertainty with optimism, hope, and confidence in our abilities to make the most of every situation.

It is about feeling empowered.

I may not be in control of the circumstances, but I am in control of how I ultimately choose to respond. I know at any given moment, I can allow myself to behave like a victim or like a bad-ass.

That is what I learned from being on the road for two years. It has suited me well in pursuing something as uncertain as a self funded career in art. Uncertainty is just everyday life; you can either fear it or embrace your ability to excel in it.

You don't have to go on a road trip, quit your job, or do anything remotely like I did to embrace uncertainty. Do it at your pace, step by step. Just be aware of your willingness to embrace uncertainty and move forward in your creative life.

THE ROGUE ARTIST SURVIVAL GUIDE

Do you...

- Feel like its all or nothing?
- Over generalize?
- Jump to conclusions?
- Blame the issues?
- Tend to be negative?
- Expect disaster?
- Controlled by feelings?
- Stick to shoulds?
- Label everything?

Yes → Then stop.

HOW TO FACE UNCERTAINTY HEAD ON

If you're preoccupied with *what ifs* and worst-case scenarios, worry becomes a problem. Unrelenting doubts and fears can be paralyzing. They can sap your emotional energy, send your anxiety levels soaring, and interfere with your daily creative life. Honestly, it just plain sucks.

You can quickly get stuck in the ridiculous habit of worrying about things chronically because you think that worrying is productive.

For example, you may think:

"Maybe I'll find a solution."
"I don't want to overlook anything, maybe I'm missing something."
"If I worry a little longer, maybe I'll figure it out."
"I have to figure out a way to avoid things not working out."
"I want to be responsible, this is important, and I must think about it."

Some people feel like a victim to their worry and find themselves worrying about how much they worry. Stress and anxious thoughts can feel uncontrollable.

So if you find yourself worrying about something, what can you possibly do? There are a lot of ways to face uncertainty. From distracting yourself, reasoning with your worries, or trying to think positive, but not every worry is created equal.

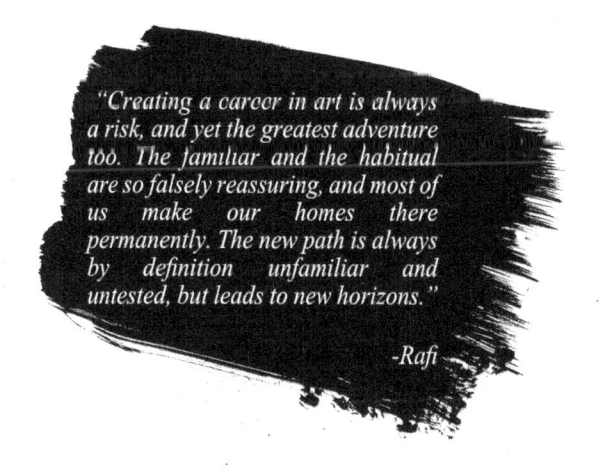

> "Creating a career in art is always a risk, and yet the greatest adventure too. The familiar and the habitual are so falsely reassuring, and most of us make our homes there permanently. The new path is always by definition unfamiliar and untested, but leads to new horizons."
>
> -Rafi

Luckily, there are patterns of worry habits that are easy to identify.

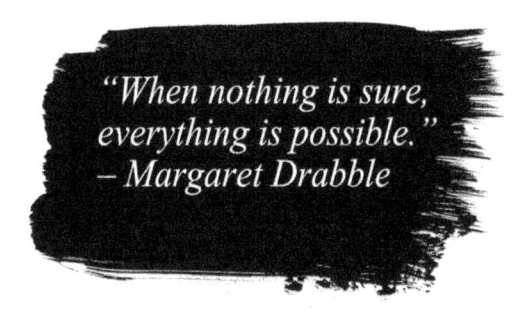

> *"When nothing is sure, everything is possible."*
> – Margaret Drabble

Worrying about stuff is not all that original, and chances are we learned it from someone else. Because of that, worry takes on very familiar forms. Take a look and see if you do any of these:

It's All Or Nothing: Looking at things in black-or-white categories, with no middle ground. "I can't get this painting right, I'm a total failure."

Overgeneralize: Making a generalization from a single negative experience, expecting it to hold true forever. "My art got rejected. I'll never make it."

Minimizing The Positive: Coming up with reasons why positive experiences don't count. "I did well at the show, but I was just lucky."

Jumping To Conclusions: Making negative statements without actual evidence. Acting like a mind reader, "I can tell they secretly hate me." or a fortune teller, "I just know something is going to go wrong."

Blaming The Issue: Assuming or giving blame for things that are outside your control. "It's your fault I got rejected. You should have never let me go through with it."

The Negative Filter: Being Focused on the negatives while filtering out all the positives. Noticing just what goes wrong and not what goes right.

Catastrophizing: Expecting the worst-case scenario to happen. "If I don't sell any art at this art show, my life is over!"

Emotional Rationalizing: Believing that feelings reflect reality. "I feel anxious right now. That must mean something is going wrong."

Should And Shouldn't: Being strict about seemingly rational things you should and shouldn't do. Beating yourself up if you break any of the rules. "I should have known better than to think it was perfect, that's why it got rejected."

Labeling Mistakes: Labeling yourself with mistakes and perceived shortcomings that have or haven't happened. "I'm a failure, an idiot, a loser. I can't do this."

If you find yourself doing any of these, and most likely you are, then you have identified your illogical way of looking at any issue. If you are worried, then you are negatively orienting your thoughts and suffering the consequences for something that isn't even real.

After you identify your habit pattern, ask yourself these questions about the doomsday thoughts that are banging around in your head.

- Is there a more positive way of looking at the situation?
- What would I feel like if none of this was a big deal?
- How would I rather look at this situation, what kind of person would I be?
- Can I decide to look at this however I want?
- Can I choose how I look at the situation?
- What would I say to a friend who had this worry?

It gets more comfortable and easy to answer these questions in an empowering way the more you do it.

Eventually, I had the realization that worrying about uncertainty is a waste of time. In fact, I found that worrying about anything was actually my way of distracting myself from the real issues and things that I could take action on.

THE 3 STEPS TO BEING HAPPIER:

1. Notice what you are feeling.
2. Notice what you are thinking.
3. Notice that the thinking created the feeling... (it's just a thought) THINK MORE GOOD!

YOU HAVE EVERYTHING YOU NEED INSIDE

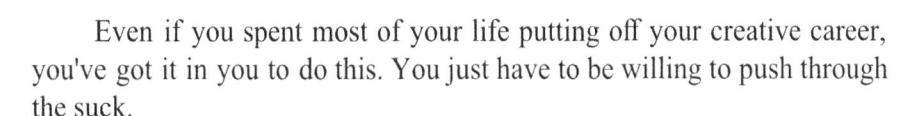

I know what you are thinking. But it's true.

Even if you spent most of your life putting off your creative career, you've got it in you to do this. You just have to be willing to push through the suck.

When you are faced with a challenge, do you doubt your own abilities to overcome the hardship? Or do you believe you can handle it?

This morning I got this comment on social media:
"Rafi...nobody wants my art. I'm starting to doubt."

I responded with, "Doubt is all part of the journey, but it is unnecessary because it doesn't help anything. It'll help if you don't make ridiculous statements like "Nobody wants my art." Just because your art hasn't sold, doesn't mean nobody wants it. If that were true, I have about 400 pieces that nobody wants. Just keep going, don't let your own head get in the way."

It is so important to pay attention to the dialogue you have with yourself. If it is discouraging and not supportive, then all you are doing is sabotaging yourself.

I'll usually play a game with myself and see how much better I can say things to myself.

- "Nobody wants my art." I evaluate the feeling. Say it better.
- "There are people that want my art." Say it better.
- "I've got plenty of art for sale." Say it better.
- "All the art I create will sell sooner or later." Say it better.
- "Everything I create is money in the bank."

I like that. New mantra, "EVERYTHING I CREATE IS MONEY IN THE BANK."

THE ROGUE ARTIST SURVIVAL GUIDE

The trick to this game is to get to a statement that makes you feel like a bad-ass when you say it. By re-framing the discouraging comments you make to yourself, you also give yourself a plethora of great responses to comments from other people.

Just remember, people are going to make their comments, criticisms, have their input, and have all kinds of reasons behind why they say what they say. No matter what anyone tells you, it will never have as big of an impact as what you repeat to yourself.

Whether or not you're telling those stories in your own mind or you're blurting them out in conversation, those stories have a power behind them.

Watch what you say.

I made the decision to become my biggest cheerleader... to develop a strong belief in my own ability to handle all situations that were thrown at me. This took time, but it gave me the tools I needed to stand up for myself, whether it was someone telling me that I could not do it or the voices in my own head trying to discourage me.

Become your own biggest cheerleader. This will improve your relationship with you, and it will enhance your ability to go all the way in whatever creative endeavor you decide. Also, remember that if you are comparing yourself to anyone else, that is not being a cheerleader. Feeling like you are better than someone else is fake self-esteem.

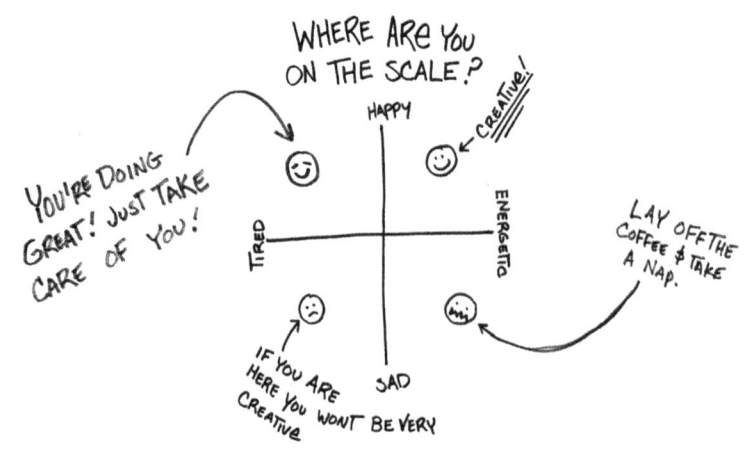

WHERE ARE YOU ON THE SCALE?

HAPPY ← CREATIVE

YOU'RE DOING GREAT! JUST TAKE CARE OF YOU!

TIRED — ENERGETIC

LAY OFF THE COFFEE & TAKE A NAP.

IF YOU ARE HERE YOU WON'T BE VERY CREATIVE

SAD

> Just because no one's ever done it before doesn't mean it's impossible.

Art By RAFI

Comparison Game

COMPARING YOURSELF TO ANOTHER ARIST IS REALLY DUMB.... YOU GET NOTHING OUT OF IT, OTHER THAN FEELING LIKE CRAP OR FEELING A FAKE ~~SENSE~~ GOOD

YEAH FAKE GOOD

CAPTAIN COMPARISON

I've noticed that some artists play the comparison game to make themselves feel better about their own art and career. They'll criticize an artist who has less experience than they do, in an attempt to feel better about themselves.

Unfortunately, this is a double-edged blade. If you use comparison to make yourself feel better, eventually some form of comparison is going to make you feel worse about your abilities and who you are.

Playing the comparison game of where you are versus where someone else is at this moment, is like being an insecure ass-hat in high school. You are always looking around, trying to be friends with people that you think are better than you. You then poke fun at people you think are less than you.

Your entire sense of self is based on the people around you. Your self perception is all about where you fit on the hierarchy. Take that hierarchy and them away, and who are you really?

Chances are, people are comparing themselves to you at this very moment. Some people will feel that they are better than you, and some will think that they are worse off than you. But are they right?

Those opinions don't matter in the grand scheme of things because it's all subjective anyhow.

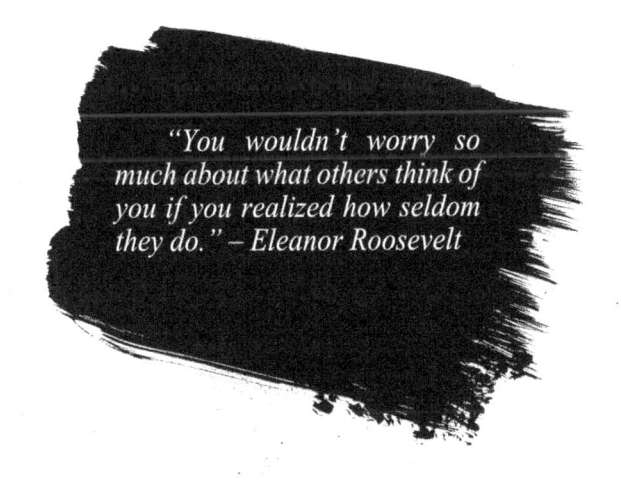

> *"You wouldn't worry so much about what others think of you if you realized how seldom they do."* – Eleanor Roosevelt

The main flaw with making comparisons is that you only see part of that person's life. The rest is all assumptions. The same thing happens when someone compares themselves to you, they have no idea all the struggles that you've gone through to get to where you are.

It all looks simple on the surface, but that is never the full story.

Most of the stories we tell ourselves about other artists are fabrications that have nothing to do with that person's actual life. It is a story that has everything to do with us and where we are.

Playing the comparison game distracts you from where you want to be and what you want to focus on. Make it a point to put your focus where it belongs... your own career, your personal growth, and your own journey.

Comparing yourself to another artist in a field where that other artist has already established years of experience, practice, mistakes, failures, and confidence can be devastating.

Listen, we all got started somewhere. Start where you are, and don't concern yourself with what anyone else is doing. Train yourself to focus on your own growth.

We will run into plenty of people out there who are going to compare our work to somebody else's work. I can't even tell you how many times I've been called Picasso or Pollock. I think it's ridiculous, but I also understand that some people make sense of the world by using comparisons even if it is nonsensical.

Whether it is a critic, another artist, or your uncle, let them make their comparisons, and you just keep doing your thing.

Only compare your work to earlier versions. Track your own growth as you practice, experiment, and push yourself to get better and better in your own creative field, on your own artistic path.

Don't confuse comparison with admiration and inspiration. I've been inspired by other artists, and there is a lot of work I admire out there. I just don't allow myself to discourage myself or inflate myself based on what anyone else is doing. That's their business.

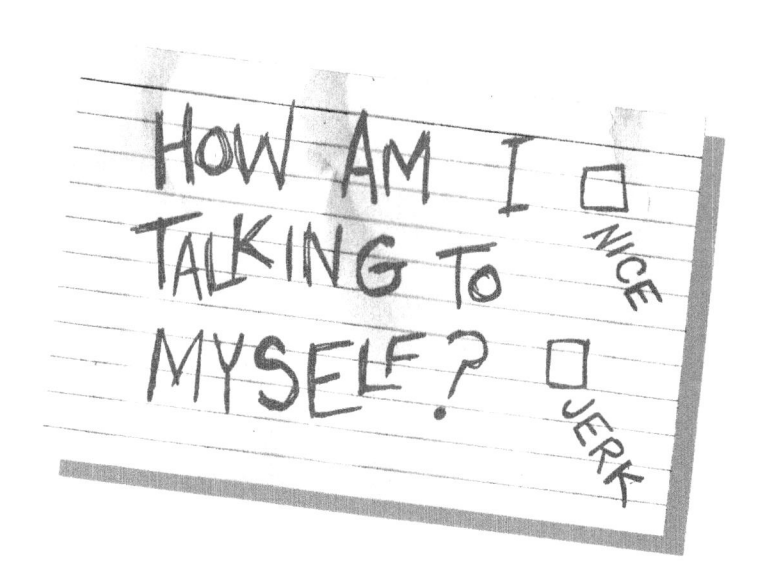

How am I talking to myself?
☐ Nice
☐ Jerk

WRITE YOUR OWN SCRIPT AS A CREATIVE

"How do I motivate myself to create art or keep going in my art career?"

I think that some of us out there are under the impression that motivation is something that you either get, consume, or find. I believe an essential factor to cover here is that your mind and body are complex mechanisms that respond to your environment and what's going on in your head.

THE ROGUE ARTIST SURVIVAL GUIDE

You may be feeling unmotivated because of your environment or because your mind is consumed by other things. If you are distracted by things that do not motivate you, then you may just find yourself sitting on the couch, staring blankly out into the nothingness, watching your artistic hopes and dreams fade.

There are times we get so wrapped up in the stories we tell, that we get discouraged. We doubt our own ability to find the motivation to do what we want to do. I find that it is all too easy to come up with these stories and then use them as excuses to stay complacent.

The following are some of the stories I tell myself at times. These have a significant impact on my motivation, especially if I'm feeling discouraged or hopeless.

- *I don't have enough time.*
- *I don't make enough money.*
- *I can't do this because I have kids.*
- *I don't have an education.*
- *I'm destined for failure.*
- *I don't know where to start.*
- *I'm not original enough.*
- *I'm a fraud, I'm not even a real creative.*
- *I'm not good enough.*
- *I'm interested in too many things at once.*
- *No one knows who I am.*
- *I can't face rejection.*
- *What if people hate my stuff?*
- *Parents, friends, teachers, relatives don't believe in me.*
- *I live in the middle of nowhere.*
- *I don't know how to market myself.*
- *I don't know how to use stuff online.*
- *I never finish what I start.*
- *Everyone thinks I'll fail, what if they are right?*
- *What if I run out of creative ideas?*
- *I don't have enough art to get started.*
- *I'm waiting for the time to be perfect.*

No matter how you adopt the stories that discourage you, it's best to remind yourself that it's just a story. Just because we repeat a story over and over to ourselves doesn't make it real, it just means you haven't explored other perspectives.

When you buy into your stories, you deny yourself the ability to express what you are truly made of. If you do not challenge the narrative, it becomes a limiting fact and that's where you leave it.

What would happen if you challenged those stories?

These yarns we spin can come in all shapes and sizes, something insignificant or something life-changing. These stories can also lead to a lot of regret. I noticed that I didn't have any regrets for the things that I tried, even if they didn't work out.

It was the things that I put off, the things that I wanted to do but just thought I wasn't good enough, and the things that I needed to get right... those were the regrets. I found myself wishing that I had at least tried them. To be honest with you, there is nothing that will destroy motivation like the stupid unfounded stories we tell ourselves.

If you are planning on moving forward with a career in creativity, you are going to need all the motivation you can get. A creative career is hard enough with all the outside factors. If you are making it even more difficult by reminding yourself constantly that you don't have what it takes, then you have an arduous struggle ahead of you.

Take a minute and think about what you've said to yourself today.

Was it critical?
Or was it kind and helpful?
How did you feel after you engaged this story?
Do you feel motivated to reach for the stars?

Your thoughts are the source of your emotions and moods. The stories you tell yourself can be destructive or beneficial. They influence how you feel about yourself and how you respond to circumstances in your life.

THE ROGUE ARTIST SURVIVAL GUIDE

THE STICKMAN

IS RUDE...

The Stickman In Your Script.

Klee and I call the negative storyteller in our heads the *stickman*. This helps us remember that the stories are not the voice of reason, but merely silly stories that aren't necessarily true. They are tragic comedies told by a ridiculous *stickman*.

Brené Brown, a professor at the University of Houston Graduate College, refers to the negative voices in her head as her gremlins. By giving her negative thoughts a name, she's both not taking them seriously and poking fun at them.

For the most part, we all take those stories so seriously and never question their validity. We are never taught to question our own mind, or question where those stories actually come from. In fact, my advice here will sound like crazy talk to some people.

I am suggesting that you remind yourself that *you have voices in your head that are lying to you*. I am also suggesting that you disassociate yourself from those voices so you can respond accordingly. We relate the stories to ourselves because we tend to use words such as "I" or "me."

"I'm a fraud, I'm not even really creative."

Klee says, "I woke up to the *stickman* in my head telling me that I'm a fraud today and that I'm not a real creative."

Her initial response to the comment in her head gives her the breathing room to be able to evaluate why she might be feeling that way, and not take it personally. It opens it up to the conversation, instead of it becoming law.

Klee will say, "Hey *stickman*, do you need a hug? Cause that's rude. Besides, I'm as real as they get."

See if you can identify the *stickmen*, don't take them so seriously, and don't allow yourself to get discouraged. You'll find that you will be much more motivated to keep going when you don't buy into what the *stickman* is trying to tell you, sometimes he's just rude.

HOW DO YOU TALK TO YOU?
TALK NICE TO YOU
BAD
GOOD
CYCLE OF DOOM
CAN BE CYCLE OF AWESOME
SELF TALK. WHAT YOU BELIEVE
WRITE A BETTER SCRIPT.
SELF IMAGE. HOW YOU THINK OTHER'S SEE YOU
THE WAY YOU SHOULD BEHAVE BASE ON SELF IMAGE

Writing A Better Script.

Spend a few days listening carefully to your inner dialogue and storytelling.

- Are you supportive of yourself?
- Are you critical or negative?
- Would you speak that way to someone you love?
- Don't you think it's about time you have a better relationship with yourself?

The stories we tell are the script that we use to frame our lives. If we are continually telling negative stories about ourselves, then we begin to develop an automatic adverse reaction to most circumstances. As a Rogue Artist, our inner dialogue is the most powerful tool at our disposal.

We can't always control what happens to us, but if we fear all the outcomes and tell ourselves terrible things, it is devastating. It's almost like a self-fulfilling prophecy; the more negative we are, the more negative crap seems to follow us around.

Conversely, if we engage in positive stories, we begin to view the world more positively and will ultimately feel better about ourselves. We're then more likely to turn the flashlight of our focus on opportunities and solutions rather than the problems.

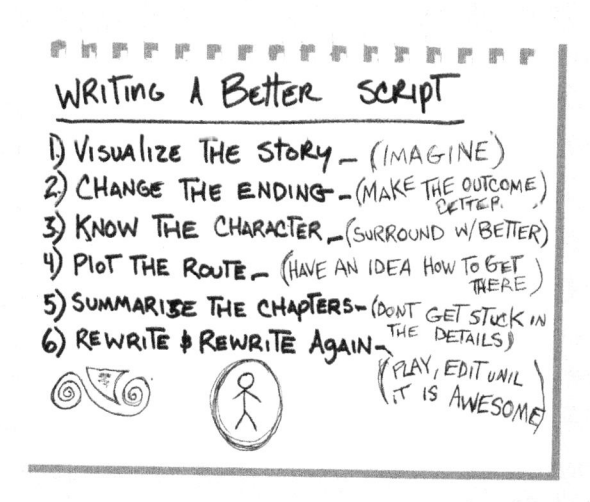

> **WRITING A BETTER SCRIPT**
>
> 1) VISUALIZE THE STORY — (IMAGINE)
> 2) CHANGE THE ENDING — (MAKE THE OUTCOME BETTER.)
> 3) KNOW THE CHARACTER — (SURROUND W/ BETTER)
> 4) PLOT THE ROUTE — (HAVE AN IDEA HOW TO GET THERE)
> 5) SUMMARIZE THE CHAPTERS — (DONT GET STUCK IN THE DETAILS)
> 6) REWRITE & REWRITE AGAIN — (PLAY, EDIT UNTIL IT IS AWESOME)

We can't always control what happens in our lives, but we can control how we respond to it.

Having an inner critic bash you 24 hours a day 7 days a week is honestly a waste of time. There are plenty of people out there who are going to bash you and try to put you down when you try to pursue a creative career.

I remember when I first started to reevaluate the way I talked to myself, I was surprised at how negative and unsupportive I was. I was repeating a bunch of bogus stories in my brain jar, meant to discourage me.

What was even more impressive was the pushback I got when I tried to be kind to myself. It almost felt wrong to call me a nice thing. I concluded that I had spent so many years calling myself a loser, that anything positive was uncomfortable.

The other pushback I experienced was feeling arrogant, vain, narcissistic, self-centered, egocentric, arrogant, cocky, boastful, smug, stuck up, and big-headed.

Why was it so difficult to just believe in me? To just be nice?

What I was experiencing was a miscommunication of ideas. On the one hand, we are told to love ourselves; on the other hand, we are advised not to be self-centered or vain.

I remember being in the gallery one day talking to another artist. I was pointing to one of my pieces hanging on the wall, and I exclaimed, "I love that piece, it's awesome." and she looked uncomfortable.

I asked her what was wrong and she told me, "That's very boastful of you." and I responded, "Sure, but I think that piece is awesome, is it wrong for me to like my own art?" She said, "No, but you should probably not let anyone know you do."

This conversation gave me an insight into why I struggled with the idea of loving myself. It is more accepted in society to call yourself a loser or stupid than it is to call yourself awesome.

In the end, I just said, "Well, I think you are awesome, and I am too. So we'll just agree to disagree, but not really disagree, because I know you think I'm awesome too."

It's important to note that when I say to be kind to yourself, in no way shape or form does that require you to put someone else down to lift you up.

If you find that you are comparing yourself and saying that you are "better than that person," then that's just rude. Not only is it rude, but it's not real.

It's ok to become your biggest cheerleader and develop a positive relationship with yourself. You are going to need all the backup you can get in traversing a creative career.

Some people may find it easier than others to adopt a positive outlook and tell better stories. Others may have to give it more time and put more effort into it. Either way, it's a worthwhile step toward bettering yourself and improving your sense of self-worth.

In having productive, positive inner conversations, your stories have no downside. Give it a try.

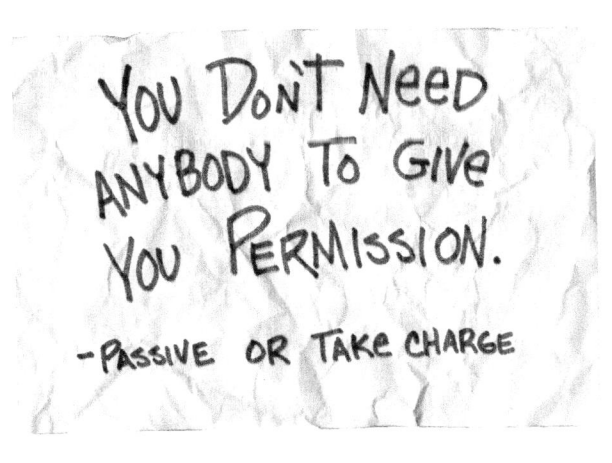

> YOU DON'T NEED ANYBODY TO GIVE YOU PERMISSION.
> — PASSIVE OR TAKE CHARGE

THERE Will Be Haters,
DOUBTERS, NON-BelIEVERS,
$ FINGER POINTING...
$ THEN
THERE
WILL
BE
YOU...
RAFI
PROVING THEM WRONG.
Believe IN YOU

LET THE CRITICS BE CRITICS

We've all been there. Someone decides to go on a tirade about your choices in life to pursue something creative. They say some bunk crap about you and whatever you are creating. Sometimes they make it personal, and it really gets under your skin.

Earlier, we talked about the uncertainty, which is riddled with fear of the unknown. This is the place where your most terrifying nightmares can come from. This is also a place where some of your most potent creative motivations can live. Unfortunately, out in the unknown, we also have the critic.

Don't get me wrong, I love getting constructive criticism and feedback from people who genuinely want to help me improve. Even if I don't agree with them at times, the input is appreciated.

I'm talking about people who make deliberate personal attacks on you and your art. They say something nasty that doesn't benefit you at all. These are comments that are meant to hurt.

Some hurtful comments don't just come from nameless trolls on the internet. The motivation behind them is not always the same, but they are all difficult to deal with.

They can cause you to lose your footing a little. Doubt and fear of the unknown may quickly surface as a result of reading or hearing one of these gems. Usually, it will be after a big event where you really put yourself out there in a vulnerable way.

After a negative comment, we can easily start to focus on everything that could go wrong. Our brains are wired to protect us in dangerous situations and that includes verbal attacks.

It becomes laser-focused on protecting you from danger. That works great when you have a drunk monkey chasing you with a knife. Unfortunately, it also causes a negative comment to stick in your mind like a bad song.

Negative Comments

Our own ~~familys~~ (family) can say really cruel stuff. I make it a point to always point out the flaw in their argument (they are usually not talking from actual experience).

"Great input! So how long have you been an artist?"

Well Meaning Negative Comments.

Sometimes, friends and family may make some horrible sounding comments because they are making a risk assessment and are trying to dissuade you from pursuing something that they have deemed dangerous. Mostly, their comments are their attempt to make you come to your senses.

The problem with most risk assessment is that until you are standing in the middle of what you are doing, you will not have an accurate estimate of what is actually going on. There may be opportunities that you can't imagine or roadblocks that you never predicted.

Whenever you tell someone that you want to pursue any kind of creative field, you may be met with a plethora of deadly risk assessments. People will point out everything that could go wrong. Most times, they have no idea what they're talking about. They can just as easily say that everything will go right. It's all the same, one way or the other. It is usually speculation that has never been tested out by the person spewing it.

The way I see it, every argument people pose as to why I won't succeed is an opportunity for me to show myself who I am. I think the secret here is not to wage war or become contrary.

To do this, you have to make sure you don't take their concerns personally. Remember, they are posing their assessment from what they believe is possible for them, not you... even if they think it's you that they're talking about.

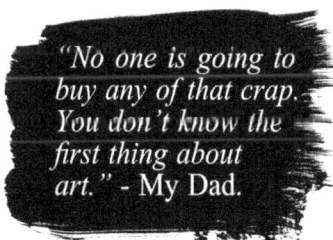

> *"No one is going to buy any of that crap. You don't know the first thing about art."* - My Dad.

If you take any comments personally, chances are there is a part of you that believes the comment to be true. Any feedback that pushes your buttons is an opportunity to evaluate the button.

THE ROGUE ARTIST SURVIVAL GUIDE

When Someone Pushes Your Buttons, Do You React?

Or Do You Respond?

They Are Your Buttons.

Listen, I am not going to sugar coat this. Dealing with rejection, criticism, and personal attacks is probably the hardest thing you will do in your creative career. When you put yourself out there, you are putting yourself in a position that is vulnerable to all sorts of commentary.

I think there is power in vulnerability. On YouTube, I try to remain as authentic and vulnerable as possible. I give my opinion about what it's like to have an art career; I show my failures, my wins, and when things are not easy. I talk about being nervous, scared, or when I'm feeling like an impostor. There is no script, and nothing about our videos is perfect. Yet, that is how I like it, that is authentically me.

We have slowly gained an amazing following on YouTube, but have also gotten some really nasty comments ranging from not liking my stupid face, to thinking that Klee shouldn't speak as much in my videos.

"Why does she keep talking in the background, doesn't she know how to shut up?" (YouTube Comment)

I responded with, "I know, right? Pretty soon, she'll be wearing pants, be allowed to vote, and have valid ideas and shit... what is this world coming to?"

To which he responded, "You're nothing but a man-gina wearing a dress!"

To which I responded, "Dresses are comfortable. You should try it."

I then deleted his comments and blocked him from our channel because I didn't want our followers to have to deal with an idiot.

That was one example of a comment that I was able to have fun with. I've gotten to a point where most comments don't really bother me, but there are still some that can knock the wind out of my sails. I suspect that there will always be something that will push my buttons.

When something really bothers me, I know it is attached to my own insecurities. That is the beauty of trolls, they know how to get under your skin. The choice is to either hide away from the world or put yourself out there and be vulnerable.

"Vulnerability is the core of shame, fear, and struggle for worthiness, but it appears that it's also the birthplace of joy." Brené Brown, author of Daring Greatly.

There is a quote from Theodore Roosevelt that sums up the critic:

"It is not the critic who counts; not the man who points out how the strong man stumbles, or where the doer of deeds could have done them better. The credit belongs to the man who is actually in the arena, whose face is marred by dust and sweat and blood; who strives valiantly; who errs, who comes short again and again, because there is no effort without error and shortcoming; but who does actually attempt to do the deeds; who knows great enthusiasms, the great devotions; who spends himself in a worthy cause; who at the best knows in the end the triumph of high achievement, and who at the worst, if he fails, at least fails while daring greatly, so that his place shall never be with those cold and timid souls who neither know victory nor defeat."

We creatives are in the arena when we put ourselves out there. We are going to stumble, we are going to fail, we are going to fall short, we are going to make the same mistakes over and over again. We will expose every button of insecurity and self doubt that we have.

We are the ones putting ourselves in the cross-hairs of the person who points from the sidelines. They may say they could do it better, they may laugh as we fall, they may point at all of our flaws, all from a safe distance, but the critic is no one without the creative gladiator.

So let them talk and point, but they will never know what it truly means to live in the moment of creation. Let them push your buttons, it will allow you to investigate your own insecurities. If something that someone said bothers you, it means you have some inner work to do.

THE MAN IN THE ARENA

"It is not the critic who counts; not the man who points out how the strong man stumbles, or where the doer of deeds could have done them better. The credit belongs to the man who is actually in the arena, whose face is marred by dust and sweat and blood; who strives valiantly; who errs, who comes short again and again, because there is no effort without error and shortcoming; but who does actually strive to do the deeds; who knows great enthusiasms, the great devotions; who spends himself in a worthy cause; who at the best knows in the end the triumph of high achievement, and who at the worst, if he fails, at least fails while daring greatly, so that his place shall never be with those cold and timid souls who neither know victory nor defeat."

Theodore Roosevelt

Most times, when you feel vulnerable, it's like you are falling down a well... slowly tumbling down in a sea of hands that have the option to either lift you up or push you further down. You can easily feel a sense of uncertainty and like you have no control, like your emotions are at someone else's mercy.

I would argue that although you can't control what someone may say or think, you always have control over how you respond. Even if you have a knee jerk response, you can still gather yourself and respond in an empowering way. Be prepared to have your buttons pushed, and expect buttons to surface that you are not aware of. Discovering and facing your buttons, gives you the opportunity to do something about them.

Whether you are an aspiring artist or a veteran, be prepared for the uncertainty and remember that YOU are in the arena. Be confident in your ability to face adversity your own way.

I like to say that if I get dropped off in the middle of a jungle of nasty critics, two weeks later I will have built a happy tree-house. I'm talking about the ability to be confident in your choices, yet be flexible and willing to make mistakes.

To fail, dust yourself off, and stand back up even when everyone is telling you that you suck, is the most powerful thing you can do for yourself as a creative.

It comes down to this... if you don't want to be criticized or judged in life, then don't ever do anything amazing. Stay invisible and safe.

If you want to be a bad-ass creative, then chances are some folks are going to finger point and flap their lips about you. Use it as an opportunity to look within yourself and improve your own critic in your head.

Listen, critics have the right to criticize. Haters have the right to hate. Naysayers have the right to naysay. People have the right to make their lives as miserable or as excellent as they want. You can judge and criticize them too, or you can focus on what you got going on.

Some really talented artists I know don't move forward in their careers because they are too busy complaining about people who put them or their art down.

They whine and complain about the system, the galleries, the people in their town, other artists, their parents, everything.

They get stuck in blaming others for their misfortune, or things not going their way, instead of figuring out a solution. They get stuck, running in place, and going nowhere.

I can't tell you how many times I've had full-grown adults tell me that they didn't pursue something because their parents weren't supportive when they were kids.

C'mon, really? Are you still using that lame excuse?

One of the most destructive things we can do as creatives is play the blame game. If we are going to do that, we might as well just give up. When you do any finger-pointing, you are just giving away your creative power.

When A Harsh Critic Attacks.

How do I take harsh criticism? Not well, sometimes. However, I do have a trick up my sleeve that has helped me get better and better at dealing with poo-flinging critics.

I think it is a necessary plight that one will have to get used to when you are putting yourself out there. I am an artist who creates art, music, writing, YouTube videos, and puts them all out there for the world to see... I get a lot of negative criticism.

Listen, sometimes even a helpful criticism can be hard to hear, and our first response may be to run away, flailing our arms helplessly, but sometimes it's valid. If the criticism is entirely invalid, totally off, and only meant to hurt you, then that's what I'm talking about here.

So what do I do when someone is all *"Blah blah blah you suck Rafi blah blah blah!"?*

I *don't* take it personally. I believe that it takes a miserable person to try to make themselves feel better by trying to bring someone else down, and that misery doesn't belong to me.

If someone says something nasty to you or harsh, don't take it, it's not yours, and it doesn't belong to you. Understand that people who are in pain can say some really hurtful things, especially people that are close to you and may know which buttons to push.

Think about a time when you may have said something terrible to someone.

- Were you in your right mind?
- Were you in pain?
- Were you feeling like a victim?
- Did you say something mean on purpose to hurt them?

I'm not saying to feel sorry for trolls and ass-hats. I want you to understand that what comes out of anybody else's mouth about you, has nothing to do with you. Usually, if something that someone said is really bothering you, it is because, to one extent or another, part of you believes it's true.

Understand that it is YOUR buttons being pushed. Why is it that one person can be called ugly and not even react a little, but someone else will blow a gasket? It's because we all have our own little triggers based on our own insecurities. Figure out what's behind it and sort it out.

Are you going to simply stop being who you are because someone spewed some garbage at you? Of course not. On the whole, very few people will talk smack in my life, and they either get ignored, deleted, or blocked. I personally take the encounter as an opportunity to get rid of the insecurity that I've so graciously been made aware of.

Listen, people talk crap all the time. Most of them are not putting themselves out there in the muck, sweating, bleeding, and enduring the terrifyingly exhilarating ride that is fulfilling your dreams.

They are going to say you can't sing, you can't paint, you're not funny, you're are not good enough, and more. The naysayers can quickly destroy your hope and get you to stop. Don't EVER let someone who is not putting themselves out there in the muck discourage you from going all the way. If they are not doing it themselves, facing critics of their own, then they have no right to talk.

If you're not able to push all of the negative words aside right away, don't get discouraged. It takes practice, but it gets easier and easier.

As *Rogue Artists*, we roll with the punches, and don't allow ourselves to take anything personally, especially when we feel that it is directed at us.

A lot of people will suggest growing a thicker skin or putting a wall up, developing a self-defense mechanism, and I would have to disagree.

When you do that, you end up burying the real feelings under a layer of protection. That's dangerous because although on the surface it may seem like it's not getting to you, we all know the truth hardly ever sits on the surface… unless you are authentic.

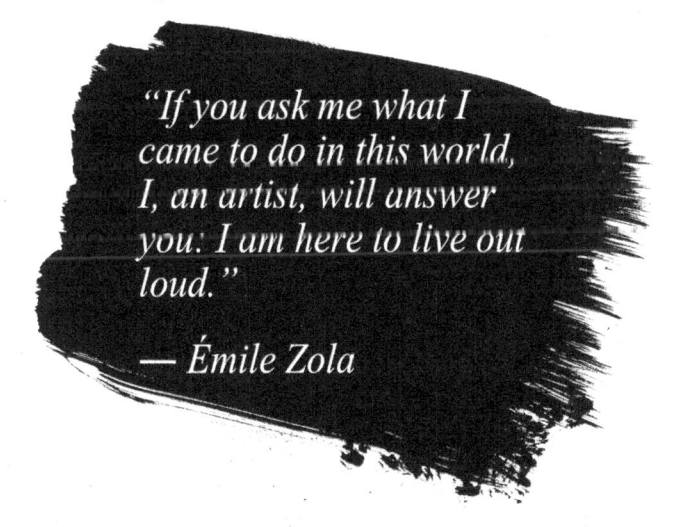

> *"If you ask me what I came to do in this world, I, an artist, will answer you: I am here to live out loud."*
>
> — Émile Zola

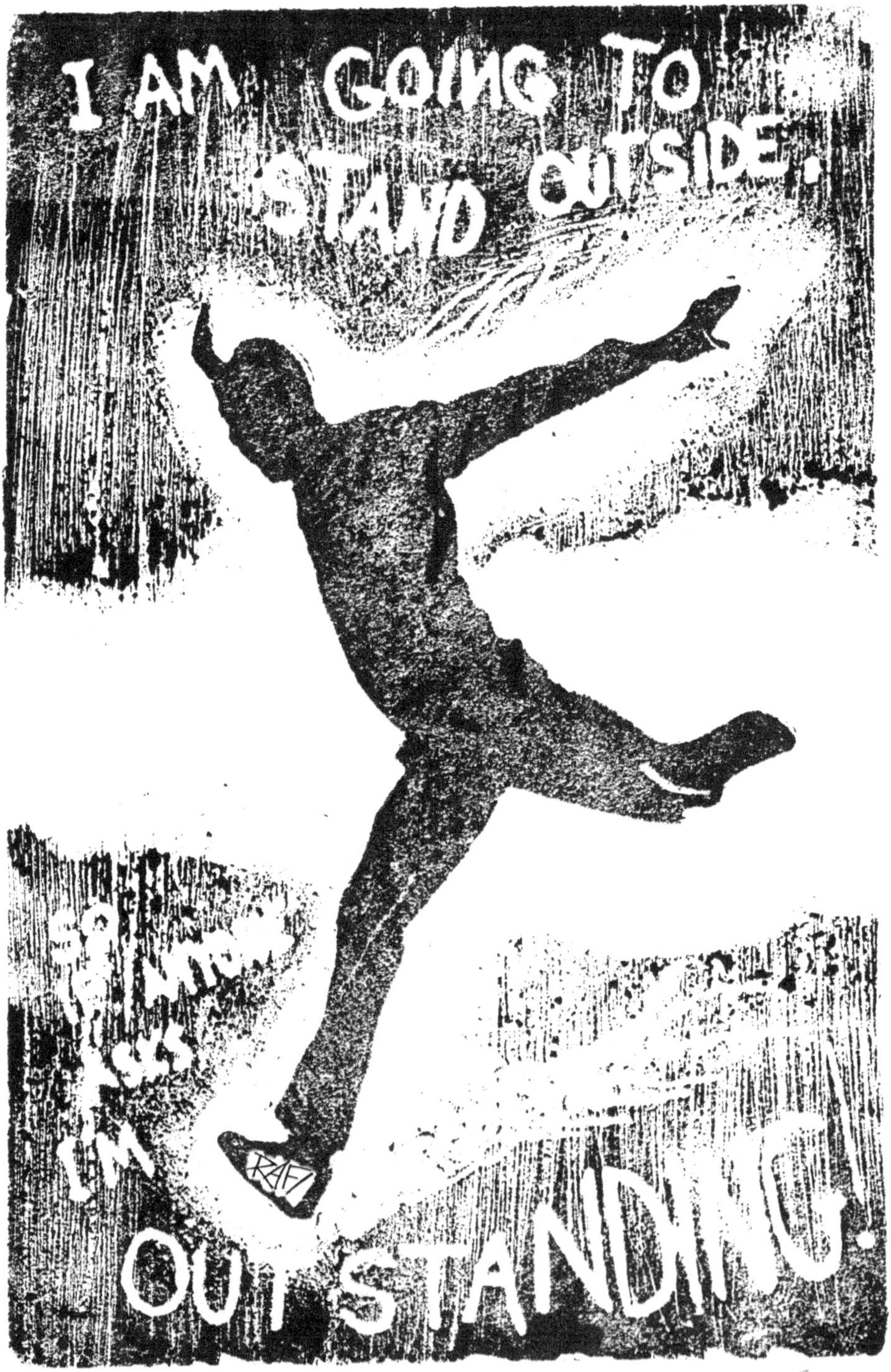
I AM GOING TO
STAND OUTSIDE.
OUT STANDING!

PROBLEM-SOLVING VS FINGER POINTING

When you convince yourself that it is someone else's fault when you experience an undesirable outcome, you end up giving up your sense of power in the situation or circumstance.

Instead of being proactive, flexible, and making the necessary changes to resolve or change the situation, you end up feeling like a victim. If you get stuck on the idea that it's someone else's fault, you leave yourself zero options other than just blaming them. Honestly, that's not going to get you very far.

I'm also not saying to blame yourself. I'm saying to look at the situation objectively without throwing ANY blame around. If you blame yourself or another person, you will be focused on something you can't do anything about. If you move past blame altogether, you can focus on a solution.

If I'm feeling like a victim to a person, place, thing, circumstance, weather, or anything, I pause and remind myself that I am not a victim to anyone or anything. I get to choose how I respond to each and every situation that comes up. That is where my power lies.

If someone says, "The gallery rejected my art, that's why I can't show my art anywhere." I call bullshit. There are so many options to show your art, you don't need a gallery to say yay or nay. If you are not showing your artwork, it's because YOU are not showing your art.

Take Responsibility.

Hand in hand with not blaming others is taking responsibility. It's important not to allow yourself to blame yourself when taking responsibility. It's not about feeling guilty about something or feeling bad; it's about taking ownership.

Taking ownership of your own actions and their consequences will allow you to make a choice. Making a choice and taking action when things don't work out will enable you to take ownership of your life. It is only when you have ownership of your life, that you can adjust your actions accordingly.

Even if it seems blatant that it's someone else's fault, remember this thought: "Alright this happened, and I'm not going to get anywhere by laying out blame, but I am going to get somewhere by taking action at this very moment in time and moving forward from here."

Take action now, don't wait around for permission.

Whether you have a great plan, or you only know the first step, it is essential just to start. Sitting around, thinking about doing something is just that, sitting around and thinking about doing something.

How To Take a Compliment

WRONG!
- ✗ Makes you feel bad
- ✗ Makes them feel bad
- ✗ Dismisses their opinion

RIGHT!
- ✓ Makes you happy
- ✓ Makes them happy
- ✓ Improves your sense of self
- ✓ Shows your appreciation

Don't be dumb... Accept compliments

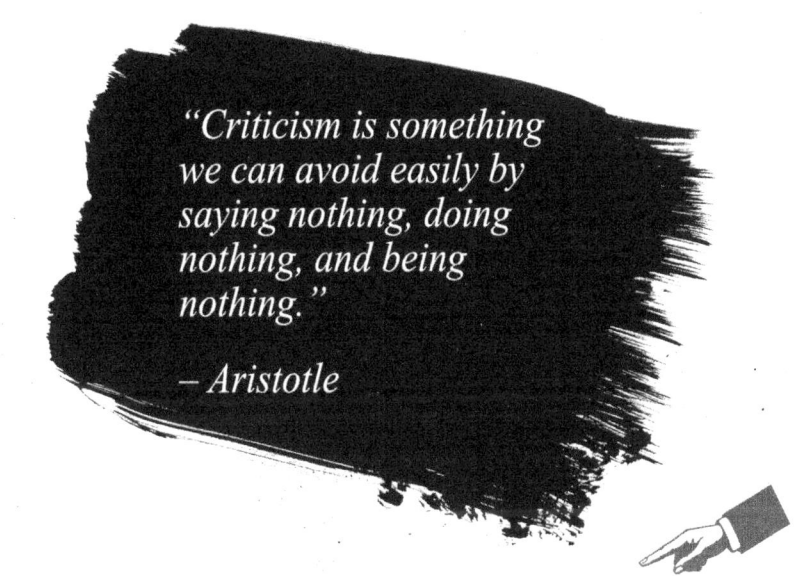

> *"Criticism is something we can avoid easily by saying nothing, doing nothing, and being nothing."*
>
> *– Aristotle*

THE NOT SO GOOD, THE BAD, AND THE UGLY

The ugly side of the art business is like the nasty side of anything. The most common underlying sources for ugliness in the art world are deep insecurity, greed, victim-hood, and overcompensating for insecurities.

Bullies usually pick on someone weaker than they are. This ultimately occurs because there is or was someone picking on them. They may have spent years feeling powerless to someone else. When you live this way, you may have an understanding of the world that might be a little warped by the experience.

Power struggle relationships are all about domination and control. The bully gets their sense of power and self-esteem by making someone else feel powerless. Because the bully is constantly relying on someone else to be weaker than they are, it is a very codependent way to feel good and is an illusion.

Whenever someone feels the need to put someone else down, usually, it is attached to the need to lift themselves up.

Although many of us know that lifting yourself up is a matter of paying attention to and improving your relationship with yourself, some people require someone else to be kicked down a notch to feel superior.

It is a false sense of self-esteem and completely unpredictable. Unfortunately, a lot of people may not even be aware of the core of that behavior.

There are all kinds of bullies in the art world. They come in all shapes and sizes. Some bullies are obvious, but some just seem to throw their weight around out of entitlement.

No matter what the degree, if you are walking away from any interaction feeling like a victim in any way, then you need to regain your footing.

Who Are These Critics Anyhow?

If you are putting yourself out there, you are going to run into rejection, haters, feeling invisible, and trolls. The question isn't, "How do I avoid encountering these?"

It is, "How do I handle it when I do?"

It would be fantastic if I could tell you that avoiding antagonists is possible… but it's not. When putting yourself and your work out there, you are inevitably going to run into all of them.

The only way to avoid haters and critics is never to put yourself out there. If you are doing ANYTHING with your life that is extraordinary, you are going to have people that love it and people that hate it.

Not all haters and critics are created equally, and it is crucial to identify which is which so you can respond appropriately.

The Constructive Critic. This is somebody who genuinely has an opinion about your art, and they are just expressing that opinion. They are not mean about it or rude. They are usually trying to give you some kind of help or advice from their point of view. Try not to take it personally and engage in a conversation if you can, you may get a different and valuable perspective.

The Nonconstructive Critic. This is the person that is going to say some stupid thing about your art that gives you no benefit whatsoever. Usually, they are trying to show off how smart they are, or they are just being rude. Don't listen to them, and don't take it personally. It can be an artist who uses this tactic to feel better about themselves and their own art, or some random jerk face. Pretentious people need to put something else down to lift themselves up. It's a false sense of validation for them, which crumbles when you laugh and walk away.

The Hater. This one is interesting to me. A person that simply cannot be happy for another person's success. So rather than be satisfied, they make a point of exposing and focusing on what is wrong. This is somebody who basically just goes around hating on things because their life sucks. Because of this, they want to knock someone else down a notch. The nonconstructive critic and troll are close variations of a hater. Needless to say, their opinion just doesn't matter, so don't take it personally.

The Troll. Someone who deliberately tries to piss people off online. Their goal is to instigate, get a reaction, and shock people. These sad souls may even follow you online, just to troll you. They mostly thrive in the anonymity of being on the internet. Definitely don't take anything a troll says personally. Don't feed the flames by engaging either. That is what they want. I know a troll, and she seems to get a twisted sense of validation when an argument erupts because of what she posted. Ignore it, block, delete, and move on.

No matter what you run into, don't ever allow anyone to make you feel wrong about who you are. Ignore the hater and walk away or laugh at their idiotic behavior, but make sure you feel empowered in your interaction. Most importantly, don't take any of it personally. Take appropriate action to get them out of your life if they are toxic to you.

BE THE BLUE FLAME

How To Deal With Art Bullies And Other Conflicts.

You may have some conflicts as you navigate your new creative journey. There are all kinds of personalities in the art world that are going to test us. Knowing how to deal with any conflict ahead of time will give you more confidence in moving forward. That way, if it comes to verbal fists-to-cuffs, you know you have your oral brass knuckles on the ready.

Even if it is a bully, the person may not be aware that they are one, but it doesn't matter. This is about personal power. Here are some of the things that I focus on when running into any conflict situation.

Be The Blue Flame. They may be in a heightened emotional state, and you might also be. It doesn't need to be a be-all-end-all conflict. Keep your wits about you and don't become the red flame. Just speak up confidently. Most bullies are expecting someone to explode on them or cower, but they won't expect strong confidence. Deep down, they doubt they deserve your respect. They may even admire you for speaking with self-assurance and confidence. So when they bombard, don't counter punch. Just stay strong, firm, courteous, and awesome.

Stay Connected. Bullies operate by making their victims feel isolated and hopeless. When you feel alone, you feel powerless. Having a creative career can already be isolating. Maintain connections with supportive, creative people. I think that the whole gatekeeper system would crumble if we artists realized that the art world system that is in place is based on middlemen making a profit.

Use Simple, Unemotional Language. I tend to be very matter a fact and unemotional in my confrontations with art bullies. When you do this, it sends a clear message that you are not going to be victimized. I don't make excuses or seek forgiveness, but I don't get emotional and challenge them either. A challenge gives a bully the attention and sense of power they are seeking.

"Beautiful"

Definition:
A person who is reading this

Don't Be A Balloon, Be A Human. Don't let them deflate you or inflate you to the point of bursting. If they're attempting to belittle you, call them out on it. "Did you just try to shame me right there? Not cool, not cool." If they're attempting to hurt or enrage you deliberately, call them out on that too. "Are you trying to invoke my inner hulk? You're better off dealing with me."

Set Boundaries And Limits. The trick is to remain polite and friendly while still setting your limits firmly. Don't let the art bully get under your skin, that's what they want. Practice your response, so you're prepared for the next time something happens, and you can respond swiftly without getting emotional. Practice feeling confident and strong when interacting with this person. Keep it simple: "I don't think your tone is appropriate."

Listen, But Remain A Little Skeptical. Listen to that person's point. Really listen. If you're not listening, you're gonna look stupid, and you might miss a chance to have an actual conversation. You don't need to dismiss their viewpoint, but you don't need to accept it as "The Word."

Remember that your points are valid, and so are theirs. There's no need to get angry or cower in fear. Everyone has a perspective based on their life experiences. No one has to come out as "right" or "the winner" to resolve conflict.

Act Quickly And Consistently. The longer someone has power over another person, the stronger the hold becomes. Often, bullying begins in a relatively mild form, name-calling, teasing, or minor physical aggression. After they have tested the waters and confirmed no conflict, and that person is not going to stand up for themselves, the aggression worsens. Nip it in the bud, and keep nipping it every chance you get. They may keep testing the waters, so stay consistent.

Ask A lot Of Questions. Asking questions allows you to get clarity on where they're coming from. It shows them you're actually listening and will enable them to think more deeply about where they stand. It also allows you to express yourself and guide the conversation where you want it. Sometimes people are afraid to ask questions during a confrontation, but I think it is a powerful tool.

Try Not To Argue Semantics. You can get lost in the minutia of back and forth points. This trade-off can be a never-ending battle if you let it. Try to keep focused on the main overarching topic, so you don't go around in circles trading proverbial punches.

Practice Not Just The Words, But The Feeling. It's great to practice empowering things you might say in the face of conflict. Just make sure you do not have an imaginary argument that leaves you feeling upset or dis-empowered. Practice the feeling of empowerment so that when the moment happens, you can actually get the words from your brain to your talk hole.

Strike While The Iron Is Freezing. Most people in conflict expect immediate rebuttals. Taking a pause will not only allow you to center yourself and process, this also acts as a pattern interrupt. You might even say, "Give me a moment, I'm processing what you've just said."

Remember, you are capable of pulling the camera lens back and separating from the emotion to get a more unobstructed view. Take yourself out of fight or flight mode so you can communicate clearly and confidently. Sometimes all you have to do is to take a pause and wait. Rather than exchanging hostilities, step back so that you are not reacting in the heat of the moment. Keep your cool. Stay in control and confident of who you are.

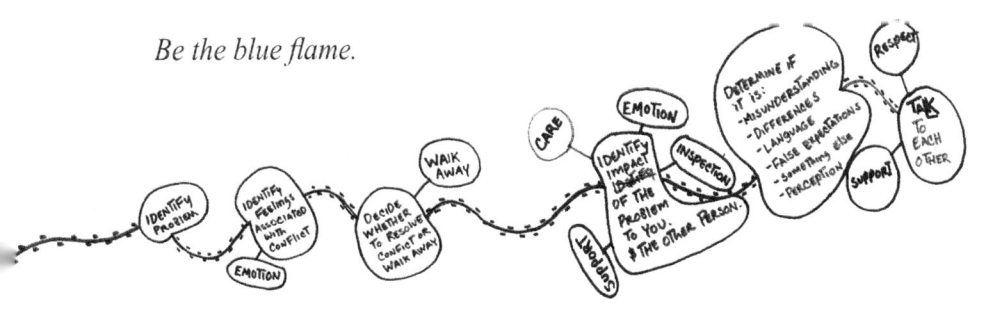

Be the blue flame.

THE ROGUE ARTIST SURVIVAL GUIDE

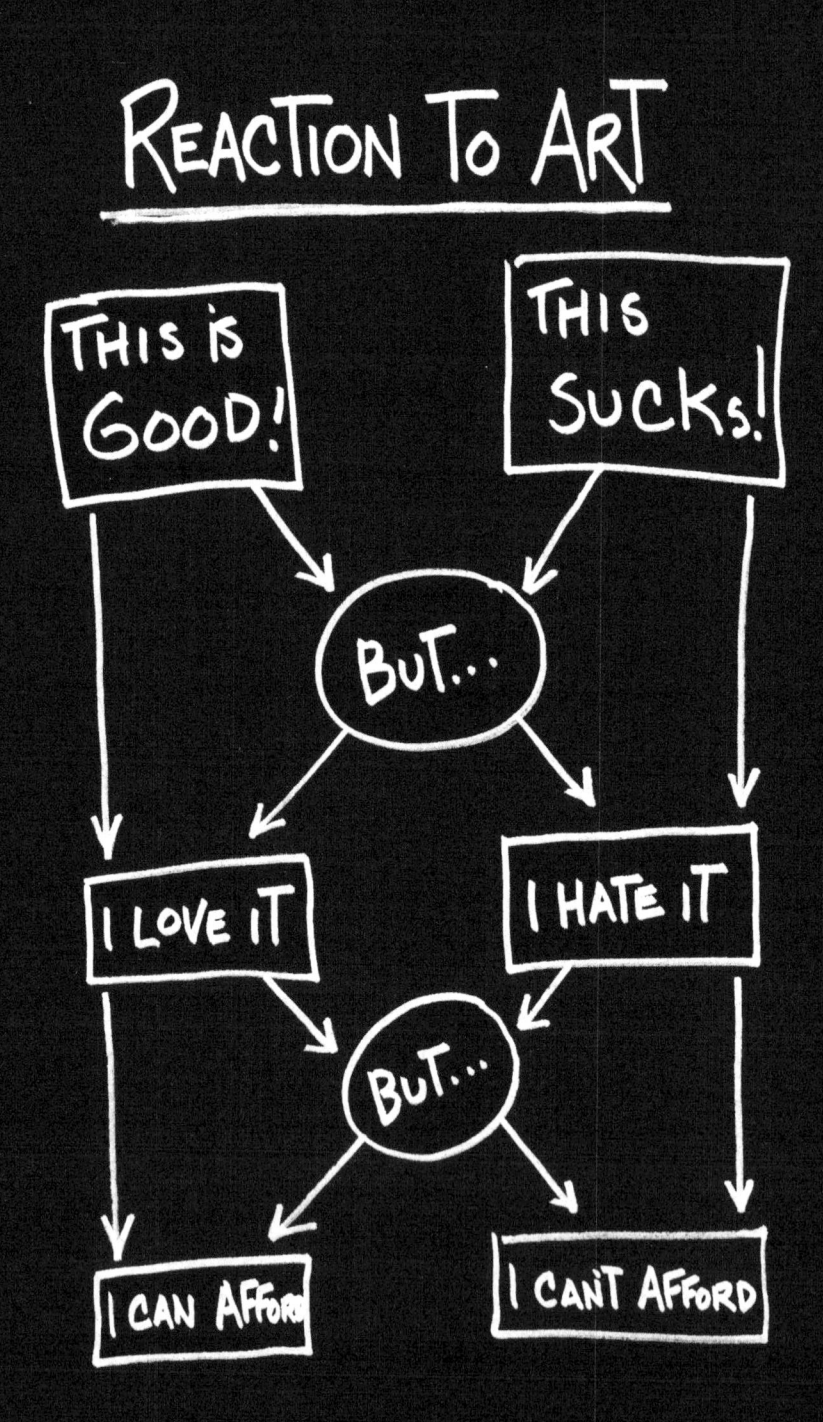

Reaction To Art

- THIS IS GOOD! → BUT... → I LOVE IT → BUT... → I CAN AFFORD
- THIS SUCKS! → BUT... → I HATE IT → I CAN'T AFFORD

> "I take rejection as someone blowing a bugle in my ear to wake me up and get going, rather than retreat."
>
> -Sylvester Stallone

GETTING REJECTED

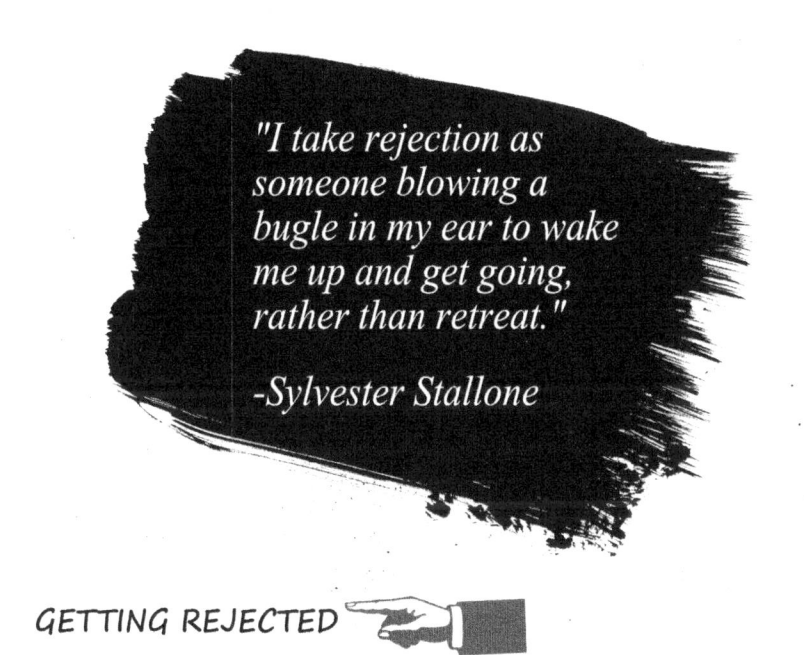

There is nothing fun about getting rejected.

Ever notice how being turned down stops some people from trying again, while others bounce back from rejection stronger than before? Everyone experiences the sweet sting of rejection, but some people use that pain to grow stronger and become even better equipped for the next round of teeth kicking.

As artists, Klee and I experience rejection *ALL* the time. In fact, if you are in any creative field, there *is* one constant in your life, you are going to be rejected time and time again.

This was one of the fears I had that kept me from pursuing an art career for most of my life. Fortunately, I've stumbled upon five steps that help me use rejection instead of rejection using me.

I Acknowledge My Emotions. Rather than suppress, ignore, or deny the pain, I acknowledge the emotions. I openly admit when I'm embarrassed, sad, disappointed, or discouraged. I have practiced confidence in my ability to deal with uncomfortable emotions head-on, which is essential to coping with the discomfort of rejection.

No matter what kind of rejection it is, trying to minimize the pain by convincing yourself *or someone else* it was "no big deal" or "it's their fault" will only prolong your agony. The best way to deal with uncomfortable emotions is to face them head-on.

I View Rejection As Evidence That I'm Pushing At My Limits. I know that rejection serves as proof that I'm living life to the fullest. Honestly, I expect to be rejected every once in a while, and I'm not afraid to go for it, even when I know it might be a long shot.

If you never get rejected, you may be living too far inside your comfort zone… just saying.

I Treat Myself With Compassion. Rather than think, "You're so stupid for thinking you could do that." I treat myself with compassion. I stand up for myself and respond to negative self-talk with a kinder, more empowering message.

Beating yourself up will only keep you down. Speak to yourself like a trusted friend or cheerleader. Drown out your harsh inner critic by repeating helpful mantras that will keep you feeling awesome.

I Refuse To Let Rejection Define Me. I stay away from making sweeping generalizations when I'm rejected. If one gallery turns me down or ignores me, I don't declare them or myself incompetent or a bad artist. I try to keep rejection in a proper perspective.

One person's opinion, or one single incident, should never define who you are. Don't let your self-worth depend upon other people's opinions of you. Just because someone else thinks something about you, doesn't mean it's true.

I AM WHO I CHOOSE.

I Learn From Rejection. If I'm rejected, I'll ask myself, "What did I gain from this?" so I can walk away with something I gained for the next try. Rather than simply tolerate the pain, I turn it into an opportunity for self-growth. I'm all about using any opportunity to learn and feel better about my life and what comes next.

Whether you learn about areas in your life that need improvement, or you simply recognize that being turned down isn't as awful as you imagined, rejection can be a good teacher. Use rejection as an opportunity to move forward with more wisdom and love.

Don't Be Defined By Someone Else

THE ROGUE ARTIST SURVIVAL GUIDE

MAKE A PERFECT MESS... YOUR CREATIVE SPACE

I see some of the creative spaces on social media that are pristine, perfectly lit, and clean... picture perfect shots of a white background with an easel, some faceless person painting, and a plant. Every time I see this, I think, "No way you are creating in there."

This doesn't mean that they are not real artists or that the pictures are staged, it just means that I am definitely not the kind of artist that can keep a studio looking spotless. I get paint everywhere. I have things stapled on the walls to inspire me, and my art studio is a safe space for wreaking havoc and artistic mayhem.

The truth is that your creative space can come in all shapes and sizes. It can be messy, disorganized, cluttered, organized, take up an entire room, or just a corner of your bedroom.

An artist's studio space is an evolving thing that is continuously in a state of change. As you evolve in your art career, so will your studio. The only rule I would say holds true to your creative space is that it needs to be respected by others. This is your sacred space, and it needs to be treated as such by anyone who interacts with it.

Throughout my life, even when I wasn't pursuing art, I always had some kind of a creative space. Whether it was a bin with art supplies under my bed, an easel in the corner of my bedroom, or a room dedicated to art, I always felt the need to have that safe space.

The only problem was that I didn't set down any ground rules for the other people that lived with me. Whether it was my ex-wife using my easel to hang laundry, my roommates grabbing my art supplies for their own projects, or my dad coming into my studio to repair his lawnmower engine, the area was not seen as sacred.

This can be really tough sometimes because most people don't understand what it means to be an artist and how vital your supplies are to you.

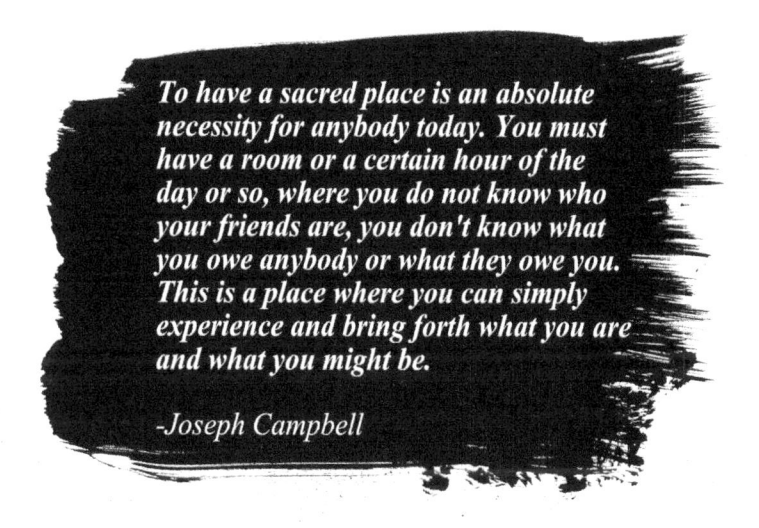

> *To have a sacred place is an absolute necessity for anybody today. You must have a room or a certain hour of the day or so, where you do not know who your friends are, you don't know what you owe anybody or what they owe you. This is a place where you can simply experience and bring forth what you are and what you might be.*
>
> -Joseph Campbell

Because it can be difficult to get other people to respect your creative space, some artists opt to rent a studio away from where they live.

I personally would prefer not to have the overhead costs of an extra studio space. If anything, I would calculate what it would cost to rent my own apartment and turn that into a live-in art studio. Of course, if you are married that may not be an option, but I would set some ground rules when it comes to your creative space, no matter where it is.

My studio started in a suitcase and grew into a small corner in my father's cluttered garage. When Klee and I got our own place, it evolved into our whole house. We have the central art and jewelry studio in the living room. We have recording equipment and instruments everywhere. We also store art everywhere in the house. Our house is a creative playground with a bedroom, bathroom, kitchen, and a place to hang out and relax.

It is an art studio with a living space, not a living area with an art studio. There is no right way or wrong way to set up your studio, just your way. What it looks like to other people doesn't matter, this is your space, make your own rules.

Keep in mind that I build most of the equipment I use, such as a spinning easel and every surface in my studio. If you can't find what you need, "Make it yourself." is my motto. Also, if you can't afford it, then build it.

Setting Up Your Art Studio.

A lot of people are curious about what I find essential in a studio, and what kind of things it should contain. I honestly think that what your studio looks and feels like is entirely up to you. The following are some of the things I find important in my studio during its current evolution.

WELL STOCKED IN UNKNOWN MATERIALS - Every artist works differently. That being said, a well-stocked studio is essential. I'm not talking about just your specific medium, I mean art supplies that involve other media as well. All artists could benefit from experimenting and playing with unknown materials.

A GOOD SURFACE TO WORK ON - This one almost goes without saying, but a proper table, desk, or other writing surface is perhaps the most essential item your studio needs. I have several surfaces in my studio from a drafting desk for drawing, tables on casters that are covered in paint, to several easels. Have surfaces that are appropriate for what you need.

GOOD LIGHTING - Natural light is always best, but when an expensive window-filled studio isn't available (or for those of us that work at all hours), a mixture of overhead lighting, movable floor lamps, and desk lamps will do. At the moment, I have seven swing arm desk lamps, twelve work lamps, and four studio filming lamps mounted around my entire space. I use LED 60 - 100 watt daylight bulbs where I need them. I like a brightly lit studio. Use whatever works for you and your creative area.

WRITING, SKETCHING, AND ARTING STUFF - Pens, pencils, markers, crayons, paint markers, colored pencils, charcoal, erasers, rulers, drafting tools, pastels, and sketch pads are just some of the things I use at my drafting table. Sometimes these materials can be overlooked because you may feel you don't need them. I like keeping a little of everything because I never know when a crayon may be the perfect material.

A COMFY CHAIR - I have several stools on casters in my studio so I can zip around from project to project. I also make sure to have at least one comfy chair or couch where I can relax and take a breather. I can chill while looking at the piece I'm working on and calm my mind about how terrible it looks.

ALL THE PAINT BRUSHES AND PAINT - I get asked all the time what kind of brushes or paint I use. The truth is, I don't know. I have a vast mixed selection of brushes and all sorts of mediums that have different uses. From cheap to expensive, I just have a lot of brushes and paint. I have inks, enamels, latex, acrylic, watercolor, airbrush paints, oils, and powdered pigments. A variety of brush styles, shapes, and materials just gives me more options. Stock up on a diverse selection so that you can paint however the mood strikes you. I usually get a lot of extra materials when there is a sale.

THINGS TO PAINT ON - I like having all kinds of materials to paint on. I use canvas, paper of all different weights (different weights of paper will provide different results), wood, or anything else that strikes my fancy. Found materials are the most challenging and fun for me. I keep all kinds of paper stock on hand, from tracing paper to heavy card stock. I make sure to have a little of everything.

MODELING CLAY AND SCULPTING - I am mostly known for my painting, but I have also created and sold sculptures. I have plaster, modeling clay, polymer clay, sculpting tools, and stone carving tools. Even if you don't intend to work in clay as a primary medium, modeling clay is great for brainstorming. Plus, it's just fun to play with when you have some downtime or are stuck in the middle of a project.

SAVE THE FLOOR - Having something to cover the floor will prevent getting in trouble if you are in a rental. A lot of artists like to use a large, basic white bed sheet which I'm not a fan of. There are a whole bunch of different painters tarps you can get at the hardware store that will give you better protection. Our studio is large, so the floors have two layers of plastic painters tarp that is covered by a canvas painters tarp.

My sacred creative space

MUSIC IS IMPORTANT - Rather than buy an expensive home audio system, get a portable wireless speaker, and stream your favorite tunes from your phone. I ended up buying an old speaker system from the thrift store and hooked it up to our virtual assistant (Alexa), which is pretty awesome. We play music, listen to audiobooks, and enjoy podcasts.

COMFORT LEVELS MATTER - Make sure you have some kind of temperature control for your studio space. A lot of times, we'll use a garage or attic and forget that it can get sweltering. That isn't fun for you while creating, and it can have an effect on your materials. While not everyone can afford air conditioning, it is often best to have a massive commercial fan at your disposal. Even though we have air conditioning and heating, we also have several fans in the studio to help with dry times.

STORAGE - Supplies can get ruined when it gets too cold or too hot, so make sure not to leave your art supplies in the sun or exposed. Some paint can go bad over time and become quite toxic, so make sure your supplies are stored in a temperature-controlled environment. This is why my first studio was in a suitcase.

HAVE A PLACE TO CLEAN STUFF - Having our kitchen right next to the studio is incredible because we can clean up without leaving the room. It is easy to make a ton of mess when you are creating artwork, and some projects will require water. There are also options for portable sinks. When I had my studio in the garage, I created a sink using buckets and old PVC pipes. Please be mindful of the environment when you dispose of materials. If you are not sure how then look it up on the internet, there are a lot of resources.

TECHNOLOGY - Camera, computer, scanner, recording devices, and more. Use them to save your work, create digital work, watch YouTube videos, or run your business. You decide what technology will assist you daily in your studio. Because I do YouTube videos, I have one computer for video and sound editing, and another computer to run my business and graphic design. Klee also has a computer where she runs her side of the company. We use technology as a tool to get ourselves out there, run our business, and create digital art.

I think, most importantly, keep the drama out of your space. This is your creative space, so don't allow anyone or anything to associate this space with anything negative. You want to train your mind to feel creative when you are there, and drama tends to zap creativity. Someone wants to argue, take it outside.

Another thing to keep in mind is that no studio is better than another. Don't ever allow yourself or another artist to studio shame you. I am very proud of my suitcase art studio days because I made it work. Yes, my studio has evolved and has more materials now, but that suitcase was exactly what I needed at the time. It was perfect.

It's easy to look around at other studios and feel like you are less than perfect because you don't have what they have.

You are perfect just the way you are, with what you have.

I have that stapled to the wall in my studio.

I think when you try to behave like someone else or have what they have because you believe that is the way you are supposed to be, then you run into problems. You can't be someone else, and it sucks to try.

I was working in the corner of a cluttered garage out of a suitcase. It wasn't glamorous, but it was mine. One of our neighbors came by and made a joke about my working conditions. I smiled and told him it's perfect for now, but an art studio is a living, breathing thing that is continuously evolving. I said, "You see a suitcase, I see endless possibilities."

Declutter And Other Magical Beasts.

Some artists will look at my studio and see clutter, but it is full of materials and things that motivate me. It is my *Sacred Space* of creation, meant to inspire by giving me the space and tools to create anything that I want to create.

Some call it cluttered, I call it intentional creative chaos. That being said, not all clutter is created equal. It is definitely possible to have too much clutter. I find it hard to create when you can't find the stuff you need, or you can't comfortably get around your studio.

I have a simple system for finding everything I need in what looks like chaos.

For example, all clear mediums in my studio are on one shelf. All mediums of one color are on another shelf. I put all my brushes in one area in different coffee cans. This makes it easy for me when I clean up and declutter. I can just toss things onto the shelves or into the bins where they belong. It takes minutes.

There is a delicate ecosystem in the studio that seems to be connected to my creative mind. When the studio is in shambles, it becomes uncomfortable. When I'm not comfortable in my space, I tend to be less creative. This is why, between projects, I will reset the studio and start fresh. It helps me reset my mind and start a new project.

THE ROGUE ARTIST SURVIVAL GUIDE

BE YOUR OWN KIND OF BEAUTIFUL

DAILY HABITS AND THOUGHTS OF A MADMAN

As someone who doesn't live a typical day because my career is not what you would call ordinary, people are often curious as to how I spend it. Being called an artist evokes visions of Venetian cafes and drunken philosophical arguments that take place at the wee hours of the night.

The reality is that it's not that charming. Most days, I'm either sitting in front of a canvas, computer, camera, microphone, easel, drawing desk, or work table for hours. My hands will stiffen on or around a paintbrush, pencil, tool, or keyboard by the end of the day. Sometimes, it'll be days before I leave the studio, and only because we started running out of food.

We do go outside and enjoy the world occasionally. Our tagline is "Endlessly Inspired By The Stuff Of Life" for a reason, but our life is not the permanent vacation a lot of people think it is. Being an artist is not easy.

It isn't like most stable professions where you leave your job at the door. Your work space is mostly located in your imagination, and you take that with you everywhere.

You are always on, finding inspiration for your next piece, and there is nothing mindless about it. Artists are also notoriously bored easily, which means we continuously have to be working on something, or we get demotivated.

It's also extremely unpredictable. There's no clearly defined workday, no boss telling you what to do, and no incentive to propel you up the corporate ladder. When the sales aren't booming, even the most confident of us artists question our choices. It is a constant rollercoaster of emotions that can cause you to give up, no matter how long you've been at it.

Because of this, I have a few daily routines that help me keep perspective and not go stir crazy in my own skin.

I Start My Day With A Short Meditation.

Every morning I wake up to coffee and 5-10 minutes of meditation. Meditation helps me focus and get a grip on any distracting thoughts that I may have bouncing around in my cranium. When I have a lot of projects, deadlines, or feel broke, I can easily get overwhelmed. Meditation helps.

Some of you may picture me surrounded by new-age paraphernalia, candles, chimes, and a goat in the background. Some think meditation is a woo woo act or only for spiritual people.

It may be all those things, but it's scientific as well.

I sit with my coffee, try to silence my thoughts, and clear my mind for at least 10 minutes. I spend most of that time swatting away thoughts, but mastering an empty head is not the point.

When you meditate, you are practicing your ability to focus on what you want to focus on. Whether it is nothing or something, you are giving yourself the ability to pay attention.

Meditation allows you to notice your thoughts.

I think a lot of people don't realize how many random thoughts they have in a matter of 10 minutes. Experts estimate that the mind thinks between 60,000 – 80,000 thoughts a day. That's an average of 2,500 – 3,300 thoughts per hour. That is 410 - 550 thoughts during your 10 minutes of meditation. That's insane.

Most times, we aren't even aware of the thoughts kicking up dirt and running amok in our own head, secretly whispering in our ear, influencing our choices, and telling us what to think.

When I have a lot going on, I don't have time to be chased down a rabbit hole and go into a downward spiral dictated by random thoughts. I want to know what I'm focused on. I want to choose what I focus on.

Like anything else in life, it will be more difficult when you first start. You may not be used to this kind of relationship with your brain. Most likely, your mind will fight back. It's used to running the show and may behave like a petulant child.

Just pick a sound, image, breathing, or anything to focus on. Put your full focus on it. Try to clear your mind of everything else.

When thoughts come in like "This is stupid." or "What do I have going on today?" just push them away.

Meditation helps train you to understand that you don't have to think random thoughts simply because they popped into your noodle.

When other thoughts pop up, just focus back on your focal point and nothing else.

Thoughts are going to try to get your attention, "Hey! Look at me!" Just respond with "Not now." and push them away.

That's it, that's meditation in a nutshell.

It can be easy to rush through life without stopping to notice much. I knew a guy who had a bed of flowers in front of his house for 5 years. When I asked him who planted them, he responded, "What flowers?"

Take a moment and stop the fast paced world from taking over. Get comfortable slowing down and taking notice of the things you appreciate in life. We're more creative when we're comfortable and at ease. It's as simple as that.

Meditation has been scientifically proven to lower stress levels, lessen feelings of anxiety, depression, and reduce negative self-talk while also boosting mood and overall well-being, thereby putting you in your most energized, creative mindset.

10 minutes… that's all it takes.

I Create Something Every Day.

For the last eight years, I have worked on something creative every day of my life. Whether it is a five-minute sketch, a painting that will take me several days, or an installation that will take months, I am continually creating or designing something.

As artists, that's what we do. We create, but sometimes we make brilliant excuses not to.

We can easily make anything else a higher priority. Whether it is the kids, our spouse, the laundry, traveling, not having enough time or anything else in life, any reason you have is bull. Take five minutes and sketch something out.

Sometimes we tell ourselves that art supplies are too expensive. Or we tell ourselves that we are not good enough and are wasting our time. That is also bull. How are you supposed to get good enough if you don't give it time?

I challenge myself to create something every single day. Even when I'm not feeling up to it, I choose to spend five minutes creating a piece of crap turd... as long as I'm creating something.

As of the writing of this book, I have sold over 2000 paintings, several sculptures, and the random art that has no label. I have created over 3000 other pieces that either haven't sold yet or no one will ever see.

Beyond creating a lot of artwork, this challenge has changed me. I am more confident in creating and sharing my art. It has helped me identify my style, the plethora of tools I like to work with, and my voice.

It has connected me with new people, opportunities, and has helped me identify as an artist. It has challenged me in ways I'm not sure I can adequately express. As I kept pushing myself to create, I started to find out more about me and the direction I wanted to head in.

I Write Or Sketch All My Ideas Down.

I got in the habit of writing everything down, whether it is:
- An idea.
- Painting sketch.
- Notes for my book.
- Video ideas.
- Something that inspires me.
- A plan for greatness.
- A to-do list.
- Random marketing ideas.
- Some philosophy I want to research.
- A new perspective.
- Something I saw that I want to remember.
- Song ideas.
- Or just some excellent random thought I had in the shower...

It allows me to clear it from my brain space and not have too much bouncing around up there.

THE ROGUE ARTIST SURVIVAL GUIDE

When I write things down, it frees my mind to focus on what I want instead of trying to store all that extra data. I also have books full of notes and other awesome tidbits of information that are fun to go back through.

Most of this book is composed of notes I have collected for over a decade, just a collection of random chicken scratchings of things that I found interesting and have learned in my life.

I also never run out of creative ideas because I have books full of all kinds of foolish schemes for new creations. Most of them are garbage, but every once in a while, something incredible can come of it.

I have journals and sketchbooks for future art projects, video projects, music projects, and writing projects. Organize it however works for you, just write it down, you'll be happy you did.

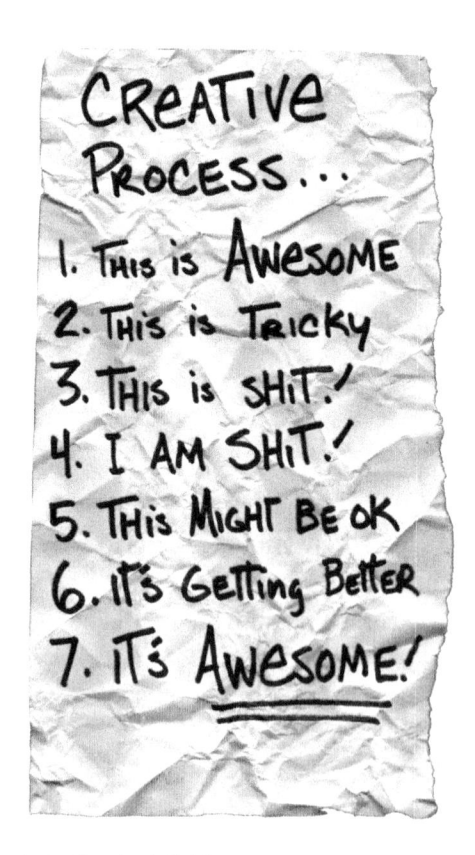

> CREATIVE PROCESS...
> 1. THIS IS AWESOME
> 2. THIS IS TRICKY
> 3. THIS IS SHIT!
> 4. I AM SHIT!
> 5. THIS MIGHT BE OK
> 6. IT'S GETTING BETTER
> 7. IT'S AWESOME!

I Plan My Day Accordingly.

This is my media schedule

Cigar-chomping leader, Colonel John "Hannibal" Smith would say, "I love it when a plan comes together." This statement usually came on the heels of all hell breaking loose. I think my little brain soaked in some unlikely wisdom from watching the A-team get out of bad situations by the skin of their teeth every week.

You can plan things out, but always be ready for the shit to hit the fan. In other words, be flexible with your planning.

When I was younger, my best friend's mother would plan things out for us. If things didn't go according to her plan, she would lose her shit and would panic. I hated doing stuff with his family because at some point during our outing, she would have a breakdown. We would all just stand there awkwardly, trying not to make eye contact until she calmed down.

I think it's important to have a plan, but don't go overboard.

THE ROGUE ARTIST SURVIVAL GUIDE

I always try to have a loose plan of how I want to spend my day. I have a to-do list, but it remains malleable and flexible. This allows me to check things off my list as I get them done, but move them if I have to.

My to-do list usually involves commission lists, deadlines, show dates, people I have to email, and other typical day-to-day things when running a creative business.

I never schedule specific art creations, but I will write down shipping deadlines for a commission. Even these deadlines are malleable because life happens sometimes, but I try to stick to my deadlines as best I can.

Some people like planning their entire week, or they like planning the day down to the hour. I don't work that way. I basically write down deadlines when they are due ahead of time, but I will plan out my day after I meditate. If I have a large project or commission I am working on that will take several days, then I will block out time for that. Just remember that shit happens, so stay flexible.

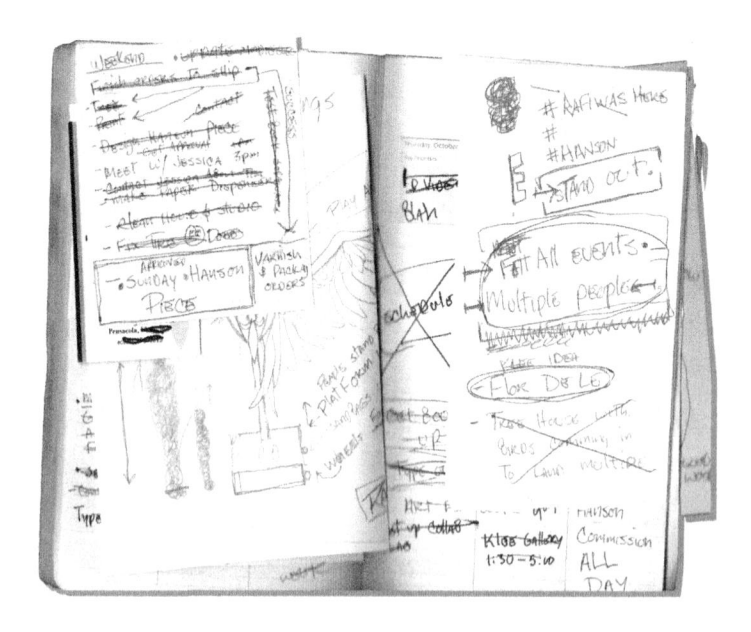

How To Make A Living As An Artist.

1. Create a lot of art.
2. Keep Pushing Boundries.
3. While Creating, Put Art Out There.
4. Show A Lot of People.
5. Be Patient. Be Friendly
6. Keep Going.
7. Keep Going.
8. Keep Going.

Fantastic 4 List.

I have also gotten in the habit of using something I call a Fantastic 4 List. It is 4 important things that I want to get done sooner than later.

The things on this list could be as simple as sending an email, making a phone call, or putting a layer on a painting. It just needs to be significant for me to grow in my career.

I am in the process of accomplishing everything that I have ever set my mind on thus far, simply because of this system. I have created a full-time art career, am in the process of publishing my own book, have grown our YouTube presence, and am continually reinventing what is possible for me.

Having a Fantastic 4 List allows me to continually keep track of the things that I want to reach. Instead of tackling a large overwhelming project all at once, it enables me to break it down into smaller, manageable chunks.

For example, early in my career I wanted to get into our local farmers market with my art. It was a juried market with an application process where there was a big possibility that my work would be rejected.

It was significant to me that I try because I was totally being a chicken about facing rejection.

I broke down the steps into four manageable chunks and put them on my fan 4 list.

1. Research The Market Website For What To do.
2. Fill Out Application And Send.
3. Confirm That They Received Your Application.
4. Follow Up For Results Of Jury Determination.

On the first day, I did numbers 1 and 2. For the next day, I moved 3 and 4 to the top of the list.

My day two fantastic 4 list looked like this:
1. Confirm That They Received Your Application.
2. Follow Up For Results Of Jury Determination.
3. Get Canopy For Market Show.
4. Design And Build Stuff To Display Art At Show.

That day, I called the market office and sent an email. I got no response. The whole list got carried over to the next day. I called several times again, sent another email, and got no response.

By the fourth day, it was bothering me that my list wasn't moving.

I printed out a copy of my application, went to the market offices, and asked to speak to the market manager. The receptionist said she wasn't available, and I said I was willing to wait.

A half-hour later, the market manager greeted me in her office. I handed her my application and asked if she would be willing to tell me my odds of jurying in and getting started before the end of the month.

She said she would call me the next day by noon. I asked for her direct line so I could get a hold of her if I missed the call.

I got home and crossed out line 1, and the list moved to the next day.

1. Follow Up For Results Of Jury Determination.
2. Get Canopy For Market Show.
3. Design and Build Stuff To Display Art At Show.
4. Research Info On Offering Prints.

I waited until noon-thirty and called her direct line. No answer. I called again around an hour and a half later. She answered and asked how soon I could start at the market. It took several days to cross off the things on my list, but I was in.

When you are done with a project, list your next project when the room opens up on your list. My next project was offering prints of my work.

If it wasn't for the fact that I wanted to cross things off my list, I don't think I would be as bold as I am.

People tend to think about new directions and big projects that they want to work on all the time. Some of these seem overwhelming because you feel you have to take care of it all right away. Sometimes life happens, and you forget. The fan four list always helps me stay on top of the extra things.

I usually like adding things that are slightly outside of my comfort zone, something that I'm somewhat afraid to do. I'll list items that will push me to the next level of my career or life.

THE ROGUE ARTIST SURVIVAL GUIDE

I Leave Space On My To-Do List.

When it comes to my main to-do list, I leave a lot of space on the page. Some people fill up their To-Do page and have to follow a clockwork schedule, and if that works for you, great. As an artist, things tend to get unpredictable.

Being flexible is understanding that there may be a whole bunch of small tasks that you didn't think about, that may come up throughout the day.

Write them down even if it is after the fact. That way, you can look at your list and really get an idea of what you accomplished that day.

I Put First Things First.

It is effortless to get overwhelmed once your creative career gets going. I think we all tend to take things a little bit more seriously once money gets involved. Taking things seriously is not necessarily a good thing.

In my own art career, I always have to remind myself why I started this whole thing in the first place. I sometimes find myself heading into the same mentality that I had in my old corporate job.

I can easily stress out over deadlines, start setting impossible target dates, and feel like I'm losing a handle over my business. Everything loses the fun and enjoyment it once had, when you get overwhelmed.

It is essential to step back, reevaluate, and remember why you decided to do what you do. In those moments, I look at my list and make sure that everything is being done for the right reasons. Is it something I enjoy? Is it helping me grow as a person? Am I creating for the *LOVE* of creating?

If I find anything on my to-do list that I'm doing out of desperation, because I desperately *THINK* it will make more money or get me somewhere, I make sure to remove it from my list. If it is something I legitimately want to do, it will find its way back eventually when I'm in a better frame of mind.

In this roller-coaster of emotions that is an art career, it is easy to lose yourself in desperate thoughts, and find yourself compromising who you are and why you do what you do. Take time to stop and really think about what you are doing.

You'll have moments where you feel like everything you do is meaningless, like nobody cares, and you are wasting your life. This is a feeling I am very familiar with, and one that will show up no matter how long you've been doing this art thing.

Trust me when I tell you, starting a creative career can be exactly like any other old job that you hated. The difference is that you're the one in charge of your destiny.

It can seem so much easier to have someone tell you what to do. When you have your own creative business, you have to be the one to determine everything, take all the risks, and make all the hard decisions. This can all be overwhelming, and is the main reason that people can lose sight of what is important. *The love of creating your art.*

THE ROGUE ARTIST SURVIVAL GUIDE

Whenever I find myself feeling at odds with my art career, I know that something in my thinking is off. I make it a point to stop and reevaluate what direction my career is heading. I also evaluate how I feel. *Am I happy? Am I making the most of my life?*

I personally don't think that there's anything wrong with creating art all the time. That being said, if you are not enjoying yourself, then you may have a problem. If you find that you are creating just for the sake of making money, chances are it's become something disingenuous, and you may be off track.

There is absolutely nothing wrong with making money. I want you to make all the money, but I want you to make money doing what you love. If you are just focused on money (which is very easy to do) and that is guiding your creative direction, then you may lose sight of where you are heading. It's easy to feel desperate when times are hard, but remember what we talked about in an earlier chapter… *we make stupid choices when we are desperate.*

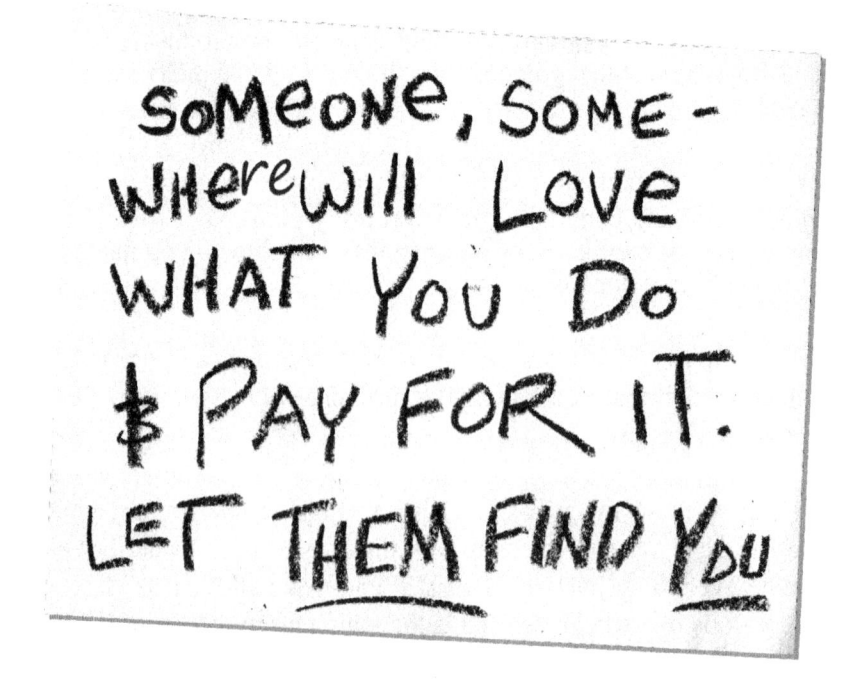

> SOMEONE, SOMEWHERE WILL LOVE WHAT YOU DO $ PAY FOR IT. LET THEM FIND YOU

> Be Happy...
> Not because everything is good, but because you can see the good in everything.

> **Rules (suggestions) To Starting an Art Career**
> 1. Create Art.
> 2. Put Art Out There.
> 3. Be Patient.
> 4. Persist Through The Bull!

I Define What It Means To Be Successful For Me.

Success is a funny thing, isn't it? Some people believe success to be the opposite of failure. Yet most times, you have to fail over and over to achieve any form of success.

In the dictionary, the definition of success is: *The accomplishment of an aim or purpose.*

I like that. It's simple and to the point.

Around the time I first started this art thing as a career, my aim or purpose was to sell my first piece of art.

After a month of putting myself out there and not selling anything, you could have said I was failing miserably. Then a week goes by, and I sell my first piece for $20. Is that a success?

Some people will look at that and say it was an absolute waste of time. Others mocked me and said I needed to get my head out of my ass and quit while I was ahead. Were they right?

A week later, I sold about $1800 worth of art. Were they still right?

The entire month I was putting myself out there without selling a thing. I was excited, and I felt triumphant. My original goal was to put myself out there and face my fears. That was it, I had no intention to sell any art.

Although I wasn't selling anything, I was kicking my goal's *ass*.

I was showing my art two days a week, dealing with insecurities, nasty comments, praises, and every other commentary under the sun. I was doing it. I felt incredibly proud of myself.

When I sold my first piece of art, I celebrated. Up until then, I wasn't sure if I could sell anything. $20 or not, that was a win for me.

Success is a moving target. You are going to evolve, grow, change direction, and want new things in life. No one else can determine the destination for you.

They are a spectator, they have no idea what you are aiming for. They have no idea what success means for *you*.

So much of the way that society views success is built around the concept of having lots of money, being a celebrity, and owning the right kinds of things. In fact, one of the past definitions in the dictionary for success was: *Attaining wealth, prosperity and/or fame.*

Listen, I am neither able nor willing to authorize the ultimate definition of success. It's just not possible. Every person on the planet has their own definition of what it means to be successful. No description exists that is suitable for all humans.

Success is whatever you decide it is. It looks like whatever you decide it is supposed to look like. Sometimes my day can be kind of annoying, but I wouldn't want to spend my day any other way.

What does it mean to YOU to be successful right now where you are? I contemplate this question often, if not daily.

Only you are an authority in your life. Go out and live your life, being bold in your beliefs. Have courage and love in everything you do. Your life is an occasion, stand up for it, and define success for yourself by being truly alive.

I Change My Mind If I Want To... Dammit.

Just as there is no roadmap to creating an art career. It's also not something that you can plot in a straight line from point A to point B. You're going to find that you have to make adjustments as you go.

You are going to make mistakes, you're going to run into roadblocks, and you're going to fail at different endeavors that you take on. It's important to remind yourself that you are allowed to make changes.

You can decide that you no longer want to finish a project that you started. You can start on an old project that you had given up on years ago. You can decide to change your mind about your feelings on a particular subject, or you can choose to head in a completely new direction on something.

People don't understand this sometimes, because it doesn't fit whatever status quo they have in their heads. When I decided to start designing my own line of fun T-Shirts, a family member responded with

"You're doing t-shirts now? I thought you did art."

"I do both."
"I thought you didn't want to do t-shirts."
"I changed my mind."

You are allowed to change your mind and do *whatever you want.*

I feel like people are expected to have one opinion or another, and stick to it with their dying breath. That's stupid. We learn new things, get a new perspective, have new experiences, evolve, change, grow, and get more information as we live. We change our minds because we can.

The problem is that we don't want to be seen as wishy-washy, uncertain, or weak-minded. If we change our perspective, it can be seen as a sign of defeat.

I've watched people argue a point for hours even though they had changed their minds, but were unwilling to lose the argument.

Changing your mind means that you are flexible, that you can actually think on your feet, and that you are willing to see the bigger picture.

It also requires authenticity, to be willing to tell the truth, and the knowledge that you don't know everything.

Listen, I'm a pretty smart guy, but I don't really know anything that is outside of my own head. That makes me really dumb at times.

I consider myself a *brilliant dumb guy* as a reminder that I don't have all the answers. I know how I feel about things in a moment of conversation, but I may change my mind midway and decide I think something else.

This can be unsettling to people that you may be engaged in conversation with. In my experience, it is not a common practice because most discussions are seen as a mini power struggle. We are used to believing that changing our minds during a debate is admitting defeat. On the other hand, I find it quite freeing. I don't see it as defeat, I see it as courageous and bold.

My question to myself is, "Do I have the courage to be vulnerable enough to admit that I changed my mind about something?"

Because we all live in our heads, the things we know to be accurate are really just our opinions.

We all have a bunch of opinions that we are throwing around at each other, but at the end of the day, they are just opinions... and ideas can change.

You are allowed to change your mind, dammit.

INDIVIDUAL DREAMS MAY VARY

I AM NOT FOR EVERYONE & NIETHER ARE YOU.

IF your work APPEALS TO EVERYONE Then it MOVES NO one.

MAKING DECISIONS →
BECAUSE I WANT TO (NOT How much money is in it)

COURAGE - TO LOVE MORE Than you FEAR.

I Drink Plenty Of Water And Make Sure To Eat.

It's no secret that artists can be forgetful, especially when we are wrapped up in a project. We can easily forgo the things that sustain us in life. It is imperative to remember to take care of yourself physically because if you don't take care of yourself physically, you're not going to get much done mentally. I don't think I need to say much more for this. Eat right, stay hydrated, exercise, move around, just take care of yourself. It's important.

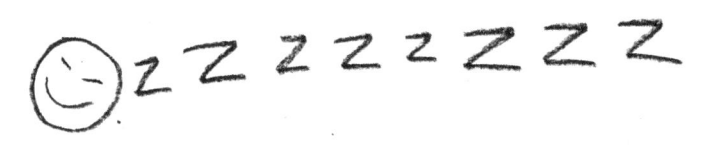

I Take A Nap If I Want To.

Sleep is the one area where I have to wonder sometimes if I am a glutton for punishment. I can go days pushing myself to the limit in the studio. It sometimes gets to the point where sitting down for 5 minutes means falling asleep. This is not good, and I don't recommend it.

I've had to learn to give myself permission to take a nap when I'm tired. It is virtually impossible to stay creative if you are continually pushing yourself to be productive. You can tire yourself out, and eventually it will lead to burn out. I've tried exercising, drinking coffee, Red Bull, sitting up straight, eating, and other tactics to make myself wake up. I'll spend more time, energy, and stress on trying to beat the problem instead of just taking a nap.

Take a nap, you'll feel refreshed, and then you can carry on with your awesome self. People out there that actually study sleep habits (yes, they exist) have found that the length of your nap has a significant effect on how awake you feel afterward. It all has to do with sleep cycles.

Beware of sleeping for longer than 90 minutes; you can go into "sleep inertia" and once you enter a new sleep cycle, you won't get any added benefits and just feel tired when you wake. It's your body, so you decide what sleep you need. Rest is cumulative, which means it adds up over time based on habits, not binge sleeping. When struggling to be productive because you are tired, it is sometimes much easier to just take a nap.

I Learn From My Mistakes And Don't Wallow In Them.

Let me start out by saying that you are definitely going to make mistakes. You're going to make all the mistakes. A lot of them. A lot of mistakes. *Mistakes… mistakes… mistakes...*

In my opinion, if you go into any situation afraid of making a mistake, you are preparing yourself for nothing but flailing. Also, if making a mistake means that you should punish yourself over and over for the rest of your life, then you are probably suffering and ill-prepared to face more. Running away from the mistakes you made is also a waste of time. We have a finite amount of time on this planet, and there are better ways to use it than wallowing in your mistakes. Understanding that *you are not* your mistakes is a big step towards accepting them. Whether it is a mistake in your career, your personal life, or with relationships, remember that you made a mistake, but you are not the mistake. It is not a reflection of the person you are, it is a mistake.

Every day I encourage myself to make mistakes. I use materials I don't regularly use, I experiment, I do things I have never done before, and I push myself to allow the mistakes to happen. You can get so far in anything you do if you just accept the fact that mistakes happen when you are pushing the envelope. You made a mistake, learn from it, and move forward.

I Remember Who "I" Actually Am.

One of the most important things I try to do daily is to give myself a moment to reflect on my identity. Recently, I had a friend who was fired from a job he held for several decades. He admitted to me that he felt lost and didn't know who he was without his position. He desperately searched for other work that would fill the void, and felt like he had no purpose. I remember saying to him, "You are so much more than your job, in fact your job has nothing to do with who you are."

As artists we tend to share our vulnerable parts with the world through our art. We can easily identify the art as a part of us. The label of "artist" also becomes part of our sense of self identity. An art studio can become an extension of our being.

We refer to parts of our body as "my arm, my hands, my brain, my eyes, and my nose." It is all a physical part of us, we identify personally with it, and we do not want to lose that connection. I want my hand to stay where it is and not go away, because that would suck.

Unfortunately, we seem to make a similar connection with the things we identify with that are outside of us. Labels, possessions, positions, status, careers, family, roles, and titles will usually have a huge influence on how we perceive our own value. When I was a kid, I was my cool toys. As I got older and older, my identity shifted to other things. As a teenager, I was my cool friends, I was my awesome car, I was my unique clothing, I was my bad-ass hair style, and I was my family business. As an adult, I was my job, I was my family, I was my house, and I was my financial status and security.

When I lost all of that, I realized that identifying yourself with things, people, positions or what you have accomplished, is a dangerous game. I also realized that most of my life was spent trying to desperately hold on to that sense of identity. I was terrified to lose the things that made me who I was. If you lose that thing, then who are you?

That is the question I try to ask myself every day. I can get lost in the fear of holding on desperately to the things that I think help to make me who I am. What if I lose my art studio? What if I lose my art collectors? What if I lose my large online following? What if I lose my ability to create art? What if all my art burns? What if things get sour between Klee and me? These are tough questions, but necessary in order to get to the truth behind my motivations. I can identify as:

- A YouTube infuencer, afraid of losing his following.
- An award winning artist, afraid of losing his art studio.
- An awesome husband, afraid of things falling apart.

In those moments it is important to remember that I am not my label of award winning artist. I am not my studio, I am not my relationship, I am not my YouTube channel, I am not my art, I am not my reputation, and I am not what other people think of me.

Who are you without those labels, possessions, positions, status, careers, family, roles, and titles?

Many people run away from this question because they believe they are nothing without the things that make them who they are… but they are so much more. You are so much more, contemplate it.

THE ROGUE ARTIST SURVIVAL GUIDE

SOCIAL MEDIA

I get contacted by artists all the time who tell me that I am great at marketing, and honestly, I don't see it. What I am great at is sharing what I'm excited about. That's it.

I'm not into that perfect life image that most social media postings are about. You know what I mean, the flawlessly staged shot that makes it seem like everything is polished and perfect. Life doesn't work that way. Life has the ins and outs, ups and downs, and sometimes the odd roundabout. I get excited about everything in life, whether it is beautiful or has warts all over it.

I Share What I'm Excited About. Don't Worry About Numbers.

- What adventure is in store?
- What do I want to remember about today or yesterday?
- What am I working on?
- What is going on in my life?
- What was I thinking?

I use social media as a personal journal to record my life.

Whether it is a mistake, an embarrassing moment, a silly thought, a work of genius, a piece of crap, or an awesome moment... if I want to remember it, it gets shared.

Putting yourself out there, to me, means sharing your creations with the world, whether they are beautiful or ugly. Unfortunately, sharing on social media also means you may react to online metrics. It's easy to become obsessed with how many likes you have on a post. This is a slippery slope and one that I urge you to avoid.

Online metrics are empty at worst and shallow at best. they will never tell you how a person obsessed over your creation. they will never reflect how someone danced to your song in their living room. they cannot give you a glimpse into the person's mind.

I would much rather have one person love something I posted because it impacted their life in a positive way than 100 empty likes from people who are just going through the motions and barely noticed what I shared.

This is why I just share what I want to share because it is something I want to see. I appreciate the likes and comments, but I don't rely on them to feel good about what I'm sharing.

Ultimately, do what you want to do with your social media, but have fun with it. I think too many people go the marketing route, and honestly, people are tired of being marketed to.

That's why I would instead use those platforms to build creative and long-lasting connections with people, one on one. Some will be other artists, some will be collectors of my art, all will be based on my authenticity of being me.

Although we started our career doing festivals and markets with no online presence several years ago, I realized that there is a cap on local prominence. We might get discovered by other people in the world who visit our town, but mostly our world was made up of the 300,000 people who lived locally. Our *village* or town only has a population of 52,000, and I wanted to make more people aware of who we are.

I enjoyed sharing my insights with local aspiring artists and talking about the creative life. We had traveled and experienced so much that I knew we had some interesting opinions and a unique approach to living the artist's life.

I had always been very interested in YouTube and sharing online videos on the topic. This brought with it a whole different set of insecurities that I had to work through. I decided to step into it and bumble my way through as I did with my art career.

Create stuff, put it out there, and persist through the bullshit.

The internet is easier to understand if you look at it as a giant farmers market. If you set up a booth, chances are you will get overlooked the first few weeks because there is a lot of stuff to look at.

If you are consistently showing new stuff, working your booth, and communicating with people, slowly, but surely, people start to notice you.

A lot of people that do anything online post one or two things expecting hoards of people to visit their page, and get disappointed because they only got tumbleweeds, then quit. They say it didn't work for them, and they end up missing out on the opportunity to grow.

Posting a few times online and declaring it a failure is like setting up at an art market, leaving to sit in your car, and then complaining that you didn't meet anybody.

Doing anything online is almost like starting an art career. You have to love what you are doing because if you are expecting traction right away, you've got another thing coming. It's going to be tumbleweeds for a while. That's why I just share what I want to see.

When we first started posting our videos online, I'm pretty sure we were the only people out there watching them. Fortunately, we enjoyed our videos, so I kept posting.

It took about 5 years to get a little-noticed on YouTube. Even still, we don't have millions of followers, but we are sharing our opinions in the world, and more and more people know we exist.

The same thing across the board on social media platforms. I just kept sharing and growing organically. It takes time.

At this point, we do YouTube videos for artists, have a vlog channel, have a weekly podcast, and have a loyal Patreon following. I share consistently across social media, and I write a weekly blog on my website. At no point in time am I marketing us or our work, but I am sharing who we are, what we create, and our thoughts on life.

Listen, you don't need an online presence to start your art career. We could have kept expanding our reach locally, and we were doing just fine financially.

Social media postings happen almost daily. I post the same post across the board on all my social media platforms, and it takes me about 5 minutes a day to do that.

Most experts will suggest doing different posts for each platform, and that may be a great idea... I just don't want to. I'm happy copying and pasting the text across the board.

Like I said before, you don't need an online presence to become a full-time artist. We sure didn't have one when we started. But, if you want to expand globally, I think at least posting on social media is a great idea.

EXPAND YOUR REACH.

WHY SO SERIOUS? BE A UNICORN

Some of the things that are rampant in the professional art world are snobbishness, exclusivity, and a whole bunch of fools trying to take themselves seriously.

I think the reason some artists and other art professionals take themselves seriously is that they want other people to take them seriously as professionals.

This is hilarious to me, because essentially, what we do is draw pictures all day. We play with instruments, do crafts, get messy, and we basically do what children do for play.

I think something gets lost in the innocence of creation when we try to take ourselves seriously or have other people admire us as professionals. I would much rather be known as a childish, playful, and fun artist than to be taken earnestly by some art curmudgeons, snobs, or other "serious" people in the world.

THE ROGUE ARTIST SURVIVAL GUIDE

This is something to really look out for when you cross the threshold in your mind from amateur to professional. As a professional, we can concern ourselves way too much with LOOKING professional.

A lot of our decisions start to venture away from who we are; we can easily get lost in what we are known for, and what our reputation is.

We turn creativity into a serious business when the business of creativity is the opposite of serious.

It is easy to think your shit doesn't stink as an artist. Most of the art market system is set up to validate through awards and notches on a belt.

At one point, I became very serious as I started to view myself as an award-winning professional artist. This was a drag on my creativity and my overall sense of happiness. Luckily, I learned from that.

I am pretty much convinced that kids have life all figured out. I mean, think about it, chances are you were once a kid. Chances are you were even fun and spontaneous, with a great sense of humor.

Then, at some point, you were welcomed into the ritualistic daily grind of adulthood, gradually eradicating your inner child.

Let's be honest, most adults suck. They feel frustration instead of hope, and care too much about what other so-called adults think of them.

If you have been reading this book thus far without chucking it in the garbage, chances are, you are not much of an adult.

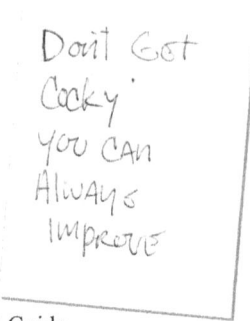

> Don't Get Cocky
> You can Always Improve

You are more of a magical creature that keeps the inner child alive and still gets excited over mundane things. You see being childish as a good thing and not a bad thing.

What I mean by being childish is:
- *You are curiously looking at the world.*
- *You make it a point to learn something new every day.*
- *You make small things enjoyable.*
- *You persevere.*
- *You stay active.*
- *You are optimistic.*
- *You see the beauty in nature.*
- *You don't hold grudges.*
- *You are adaptable.*
- *You don't care about what other people think about you.*
- *You dream big.*
- *You are kind to others, but you don't take anyone's shit.*
- *You aren't rushed.*
- *You have more fun.*
- *You are curious about the world.*
- *You make the mundane exciting.*
- *You say no when you don't want to do something.*

Living a life full of wonder, appreciation for the small things, humor, kindness, resilience, and big dreams, is exactly what your inner child would want you to do. So, embracing it just might be the most remarkable thing you can do for your life.

Be childish in your approach to anything in your life, especially your art career. I know right now you are saying "But Rafi, there are serious things I have to contend with like taxes and running a business. How can I be childish in a moment that *requires* being serious?"

Every year, Klee and I do our federal taxes. Admittedly, it's not the most fun thing I can think of, but we make it a game. Instead of spending a day dreading every minute, we play a game and try and make it as fun as we can.

THE ROGUE ARTIST SURVIVAL GUIDE

I'm not going to tell you how to live your life, but I will say that adding a little fun, wonder, and joy to your day will always beat taking yourself seriously.

As a child, sometimes YOU just have to be a UNICORN.

So, not everyone is a unicorn. Unicorns are mythical creatures who drink coffee in the morning and focus on the magic of life.

Usually, they are referred to as *Pollyanna,* or someone who wears *rose-colored glasses.*

Actually, EVERYONE can be a unicorn, but some don't find it practical. Some people think you have to keep your eyes open and live in the REAL world.

Honestly, the real world is just a subjective interpretation of what you see with your brain. There are meanings you've attached to said items or circumstances that are all in your head. We are all merely making this shit up as we go.

> REMEMBER WHEN YOU WERE a KID $ WERE ːHappyː FOR No Reason?
>
> Be THAT AGAIN

We are just a bunch of old kids playing pretend. It is simply the way it is. We don't actually know anything, we are just guessing. It's the reason two people will argue two completely opposing views, and both believe that they are entirely correct in their argument.

I figure if we are all just making it up as we go, why not be a unicorn and make every day awesome? Be childish? Have fun? Isn't life way too short to do anything else?

I'm currently writing this book, which terrifies me. Putting yourself out there in print is just asking for critics to destroy you. Things like this are outside of my comfort zone, a new and unfamiliar emotional risk.

This shit is scary, and most of the time whatever is bouncing around my skull doesn't help. Taking risks is scary, and some serious people are going to judge you. This doesn't mean it is a serious affair.

Usually, when I am doing something that makes me slightly nervous or is beyond what I think I can do, there is that voice of negativity that says, "You know, you're going to mess this up and make an ass of yourself."

Luckily, I know that the only way that it could damage or bother me is if I take myself seriously and worry about what other people may think. If I remember that I can have fun, even if the shit hits the fan, then I'm a unicorn.

It is easy to get bogged down in the severe nature of wanting to be seen as a professional. We artists are always chasing validation, and we tend to worry about what people think. We can be especially serious with what we share on social media or with the world.

That's why I think, every day, you just gotta be a unicorn. Even if people think you are crazy... be a unicorn. Be childish.

CHILDREN SEE MAGIC BECAUSE THEY LOOK FOR IT. LOOK FOR THE MAGIC IN LIFE.

THE ROGUE ARTIST SURVIVAL GUIDE

~~Connect~~
Airplane Mode

GET RID OF PESKY DISTRACTIONS

We are living in the age of personal technology, and for artists, that can be devastating to our creative focus. We always have our smartphone at hand to check the latest cat meme, Tweet, or silly YouTube video.

We also love jumping on the distraction bandwagon anytime we feel discouraged, afraid, or disappointed with the project we are working on.

Some of us also suffer from *FOMO* (Fear Of Missing Out). This means we can't help but distract ourselves from a project any time a notification dings. We don't want to be that one guy or gal that doesn't know what is going on with our people.

Even putting your phone on silent is distracting. I have jumped out of my skin when my phone vibrates, and I'm engrossed in a project.

FOMO or not, sometimes you have to put the world on pause and press play on you and your creativity. You are allowed to disconnect and give yourself the time to create. Besides, your friends aren't that interesting, you probably won't miss out on much.

Although putting yourself and your creations "out there" means that you may be connected to the world, it is crucial to put the world on pause.

Or on airplane mode.

Silence is the great equalizer of the noise of the push notifications, social media, friends, your family needing your attention, and anything else that can distract you from the focus you need for creating. Keep your studio space away from the rest of the world. Put your phone on airplane mode, forget emails, favors, or bills. You'll have to run your business, but set time aside for creation.

As I said in an earlier chapter, make sure your creative space is respected. Not just your physical space, but your emotional creative space too.

7 DISTRACTIONS

(THINGS TO **NOT** WATCH FOR.... well, watch, BUT DON'T GET DISTRACTED.)

📱 ← PHONE NOTIFICATIONS

💻 ← COMPUTER NOTIFICATIONS

🕐 ← THE CLOCK (JUST SET ALARM)

📝 ← THINGS FLOATING AROUND IN YOUR HEAD (WRITE ~~THE~~ THEM DOWN)

🎧 ← NOISE (WEAR HEADPHONES)

🙂 ← FRIEND OR FAMILY WHO DOESN'T GET IT

Stop The Digital World. Carve out blocks of creative time. Turn off your phone and computer. Don't worry, the world will not end if your cousin Margerie can't get a hold of you and ask you about your day.

Give Yourself A Break. Just because we are used to working for the man, doesn't mean we have to treat ourselves the same way. Make time for creating, but give yourself the time to connect and relax. It may all be one and the same, you determine what is right for you. I like taking breaks around every 2 hours and stepping outside to enjoy the day.

Turn Off Notifications. I have a lot going on in the digital world. My phone could ding, vibrate, ring, or make some other sound every three minutes if notifications were on.

We have this fear that we are going to miss out on something important, but it could be very overwhelming to be ON all the time. Set some time aside every day, or week, to check your online stuff but limit the number of times per day you check and respond to emails, texts, and social media.

Clear Your Day Up. In the morning, after meditation, I dedicate a few minutes to managing my schedule. This helps me make my day clear for myself. That way, when they come knocking at my door asking for a favor, I can make a choice based on my plans for that day. I suggest that once you've made a choice on how you want to spend your day, hold on to it and ruthlessly follow through. It will help solidify your priorities and personal power.

Eliminate Or Minimize Negative People In Your Life. These are people who play the victim, are dramatic, are stuck in unhealthy habits, seem to have a dark cloud looming overhead, or generally make you feel drained or bad about yourself. Surround yourself with those who are positive, focused, productive, fun, hopeful, and ambitious.

THE ROGUE ARTIST SURVIVAL GUIDE

~~I AM NEEDED~~

I HAVE VALUE ← TRUTH

SELF SIGNIFICANCE AND SAYING NO

One of the most important things you can do as an artist is to learn to say *no*. This can be really tough. Especially if you feel like you are missing out on a good time or feel obligated to do things for other people.

Listen, it's okay to say *yes*, but if you scheduled yourself to create at 7 p.m. and your friend wants to go out, that can be a problem. If you change your mind and go out, you may have just screwed yourself. From that point on, not only will your friend not take your creation time seriously, but neither will you.

> *Every relationship is unique, and you have to approach that relationship accordingly. There are times when you decide to create, and some people will not understand your motivations or decisions... others will just miss you, but choose carefully.*

You may have to train your friends and family to understand where you are when it comes to your art. You have to be the one to make it a priority before they will. If you continuously cave, then you are just proving to them that it is not that important.

For some, this is the case. You've already spent time training that person to believe that your art is not a priority by caving to their requests. You're going to have to change that dynamic. If not, you are going to be stuck feeling like a victim to circumstances that you created in the first place.

As hard as it was for me to admit this to myself, the reason I had a hard time saying no to people was due to a sense of *Self Significance*.

Listen, what I'm about to talk about might be extremely challenging. A lot of times, our self-esteem is wrapped up tightly in a personal pecking order that we may not even recognize.

Self Significance is when your sense of self-esteem or self-worth comes from your relationship with someone else.

For example, making statements like:

- *She has a hard time making choices without me.*
- *He needs me to pick out his clothes because he can't dress right.*
- *If I don't do the laundry, then no one will.*
- *Honestly, I'm not sure the show would happen without me.*
- *He has a hard time with this kind of stuff, I need to help him.*
- *They've been looking for someone like me for a long time.*
- *I've been there for ten years, I'm like a staple for the ...*
- *I'm the only one who understands that side of her.*
- *She needs me, I'm her best friend.*
- *We've been best friends for years, I owe him.*

It is thinking that the world will not go on without you. That someone cannot possibly survive without something that you possess.

There are times where our self-value is neatly tied up in a role we play. We identify with that role and feel obligated to fulfill it.

I understand if you are caring for a newborn, you need to pick up your kids, or you are taking care of a loved one who can't take care of themselves, you may feel a sense of obligation and responsibility, and rightfully so. Even then, personal importance can sneak in when your sense of self-worth is tied into that role.

"I am the only one who knows how to take care of him."

That statement becomes your new mission in life and your new burden. Of course, it is false, despite all the stories you tell yourself on the subject. If you weren't around, the world would still continue to spin.

For some of us, that is a harsh realization. Some of us will deny it for a long time because we don't see the harm that it does to ourselves and others.

Chances are, if you are having a difficult time getting away and having your own creative space, you may be under the impression that people need you. *That you are essential in their lives.* They may even express that you are important to them and their survival.

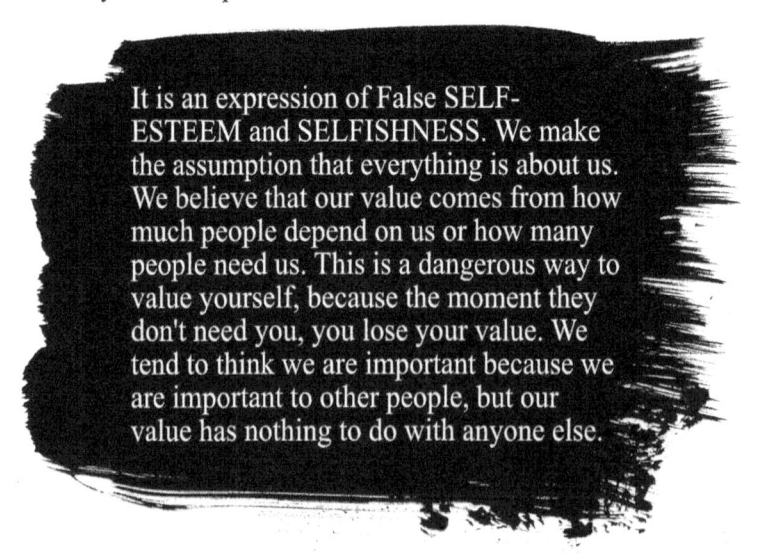

> It is an expression of False SELF-ESTEEM and SELFISHNESS. We make the assumption that everything is about us. We believe that our value comes from how much people depend on us or how many people need us. This is a dangerous way to value yourself, because the moment they don't need you, you lose your value. We tend to think we are important because we are important to other people, but our value has nothing to do with anyone else.

I can tell you right now, this sounds nice, but it is a gilded cage. This leads to resentment, martyrdom, feeling trapped, a false sense of value, depression, a false sense of duty, and is a tricky path to navigate.

For me, the realization of what I was doing to myself came one day when I almost died. I know, sounds morbid but bear with me. I realized that the world would go on. Sure, people will miss me, remember me, and wish I was still around, but the world wouldn't stop spinning. This was a sobering thought.

As hard as it might be for you to swallow, you're just not that important to the survival of the other people in your life. I'm not saying you shouldn't feed your kids or that you should be irresponsible with the people you care for, but understand that your value isn't wrapped up in the sacrifice. If you choose to do those things, you are doing them because it is YOUR choice, not because you are the only one that can. You are valuable because you are you, not because people need you.

Something I did after my near-death experience was take a close look at all of my relationships. I asked myself several questions when it came to each. I really thought about what kind of relationship I had with them. Was it a relationship based on codependency, or was it genuine? These are hard questions and will need some real contemplation.

- Do I feel that this person needs me?
- Do I feel that I need this person?
- Do I feel that I owe this person?
- Do I feel that this person owes me?
- Do I do what I do because of these feelings?
- Do I feel obligated?
- Will their world go on without me?
- What is the truth about our relationship?

After I sat down and contemplated these for a while, I came to the realization that I could either do things because I wanted to do them or I could do them out of obligation.

SELF SIGNIFICANCE

I think we learn this from society. In the movies you hear the line "I NEED YOU" & it marks the beginning of a relationship. It makes me cringe a little. I would rather have someone say "I WANT YOU" or "I CHOOSE U." I've heard people say things like "I want to feel needed" & I have to wonder how much of their identity is wrapped up in being needed. It's not who they actually are, they are so much more..

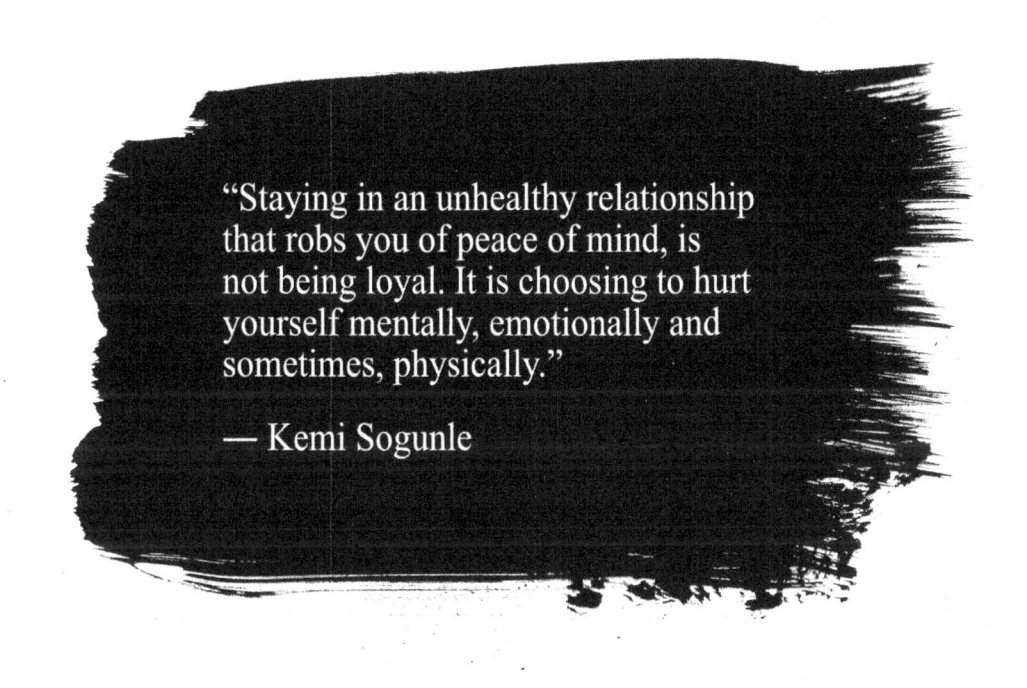

> "Staying in an unhealthy relationship that robs you of peace of mind, is not being loyal. It is choosing to hurt yourself mentally, emotionally and sometimes, physically."
>
> — Kemi Sogunle

Unhealthy Relationships.

It dawned on me that a lot of my friendships were not healthy. I had people in my life that I kept around simply because we had been friends for years, despite it not being a good friendship. I also had people in my life that I allowed to make decisions for me, despite never agreeing with their choices.

There is a fine line of emotional power at play here, so thin that it is almost indiscernible. One side, you feel like you have no choice, the other, you understand that the choice is yours.

This difference between one mindset or the other makes a huge difference in your life. Especially when it comes to pursuing your own interests and dreams.

I am constantly reevaluating my relationships and questioning my priorities. If you find yourself having a tough time saying no, it may be worth investigating your relationships a little more deeply.

Set Boundaries. This could be tough because a lot of times, people are going to push those boundaries. Consistency is key. A lot of times in these situations, we can easily view ourselves as the victim. You may feel that the person is always pulling you away from creating.

The truth is that if you have someone pushing at your boundaries, it is because you allowed it to happen. You created the dynamic that you're in with this person by not setting boundaries in the first place. Once you set a boundary, be prepared. Depending on how long this relationship has been playing out this way, there may be some serious push back.

If you stick to your boundaries, eventually that will become the norm. Unfortunately, sometimes, friends and family tend to feel entitled, so it may take longer with some. Just stay consistent.

So what if you've done all this and it's still not working in your favor?

Distance yourself.

BEING AUTHENTIC IS YOUR BAG OF CREATIVITY

The thing about facing ANYONE in the creative world is that you really have no control over the behavior of other people. You also have no control over most situations and circumstances in your life. In my opinion, the best thing you can do is be yourself in every given situation. Be Authentic.

Be authentic... What does that even mean? It means to be yourself. What does *THAT* mean?

The word authentic has been so overused that I'm almost embarrassed to use it in this book, but I'm going to reclaim it and make it awesome.

People are always talking about being authentic, but in all honesty, that's all a bit confusing.

As a creative *Rogue Artist*, I believe your power lies in being you. Every decision you make in your artistic career has to be something that stems from who you are. It has to be authentically *you* to lead you down the right path. So, I am going to try to describe my perspective on what it means to be authentic.

Material Things Don't Matter. When you are authentic, you aren't looking for happiness in things that you can buy. This doesn't mean that you deny yourself anything, it just means that you understand that you don't need the next shiny thing to make you happy. You enjoy the things you have, but you know you don't need them, and if you lose them, life goes on. Too many times, people become servants to the things they own because they feel that they need them. You also don't rate yourself or other people based on the material items that they have or don't have because you know it doesn't hold much meaning.

I often take a look around my studio and wonder how I would feel if I lost it all. I push through the initial fear and put myself in a place where I understand that I am not my stuff. This can be really hard, but it is essential to understand that if you lose everything, life goes on, and you are still you.

Experiences Make Life Richer. Be aware of how life experiences create more meaning and richness in our lives, no matter if it is an enjoyable experience or a bad one. We are all heading in the direction of a dirt nap and should relish every single minute. Being authentic means embracing all of life, warts and all. It means looking inside yourself, growing, evolving, and reaching for a sense of satisfaction in the everyday.

Really Listen. Don't listen just to respond. Don't think about what you are going to say when another person is talking. Be fully present with the other person. Share in the moment with them. Genuinely listen.

Express Thoughts, Feelings, And Views Unapologetically. Being authentic means not saying things that you don't truly mean, and not doing things that you don't really want to do. You can share your own unique thoughts, feelings, views, and creations without fear.

No People Pleasing. Authentic people know the importance of being aware, acknowledging, and expressing their own unique thoughts, feelings, views, and creations into the world. When you people please, you do things out of obligation, fear, or hope of acknowledgment, and this could cause you to lose your perspective. Do things because you want to, not because you feel that you should.

Give Love. There is power in giving love and kindness indiscriminately, understanding that we are all connected. When you are authentic, you know that by helping others, you are helping yourself. Being genuine means that you allow and encourage others to express their own truth with love and acceptance. It comes full circle.

Love Yourself. When you are authentic, you see yourself as a person of worth who deserves love, kindness, and support. Loving yourself and being unconditional is what you deserve. That means no conditions, no exceptions, no expectations, just love.

Everyone Is Unique. Not everyone is going to agree on everything all the time. Accepting differing views and opinions is understanding that it is all about perspective. It's not about being "right" and another person being "wrong," it's about different outlooks.

Take Responsibility. Authentic folks don't blame other people for what happens to them in their lives. They take personal responsibility for how their actions created an inevitable outcome. They are willing to look at how they influenced each and every situation and act accordingly.

They Trust Themselves. Authentic people can clear their minds of the constant mind chatter. They will trust their gut and take action because that's what they want. They don't wait around for permission, and they don't get confused about whether or not they can trust themselves.

Oscar Wilde said, *"Be yourself; everyone else is already taken."*

The time-tested advice of "Be Yourself" stands for a reason. It's probably the best advice you will ever receive.

Simple? Cliche? Maybe.

But as relevant as ever.

Just be yourself. Don't try to be anyone else, not even your heroes. Be the hero of your story by being the best version of you that you can be.

It can be confusing to find out who you are and define that for yourself. It starts with honesty.

Being Honest And Genuine.

People lie a lot; we all do. Small lies, big lies, white lies, and blatant lies, the fact of the matter is that we fib more than we like to admit. Most lies are petty deceits like lies told out of politeness or tact… but they are still lies. What is it about the way we are raised that gives us the license to be disingenuous?

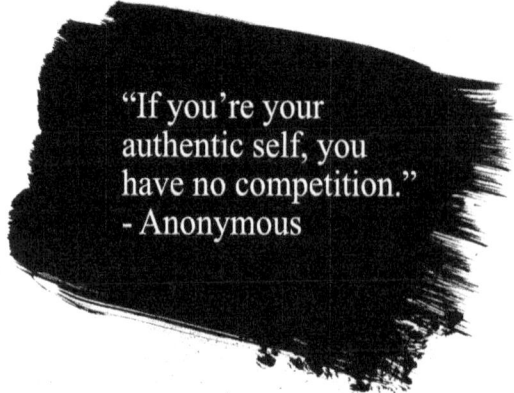

> "If you're your authentic self, you have no competition."
> - Anonymous

> **BE AUTHENTIC**
> - **B**E EXCITED TO BE YOU.
> - **E**XCEL AT TAKING CARE OF YOU.
> - **A**CCEPT ALL OF WHO YOU ARE.
> - **U**NDERSTAND YOU!
> - **T**REAT-YOU KINDLY
> - **H**ABIT-FORM KINDNESS TO YOU
> - **E**MBRACE YOUR FEELINGS
> - **N**EVER APOLOGIZE FOR BEING YOU
> - **T**ELL YOUR TRUTH
> - **I**NNER TO THE OUTER
> - **C**OURAGE IS YOU

I remember being confused by the concept of honesty when I was a kid because our society is full of mixed messages on the subject. On the one hand, you are told never to lie, but then shown that it is a necessary evil to survive.

No wonder people are so confused about what it means to be authentic.

I lied to my mom once about a test score and got caught. She scolded me and told me never to lie again, that only criminals lie. Moments later, my grandmother called. My mother desperately waved her arms, silently gesturing me to lie to my grandmother and tell her she wasn't home.

Most people lie in everyday conversation when they are trying to appear likable and competent. According to a study, it was found that 60 percent of people lied at least once during a 10-minute conversation. The average was two to three lies in ten minutes.

There are different motivations behind the crap that can fly out of our mouth. It doesn't necessarily mean that we are bad people, but we are not being "real" any time we avoid a subject by withholding or lying about it.

Make any excuse you want, but a lie is still a lie.

If you are not honest about who you are, it will be impossible to create for genuine reasons. The lies we tell complicate things, even if they seem insignificant.

It's essential to understand the things that may cause you to spin a yarn or split the blanket because, for the most part, we lie because of our insecurities. Being insecure and people-pleasing may be at the core of the deceit. As an artist, your power is in being yourself. Knowing who you are, that is your bag of goodies.

The truth will set you free. I know, I'm sure you've heard that a hundred times, but it is true. Every time you tell a lie, you are showing yourself who you are, and unfortunately, that person is not authentic.

The best way to figure out how to be genuine is to get a deeper understanding of why we and other people lie. See if you identify with any of these:

Lie To Avoid Punishment. This is the most common motivation for telling lies by both children and adults. As a kid, I lied all the time to try to get out of trouble. As an adult, I found myself doing the same thing. Instead of owning up and facing my mistakes, I avoided them at all cost. I spent so many years doing this that eventually, my self-identity was lost in the web.

Lie To Get A Reward Or Recognition. This is the second most common motive in both children and adults. *Taking credit or falsely bolstering up experience in something, to be liked or admired.* I realize I have to watch myself with people I admire because I can easily fall into this habit. Whenever I hear words blurt out of my mouth, claiming that I'm an expert at anything, usually, I know I'm full of crap.

Lie To Protect Another Person. This is keeping someone's secret and being put in a tough position where you are sacrificing your authenticity for another person's mistake. It is especially hard if you have to lie to a good friend or loved one because of it. I personally make sure no one puts me in an awkward position, the friendship is not worth it. If a conversation needs to happen, then it IS going to happen.

Lie To Win Admiration. This is where we try to make ourselves seem like more than we are to increase our popularity. From little white lies to bolster a quality to creating an entirely fabricated story.

When I was a pre-teen, I told people I was a ninja... enough said. Although I don't tell people I'm a dark assassin anymore, I keep a very close eye on this with every interaction because I know this lie is tied into my lack of self-esteem.

Lie To Avoid Awkward Social Situations. This is where we lie because we want to get out of doing something or going somewhere. I did this a lot, and my go-to was claiming I wasn't feeling well. I make it a point just to say, "I don't want to go" or "I don't want to do that."

This can be a tough one, but I find it essential to not feel like a coward when I simply don't feel like doing something... I can just be honest and say no.

Lie To Avoid Embarrassment. This is where we avoid our failures and mistakes. We pretend like an embarrassing moment never happened. The most freeing thing I have ever done in my life is own failures and be proud of them. Failures mean you are doing stuff and not just talking about doing it.

Lie To Exercise Power. This is where someone manipulates a situation by controlling the information and flipping the tables. This usually occurs while arguing and is arguably the most dangerous motive for telling lies.

I'm not trying to make anyone feel bad or say that you are a deceitful wretch, because I don't think you are. I don't think many of us are. I feel like most people that tell lies are avoiding something that might be uncomfortable.

As a Rogue Artist, you embrace discomfort because avoiding it never leads to the truth of who you are. It is almost impossible to really know what you stand for if you continuously have to keep some false story running in your brain. It's just a waste of valuable resources in that brilliant mind of yours. It's easy to get bogged down and lose sight of yourself when you are caught up in a yarn of lies.

When you are authentic, your relationship improves with yourself. The words that come out of your mouth can be trusted because by being honest with other people, you are honest with yourself.

When you are consistently truthful, what you say becomes much more powerful to you.

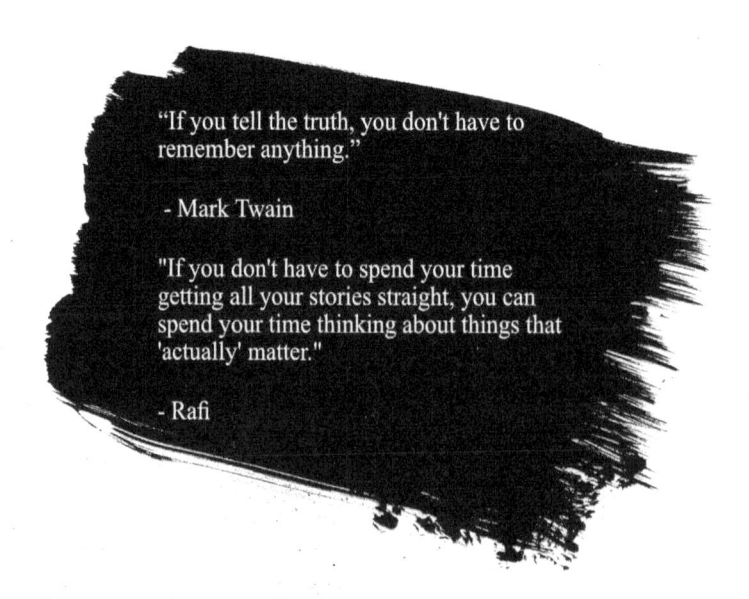

> "If you tell the truth, you don't have to remember anything."
>
> - Mark Twain
>
> "If you don't have to spend your time getting all your stories straight, you can spend your time thinking about things that 'actually' matter."
>
> - Rafi

> — ARE YOU LIVING A LIE?
> — DO YOU FEEL TRAPPED?
> — ARE YOU UNHEARD, UNSEEN, UNDERVALUED?
> — DO YOU FEEL ALONE?
> — DO YOU HIDE PAIN BEHIND A SMILE?
> — ARE YOU SOCIALLY ACCEPTABLE?
> — DO YOU PEOPLE PLEASE A LOT?
> — DO YOU ACT DIFFERENT AROUND DIFFERENT PEOPLE?
> — DID YOU GIVE UP ON YOUR DREAMS?
> — DO THE WAY OTHER PEOPLE SEE YOU MATTER TO YOU?
> — DO YOU CONSTANTLY FEEL A DARK CLOUD LOOMING?
> — DID YOU FORGET HOW TO MAKE YOURSELF HAPPY?
> — DO YOU FEEL BORED WITH LIFE?
> — DO YOU FEEL LIKE SOMETHING IS MISSING? — IF YOU SAY YES
> (BE 'REAL' & STOP THE BULLSHIT)

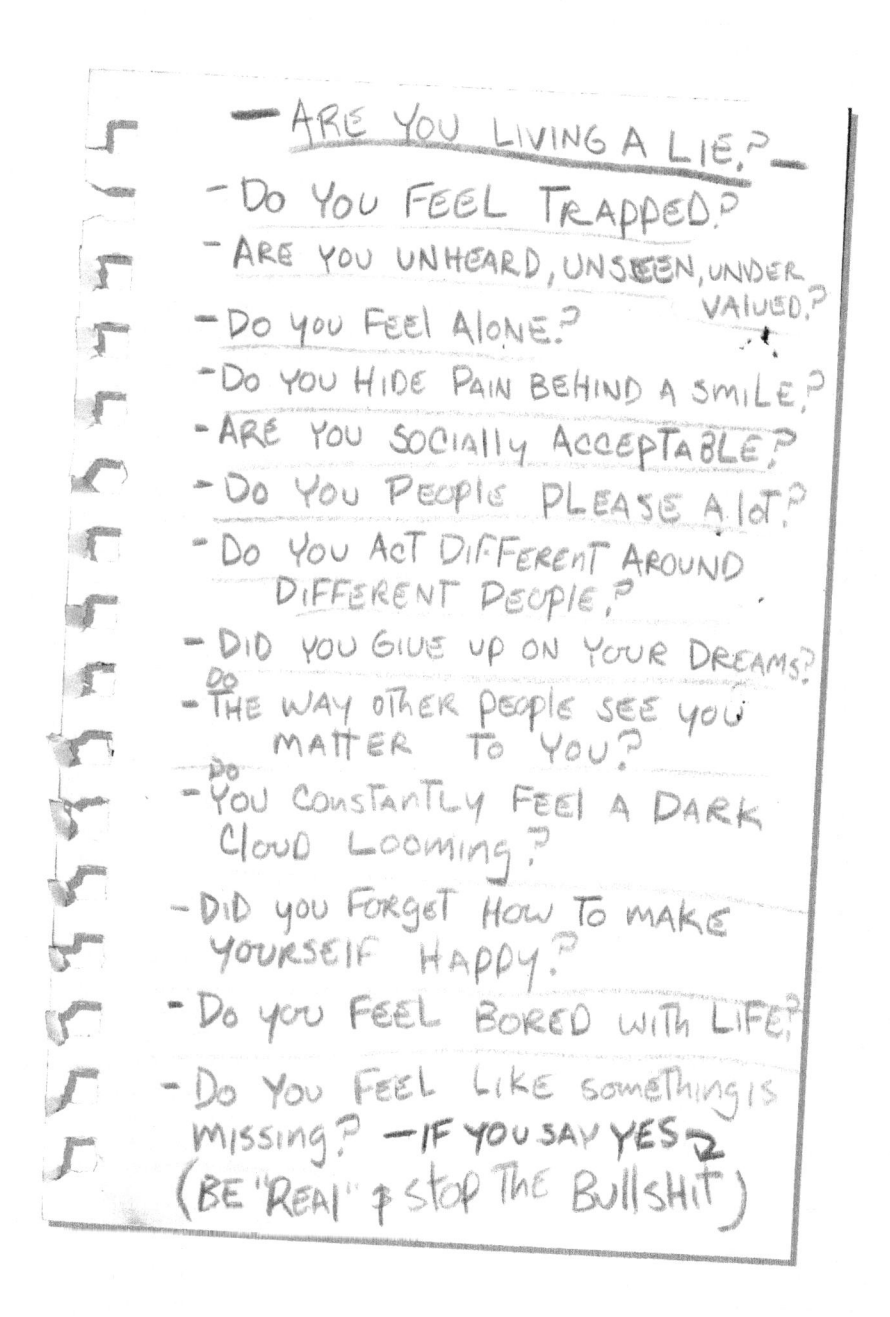

The biggest lie that we tell ourselves as creatives, is that we need validation. In fact, the lie or myth is so prominent in the art world that most of what we tell ourselves and others is based on this system of lies.
It might seem harmless to chase validation, but the repercussions are devastating.

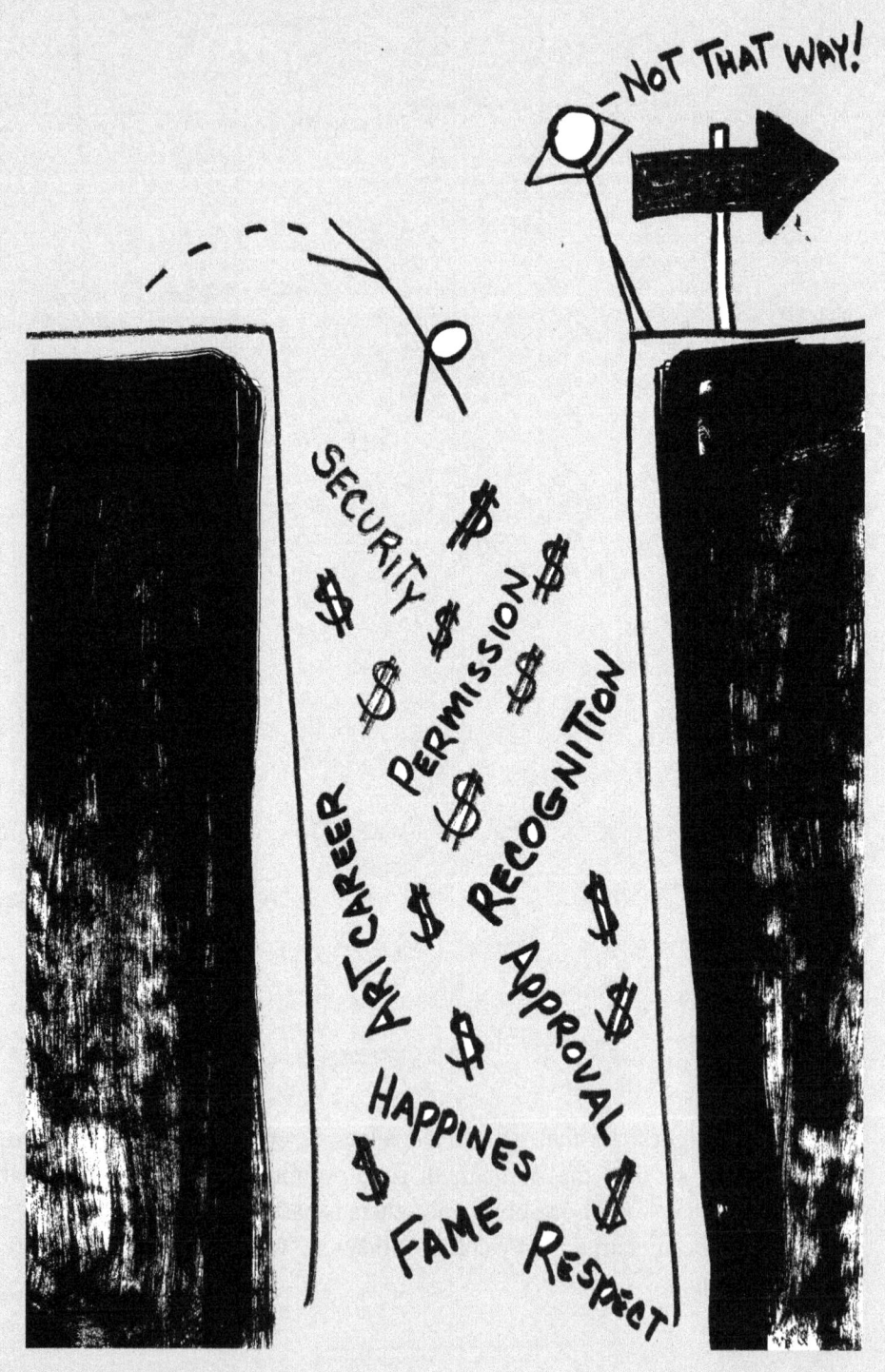

THE ROGUE ARTIST SURVIVAL GUIDE

WHAT ARE YOU CHASING ANYWAY

Usually, when people have approached me with their stories of failure, they talk about a one-time event. They'll tell me how they tried to go for it, and things didn't work out. I've had artists come to me with things like:

- I quit my job and decided to pursue an art career, and I was broke.
- No one followed me on social media, so I quit.
- I created some work for a gallery, and I got rejected. So I quit.
- No one seemed interested in my art, so I quit.
- I did a festival and didn't sell anything. I quit right after.
- I tried to talk to some art agents, and it didn't go so well.
- My pieces didn't sell at auction, no one was interested.
- My art teacher said I would never make it.
- My family wasn't supportive of my choice to become an artist.
- I invested a bunch of money and never made that money back.

Immediately I think, "Yeah, and every single one of these failures is something that I have experienced multiple times, the only difference is I didn't stop. I didn't buy into my own bullshit story."

I know some artists who spend all their time clamoring for attention from the right people, and feel like a fraud when they don't have it. For a lot of us, we have to confirm our identity by being acknowledged and recognized for who we want to be.

The Rogue Artist doesn't care. I don't mean you disregard people's opinions, they have the right to believe whatever they want. I suggest that you create amazing creations, and sometimes you create crap, but you keep creating because you want to create. You aren't chasing money, fame, or acknowledgment. You are pursuing your sense of creative innovation.

It's about creating and sharing your work with the world.

There's a really dark side for an artist when it comes to the need for validation. I know it well. At one point, I kept adding titles to my name as I kept hitting milestones in my career. This seemed to exclaim my validation as an artist out into the world. At the time, I didn't even realize how ridiculous it was.

- *Artist Rafi Perez.*
- *Award-winning Artist Rafi Perez.*
- *Award-winning Contemporary Artist Rafi Perez.*
- *International Award-winning Contemporary Artist Rafi Perez.*
- *Internationally Acclaimed Award-winning Contemporary Artist Rafi Perez.*

Luckily I stopped there; I got to the point that I hated putting my name on things because it was too long. Eventually, I dropped the fluff.

ARTIST RAFI PEREZ

Losing yourself in a drama of titles and awards can really cause you to forget why you do what you do. The need for people to validate you as an artist can lead to a whole series of problems.

I'm going to be very honest here, the system that we all know about in the art world sucks. It is a series of validation markers. Art school, galleries, juried this or that... If you let it, it will keep you in constant search of someone or something to validate your artistic genius.

Following that system, and playing the game of seeking validation is just soul-sucking. As far as shitty life choices go, I think the relentless pursuit of creative validation is in competition for the top spot with eating rusty nails and kissing your grandma's hairy mole.

I've known artists who have plans that involve brown-nosing the right people to get their art into a specific arena. One, in particular, contacted me, and we had a debate about it.

"I plan to gather collectors that are 'tastemakers' of the industry, collectors who are on the invitation list of an evening auction at Sotheby's or Christie's." He continues, "I'll do this by actively interacting with the 'right' people in the right places. The people you find in the VIP lounge of Art Basel are simply not the same people you see at markets or on YouTube. Everyone is created equal, but some are more equal than others. And at this moment, the reality is that I'm definitely less equal than some without their support."

I responded with, "I know what you're saying, and I think you should definitely pursue it. Yet, I will say, I don't chase people, nor will I ever allow myself to believe that my art will only have an impact if it gets in certain hands. I don't value certain humans over others, simply because I think they can make me or my art famous." I continued, "For me personally, it's about seeing how far I can get and experiencing every moment fully as a living breathing artist. Kissing some tastemaker's butt at a VIP event just isn't my style, for now. Maybe that will change someday, but I doubt it."

The art world is rife with the need for validation in order to succeed.

In my opinion, it is way too easy to make decisions not for yourself, but for the gain of validation from others whose respect you are seeking. In those situations, a lot of times, we hold ourselves back from trying new things because of fear of losing respect from tastemakers.

Living life like this can make you feel lost and depressed. It can feel like you have no control because other people have a grip on your life and creative career.

The problem with validation is that it can become addictive. You will do whatever it takes to get the likes, even if it means putting yourself in a position to grovel at someone's feet for recognition.

Listen, I'm not judging this kid. He can go and schmooze with anyone he wants, but I know what it feels like to be in a position like that. I spent most of my life chasing validation, money, respect, and recognition.

235

I always had to play by someone else's rules, felt like I was being tossed around, and was always afraid of being on the chopping block.

Obviously, this is stupid, and no one actually had control of my life. Unfortunately, my decisions were all guided by seeking validation, money, or recognition. Because of that, I put myself in a position where I gave others measurable control over me and my career. In return, I lost a massive part of myself. My voice, my creativity, my happiness, my freedom, was given away by me.

People think that you have to chase after something to be motivated and ambitious. I think as the idea of success got wrapped up in money and awards, things got confusing. It all became about chasing the dream, chasing the money, and chasing success.

I personally don't think any of us should be chasing anything. I think right now we are living life. I think we should just pay attention. We make hundreds of choices every day. How many of those choices are based on something elusive that you are chasing?

Pay attention to what you are chasing.

- Are you chasing security?
- Are you chasing money?
- Are you chasing recognition?
- Are you chasing likes on social media?
- Are you chasing an art career?
- Are you chasing awards?
- Are you chasing success?
- Are you chasing happiness?
- Are you chasing trends?
- Are you chasing influencers?
- Are you chasing approval?
- Are you chasing permission?
- Are you chasing fame?
- Are you chasing artistic immortality?
- Are you chasing respect?

I am ambitious about living life and expressing myself as fully as I can every moment, of every day, in everything I do. I feel like every goal above that you may want to pursue in life is a natural side effect of simply living each day as fully as you can as a creative.

Create for the sake of creating. Let your decisions be based on what you want. Put yourself out there to share your voice in whatever way you choose, and keep doing it all because it makes you happy *now*.

If you are creating art for any of the reasons above, you are in for a hard road. You won't be happy until you reach the fame, the money, or the success of your choosing and let me tell you, it will never feel like enough.

If you are creating art for the sake of creating art every day, expressing yourself by putting yourself out there, and doing what you love… for you, then you are unstoppable. Life is too short to *chase* dreams. *Live* your dream now as best you can with what you have. Eventually, the rest will follow as you grow.

Chasing anything can lead to desperation, and when we are desperate we can make some foolish decisions. People fall for scams all the time because they think there is a secret sauce, proven method, or some other bullshit that will help them get the thing they are trying to chase.

Watch Out For Scams In The Art World.

If anybody is making bold promises of sales or guarantees of large amounts of exposure for butt loads of money, then steer clear. Usually, when something is a scam, it will push at an insecurity or need for validation.

You can spot a scam if something doesn't add up. Some common ones to look out for are email scams, vanity galleries, anyone that requests bank information, cashier's check, money wire.

Things to look out for are:

- Certain contests in magazines.
- An interested buyer for a vague piece.
- Art books - kind of like those poetry book scams back in the day.
- Vanity art book publishers.
- Expensive artist website builders that target artists.
- Phone calls from strangers promising Google rankings.
- Promises of instant fame.
- Suspicious artist courses on how to become an artist.
- Festivals where you have to buy and sell tickets.
- Emails with a lot of misspellings.
- And anything that seems suspicious.

Just watch what you are chasing and don't get got.

That being said, I have heard a lot of artists say things like "I don't pay to play!" suggesting that if ANY art event charges money, that it is a scam. That is simply not true; most every legit art competition, festival, or association is going to charge a jury fee, booth rent, or service fee.

As a business, you are going to have certain expenses, just be smart about where and when you choose to spend your money. Research any art-related events you may be interested in and make sure you get all your questions answered before you agree to anything.

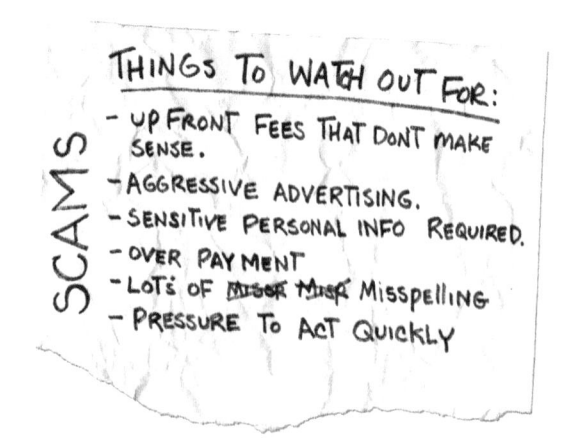

> **SCAMS**
> **THINGS TO WATCH OUT FOR:**
> - UP FRONT FEES THAT DON'T MAKE SENSE.
> - AGGRESSIVE ADVERTISING.
> - SENSITIVE PERSONAL INFO REQUIRED.
> - OVER PAYMENT
> - LOTS OF ~~MISSS MISSA~~ MISSPELLING
> - PRESSURE TO ACT QUICKLY

THE GATEKEEPERS AND MIDDLEMEN

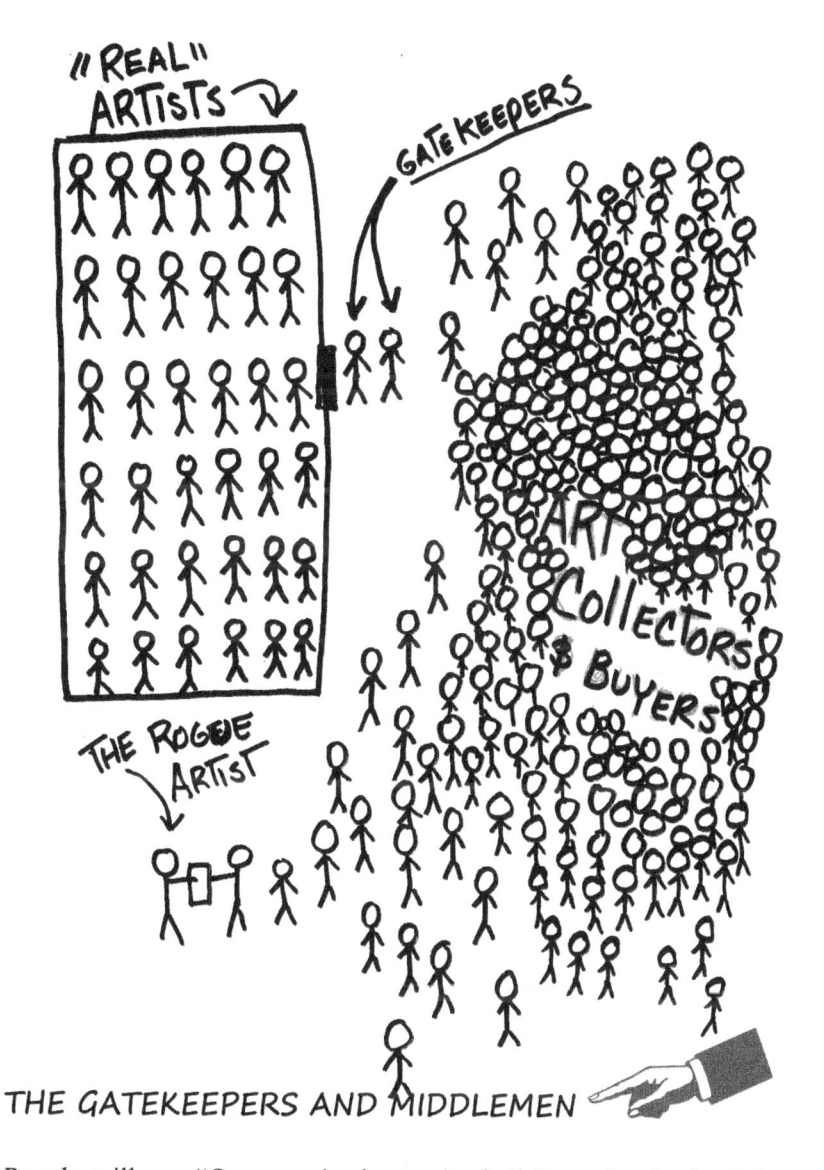

People will say "Once you're in, you're in." But who the heck has the right to decide who's in or out?

Before I continue talking about The Gatekeepers, I want you to keep in mind that the most popular art world system is ridiculous. It is set up to perpetuate artistic insecurities and bring a ranking and grading system into a career where the accolades are entirely subjective.

THE ROGUE ARTIST SURVIVAL GUIDE

In the mainstream art world, super curators and tastemakers may put together spotlight exhibits to supply an artist with validation and visibility. The promise is that being the hottest new thing in the art world is going to lead to more exhibitions, press opportunities, price raising, and a hot pursuit from galleries and collectors. There's nothing wrong with making it *BIG* in the mainstream art market, but it doesn't make or break you as an artist.

There is a distinct difference between the popular side of the art world and what I consider the REAL art world. The mainstream art world is highly dependent on the gatekeepers and go-betweens. It is also a theatrical magic show with smoke and mirrors. Most of the popular systems in the world are like that. Take the price of diamonds; De Beers created an exclusivity and demand for a stone that is not all that rare. At one point, De Beers controlled 90% of the world's diamond market, which allowed them to hold a monopoly over diamonds. The mainstream art market gives the *ILLUSION* that they control most of the artwork in the world. People have actually been quoted as saying that there is an *art shortage*, which is utterly ridiculous when you consider how many artists are out there creating art. This is all part of the illusion of exclusivity in the mainstream art market.

> THE MAINSTREAM ART MARKET TAKES A PAGE OUT OF THE DE BEERS PLAYBOOK. (WHY DIAMONDS ARE SO EXPENSIVE WHEN THEY SHOULDN'T BE.)
> 1. CONTROL SUPPLY. ← CONSIDER RARE.
> 2. LIMIT DISTRIBUTION. ← A SMALL # OF PLACES YOU CAN GET.
> 3. CREATE DEMAND. ← HYPE UP THE NEED FOR IT.
> 4. LINK SPENDING TO SUCCESS. ← "ONLY PEOPLE WITH MONEY CAN."
> 5. DEFINE VALUE. ← HAVE $ PRICING THAT IS DEFINED BY SUBJECTIVE STANDARDS.
> 6. USE EXPENSIVE PRICE AS MARKETING. ← CAUSES IT TO SEEM RARE.

The truth is that one fundamental feature of the art world as a whole is a lack of formal rules; trying to get a handle on artists or anything art related is like trying to herd a flock of geese.

The mainstream art world is continuously creating standards, rules, measures, and unregulated regulations in an attempt to convince the general public that what it says about art is the authority and final word. These sweeping proclamations make vague attempts to describe why a painting sold for hundreds of millions of dollars, even though a week earlier it sold for fifty million. It's meant to give the illusion of transparency and legitimacy to a world full of backroom deals and somewhat underhanded tactics.

According to "art experts", there are only two markets: Mainstream, and Outsider Art.

According to the internet, *Outsider art is art by self-taught or naïve art makers. Typically, those labeled as outsider artists have little or no contact with the mainstream art world or art institutions. In many cases, their work is discovered only after their deaths. Often, outsider art illustrates extreme mental states, unconventional ideas, or elaborate fantasy worlds. Outsider art is also associated with the art of the mentally ill.*

Needless to say, this is complete bullshit. Other than the self-taught part, this pretty much describes a whole bunch of artists I know. It's vague, nonsensical, and confusing descriptions like this that make the mainstream art world seem so mysterious.

Art itself cannot really have a standard of measurement, so the general public usually thinks they are missing something. Most people feel like they don't know enough about art to really understand what is going on. People who are even remotely interested in buying art will think they are not qualified to make the right choices.

Smoke and mirrors.

This is why there are so many middlemen (and middlewomen) in the mainstream art world. These are people that claim expertise when it comes to art and the art market. They know what is popular, what is important, and which art investments will get the most significant returns. These people wield tremendous power and have an influence on what kind of art is being created and sold in the mainstream art market.

THE ROGUE ARTIST SURVIVAL GUIDE

They pretty much determine what real art is *supposed* to be. This creates a sense of demand for a particular style of art or a particular artist over other art or artists. It is a brilliant system for making money for the middleman of the mainstream art world. It is also a brilliant system for inflating the prices in the art world. Klee and I call it the unregulated Art Stock Market. This is usually the art market you will read about in a magazine or newspaper.

THE ART STOCK MARKET

A lot of new artists spend their entire lives wishing to become a full-time artist and find it to be a pipe dream. That's because they set their sights on the Art Stock Market, and this market is challenging to get into, is highly exclusive, and is tightly controlled by a few players. Just to be clear, I'm not against pursuing the art stock market, although I find some of the failed tactics that artists use to get in disempowering and completely unnecessary. The Mainstream Art Market is why the starving artist myth has been able to remain so prevalent.

As a rogue artist, I take the stance of giving the Mainstream Art Market a big fat middle finger.

At some point over the years, the Art Stock Market became more about investment in both the long and short term, instead of the actual art. In the past, criminals have actually used the art stock market to launder money. Stories of art and money laundering tend to be media-friendly, and often involve the wealthy behaving poorly. Transactions are usually private, and prices can be subjective and manipulated.

It is very exclusive, highly controlled, and not as big as you would think. Sure, there are big-ticket items, but it's not the only art market out there, and definitely not where most art is sold. The problem is that when you watch documentaries, read books, or newspaper articles about the Art Market, this is the only Market that is discussed.

Because of this, many people are confused about how the art world works. The Art Stock Market is full of selective disinformation and lack of transparency, which makes things even more confusing.

People are making a lot of money as middlemen in the mainstream art market. *Mega galleries, auction houses, art brokers, and art consultants*, just to name a few. What's interesting to me is that the mainstream art market is seen as the real art market, yet when you break it down, it's not controlled by artists or collectors. It's largely controlled by the people who profit off of both.

Personally, I think it's a big farce. I have been selling art for almost a decade with no middleman, and I'm doing just fine.

As artists, we tend to work in a vacuum, and I can understand wanting to partner up with someone interested in the marketing and sales of the work.

That being said, the partner should be someone who works with the artist in a symbiotic relationship. This can be a gallery, an agent, or a manager, but the business should ultimately be controlled by the creator of the work. Unfortunately the way the mainstream art world is represented today, in some cases the axis of power has shifted to the representative of the artist. The mainstream art world is a place where business people make money on their investments and is hardly about the genuine value of the art itself.

To give you an example of this, let's take a look at Jeff Koons Popeye sculpture. This piece was purchased by Steve Wynn for 28.8 million. He was offered 60 million dollars soon after. This is an investment piece that gains value not because of the art itself, but because the people that own it increase it's value. This is known as *provenance*.

Provenance is the chronology of the ownership, custody, or location of an object. It is useful in validating that a work is authentic. It is also used to increase the value of the work, depending on who owned it.

The Art Stock Market is all about provenance and the credibility of who bought the art. It's a game of "Name That Celebrity" and not necessarily about the art itself. The more "important collector" hands it passes through, the more "valuable" it becomes. Some mainstream galleries keep this in mind when selling the art.

They pick and choose who their collectors are to increase the value of their art for when they broker the next deal. It's like an exclusive club for the rich and powerful.

The actor Daniel Radcliffe (Harry Potter) was once rejected by a Frieze Art Fair dealer because he wasn't exactly what the gallery was hoping for in a buyer.

"I went to Frieze Art Fair and saw a painting by Jim Hodges. The guy said, 'No, we're waiting for a more prestigious collector to take that.' I was like, thanks, thanks a lot," said Radcliffe.

I'm not saying the entire mainstream art world is like this. Good people are trying to navigate the minefield of exclusivity and rejection, people who are authentic and in it for the art. Still, there's no denying it's all convoluted with pretension and vagueness. You can easily get lost in the shuffle of the mega galleries, auction houses, exclusive events and what-nots.

One thing about this small part of the art world that stands out to me is the mentality about who can purchase art. Even small gallerists, collectors, and artists who navigate the mainstream art world have been tainted by the idea that having money elevates you as a person.

A common proverb among people in the mainstream art world is that unless you have a lot of money, you can't buy art.

This is ridiculous. Art is for everyone.

The false representation of *what art is* and *who it is for* can cause a lot of damage to aspiring artists and new collectors. My art world is all-inclusive. I have collectors of all financial backgrounds, from the super-wealthy to the not so wealthy. I have collectors that previously never collected a lick of art and seasoned art collectors. I am an equal opportunity art dealer and artist. I create what I want when I want, and no one tells me how to run my art business.

I may not be selling million-dollar sculptures at auction to former Las Vegas resort owners, but I make a hell of a living, and I create my own opportunities, by my own rules.

The mainstream art market would have you believe that there is a barrier between the "real" art market and the rest of the art out there. They give the illusion that artists who are not part of the exclusive mainstream art club are not real artists. Anybody outside of that barrier is an outsider artist, crafter, or amateur.

According to the mainstream art market, art that is purchased from a self-taught local artist is not considered "real art" because it is outside of the exclusive, restrictive, controlled environment of the mainstream art market.

However, if that same artist somehow manages to get into the mainstream art market, their art is then sold as "real art" even though it is the same exact art as it was before, by the same artist.

This is why so many artists are confused about what "real art" is supposed to be. They are also confused about what it means to be successful as an artist. It is the same reason that so many people hire art consultants to tell them what to buy instead of just buying something that moves them.

The system is a *big fat lie*.

This false perspective of the art world can be very discouraging for an artist because it makes it seem like you will not survive unless you somehow manage to get into that system.

When you are a Rogue Artist, you create your own art market.

I remember in the early days of my career, people were complaining about the economy and stating that art "just doesn't sell these days". Others told me it was infeasible to make a living as an artist because the art market was impossible to breach. I would respond with, "I make my own economy and art market, so it's all up to me whether I survive or starve."

To date, I've sold thousands of works of art ranging from $20 to $12,000. I have a loyal collector base from all around the world, a large following online, and yet no one really knows about me. I'm *a nobody* in the mainstream art world.

Maybe someday the Mainstream Art Market will approach me, but honestly, I don't care. There is no cap to my growth opportunity no matter what direction I decide to go in with my art, as long as I keep moving forward.

As a Rogue Artist, you make your own career, you make your own economy, and you make your own art world full of your individual collectors. You don't chase for validation, you create your personal validation.

I am not going to wait around or ask for permission to be discovered.

Could The Real Art World Please Stand Up?

When you think about it, what people call the art market in the media, is only about 1% of the actual art market. There is no mention of the everyday people that make up the actual art market. You only hear about big-name artists, galleries, museums, and celebrity collectors.

The actual art world is made up of one-on-one interactions between real people. I think we forget that sometimes in this media blasted, money-centric, quick-paced world.

I feel like the media gets it all wrong. It's not about how much money the art sold for, how wealthy the collector is, or how much prestige the sale brought the artist.

Honestly, the corporate companies I worked for before becoming an artist would print out prestige in the form of "You did real good." certificates. I would put them in cheap frames and hang them on my wall as a symbol of how important I was.

I feel like we miss the point when we confuse success with awards and accolades. You can add them to your resume, but I feel like we've lost the point of what it is all about.

It's about the friendships developed and the relationships we establish as artists. The people that connect with us through the art we create are usually like-minded folks.

It's about the creative process and the astonishing ability to face rejection every day and share your art with the world.

It is about the collector who proudly displays your artwork on their wall, or wears it on their body, or listens to it in their car. The connection that would not have been possible if that individual artist did not break through the barriers of fear and share their creations with the world.

None of this is possible without the vast amount of humans out there who buy art because of the value it has to them. Not because it has a market value, but because they are connected with it.

As an artist who ultimately chose to make his own way, I have trained myself to see the world quite differently than I used to. Where I once felt hopelessness in an impossible art system, I now see the opportunities. There is misdirection to be avoided, but I have a strong hope that everyone can pursue their creative spirit, and succeed.

I think it is easy to forget in this world that is so focused on money and success, that we artists create because of the love of creation.

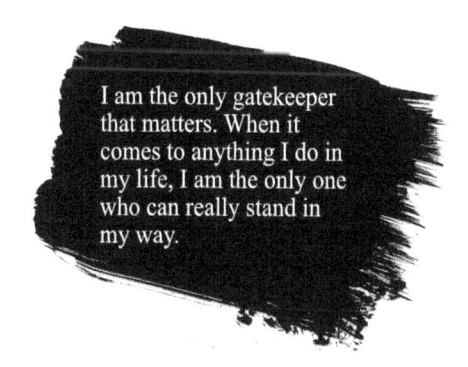

> I am the only gatekeeper that matters. When it comes to anything I do in my life, I am the only one who can really stand in my way.

MONEY MONEY MONEY

Making money with art is all about your mindset.

Poor $ Mentality
- Misses the old days.
- Thinks they're always missing something.
- Feels insignificant.
- Thinks about how to save more.
- Believes more work & sacrifice = more $

Healthy $ Mentality
- Lives in the moment.
- Figures out as they go.
- Feels significantly full of appreciation
- Thinks about how to make more
- Work smarter not harder

LET'S TALK ABOUT MONEY, BABY!

Money can be a taboo subject for a lot of creatives, but the fact is that if you are not making money as a creative in today's market, then chances are you have some garbage floating around in your cranium jar.

A lot of that garbage can come from the less than perfect money mindset we may have picked up as children. Sayings like "Money doesn't grow on trees." and "Money is scarce." perpetuate a fear when it comes to dealing with money. As creatives, some of us can struggle with feeling guilty for wanting to charge money for our art.

Some artists go as far as justifying the feelings of fear associated with money, by demonizing the idea that you can make a living as an artist.

Listen, money is part of business, and if you are wanting to make this a career, then you have to get comfortable with the subject of money.

To make some headway with the money, I think it is essential to understand where the starving artist myth may have come from. It is a mindset that took root in our culture, but it is more of an urban legend than truth.

WILL PAINT FOR FOOD.

The Starving Artist Myth.

Art For Art's Sake was the creed of bohemianism in the 20th century. This is where creations should not be made to be functional or commercial, but instead because the art is an end in of itself. A real artist didn't want to make money with their art. That was just greedy.

It fits a ridiculous model where poverty and sacrifice somehow mean that you are a good person. The reality is that whether you are having a hard time selling your creations or are living paycheck to paycheck, feeling poor sucks. The truth is that if you choose to justify feeling poor with a belief that poverty = being morally correct, then you are not likely going to make any improvements to your financial situation.

Chasing money sucks too, and is also not likely to improve your financial state. Chasing money and making money are two totally different things. The difference may seem subtle, but they are worlds apart. Unfortunately, some people haven't made that distinction and either sacrifice their well being in pursuit of the almighty dollar, or buy into the false righteousness of thinking that any act that involves money reduces the meaning of the action.

As an artist, you are building a business. Like any other business, a lot of the work you put into it won't be easy or glamorous. That includes promoting yourself, putting yourself out there, dealing with the obstacles, and generally doing all the boring stuff that doesn't happen magically. You will also have to keep going despite things being hard.

If you are waiting around and complaining because nothing is happening with your creative career, then chances are you will starve. If you are taking action and doing everything in your power to make things happen, then it'll still take time to grow, but you'll be on your way.

Making money with your art is the right thing to do. The creativity, time, materials, years of practice, unique ideas, and personal perspective have value. Do not underestimate the worth of your creative story.

As an artist, you become the CEO of your own creative empire. You choose how to run, how to market, and what the overarching message is for your business. You get to choose all of it: what you create, how hard you work, and whether or not you will succeed.

The problem is that some artists don't want to do the work. Some artists feel that they are not qualified to run their own creative empire. Some artists are afraid to fail, and others are just lazy. The truth is that none of us are qualified to run a business until we run a business.

A lousy money mentality will cause you to fear the things in business that you don't understand, and that will hold you back. When we break it down and start looking at what our attitude towards money is, sometimes we realize that there may be a fear of making money within us as well.

I think it's not so much a fear of making money, but a fear of becoming a slave to money. There is a difference between making money and chasing it.

Contemplate the difference between making a living as an artist, and chasing after the money. In my career as a professional artist, I have had to navigate these waters quite a bit. It is something I keep a close eye on. As a kid, I got started on my money mindset journey on the wrong foot.

Growing up a chubby kid, middle-class to poverty-stricken, in a ghetto of Chicago, I hoped that one day I would become a wealthy creative.

THE ROGUE ARTIST SURVIVAL GUIDE

I had no idea how I was going to make that come true, but that was my dream. My idea of success was that if I had money, and a lot of it, people would respect me and my life choices... including my parents.

I chased money for most of my life. As a child of the 80's, I learned that getting rich was the American Dream. Most of the people I grew up around wanted to be rich. My parents had shitty views on money that they happily passed down to me. Most of my friends talked about making millions of dollars, but had no plan. Unfortunately, in my experience, chasing money for the sake of money is a sure way to become emotionally bankrupt.

And that's what some people don't understand about chasing money, or even success. I almost did the same thing with my creative career. You can be on the path, reach your goals, and still hate your life.

A few years into my art career, and I started to take myself and money too seriously. I started making choices based on making more money and compromised who I was. One day I looked in the mirror and realized that although I was doing what I loved, I managed to turn it into something terrible. I was miserable. I reevaluated and put myself back on track.

This was a powerful lesson. I realized that for most of my life, I was chasing money as an answer to my dreams. I believed that if I made more money, then I would be free to do what I wanted, not realizing that I had gotten in the habit of "Money comes first, and the feelings follow."

Listen, starting any business is not easy. Starting your own creative business can feel like a nightmare sometimes. If you don't have your priorities straight, you may get somewhere you don't want to be. There is no shortcut, no easy road, and most of the time you have no clue what you are doing.

You are going to have to bust your ass and face your own fears. At some point you will ask yourself, "Is this all worth it?" If you are doing it for the money, the answer will be no.

The fact is that money isn't guaranteed, but the pain of constantly chasing after it, is.

People often chase money without fully understanding what's driving them. I wanted to be rich because I wanted to be free to make my own choices in life and be happy. I made the mistake of conflating money with happiness or, perhaps even more delusional, with freedom.

I had to stop and ask myself about my relationship with money if I was planning on changing my outcome.

Despite what people may sometimes think, money can't change the way you feel about yourself. We may want to feel powerful, be admired, be respected, be confident, and feel a sense of freedom.

Unfortunately, money can't do anything to change the way you feel about yourself. Your insecurities will survive when you make money. If you're not proud of who you are, money won't change that. If you don't believe in yourself, the money will fail you there too.

Money is not the enemy, but it is also not the goal.

My priorities are creating art, expressing myself, pushing my boundaries, adding value to people's lives, solving problems, facing fears, putting myself out there, having fun, following my bliss, autonomy, being authentic, and being honest. *Evolving as a creative and human every day, and only then, after those things, is making money a priority.*

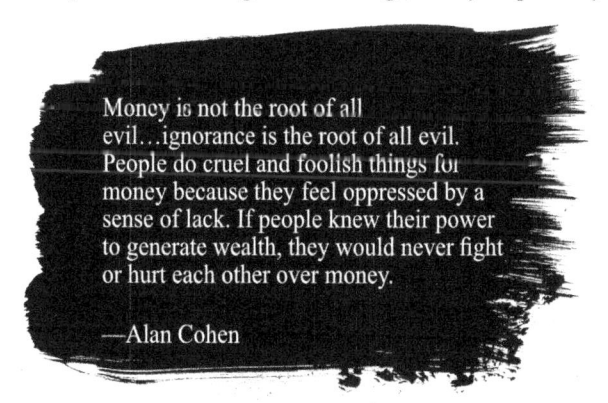

> Money is not the root of all evil…ignorance is the root of all evil. People do cruel and foolish things for money because they feel oppressed by a sense of lack. If people knew their power to generate wealth, they would never fight or hurt each other over money.
>
> —Alan Cohen

MAKE SMART CHOICES IN YOUR LIFE

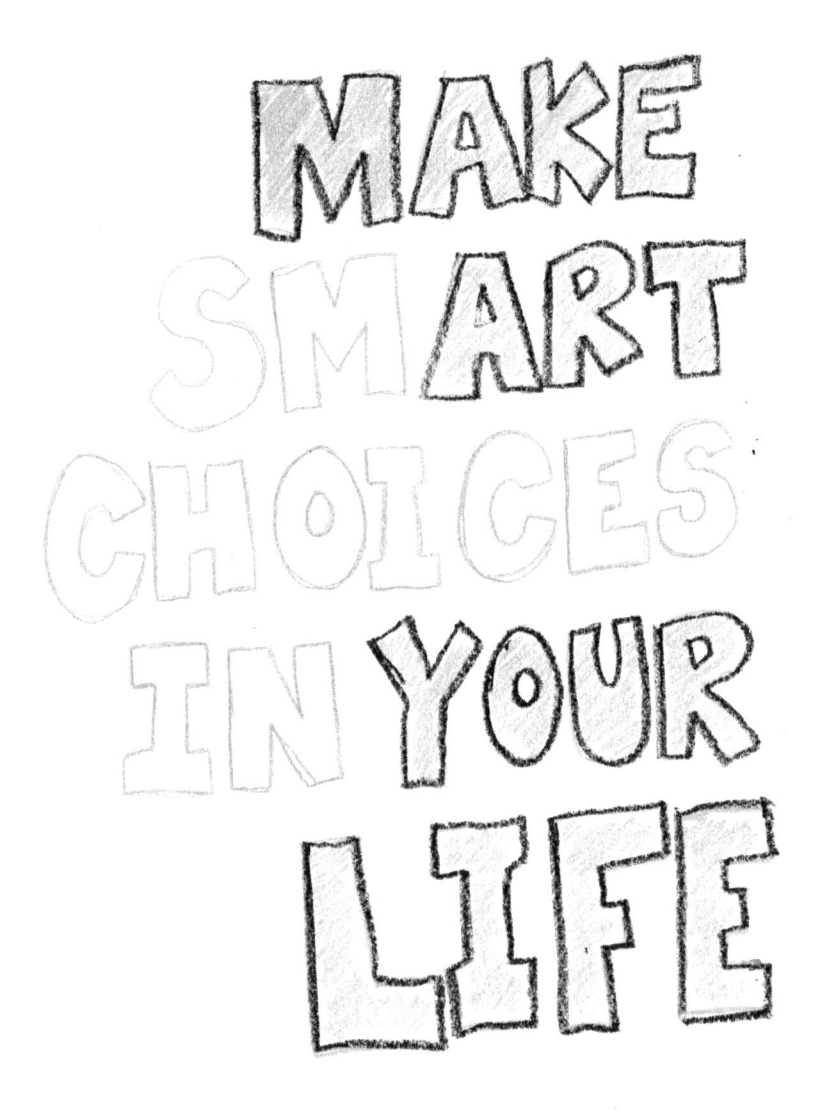

Things I focus On When It Comes To Money.

I may not allow money to be my guiding star in my creative business, but it is essential to make money, to make art. You are going to have to focus on it sometimes when running your creative business. Here are some things I think about when it comes to money.

Be Prepared For The Long Haul. There are some months where I make more money than I did when I had my corporate job. There are other months where I make zero dollars. Make sure you keep some kind of budget that breaks down your monthly and yearly bills so that you can have a realistic understanding of your financial situation.

For example, Klee and I take our total monthly bills and calculate the highest averages. We then divide them by 4 weeks. Yearly bills that haven't been added yet get divided by 52 weeks. We add these totals up, and they give us the goal of a weekly bill amount to aim for covering. We add things like entertainment, transportation, food, and savings and calculate that into the amount. The entire total is your weekly comfort overhead. If you have a job and that total is covered, then you are golden.

If you are relying on your art to cover the cost of living, then you should be realistic about the production of the work.

Covering Monthly Cost With Art. It is important to quantify how much of a cap you may have on the money you can bring in with original art. For example: If it takes you a week to create one piece and on average your paintings sell for $500 each, the total pieces you can create in a month would average about $2000.

Don't get excited yet, because there is another factor involved. Depending on how many times you actively show your art every week and what your sales history looks like, this number will change. Most times, I'll average 5% or less per active show or active online effort. So if I did a market every week that month, I would take 20% of my total number of pieces produced, and that would be my projection of sales. That makes my projected sales with four market days that month only $400.

I don't want to discourage you, I simply want you to be emotionally prepared so that when the shit hits the fan financially, you are ready. I personally always calculate the lowest averages of successful sales projections; that way anything extra is just a bonus. What is most important here is that you take a look at your money and know what your expenses and incomes are. This allows you to plan for the future.

I have asked artists how much money they made the previous year, and if I get a blank look from them, I know they are not aware of what is going on with their creative business. Honestly, if you treat money with understanding, the money will treat you back. So, understand your money. Artists who are actually making a living with their art, know how much of a living they are making.

This also causes me to get inventive and look for multiple streams of income to cover my costs every month or plan an increase for the next year. I'll include numerous streams of income in the next section.

Multiple Streams Of Income And Making More Money.

In my opinion, the more streams of income you have as a creative, the more opportunities you have to make money. It is a mental game, and each one of these takes time to build up.

If you want to make enough money to support your career as an artist, consider keeping track of the different methods you have available to you.

Create Art In Different Series. If you create pet portraits, for example, that could just be one aspect of your business or one series, and your abstracts could be a different series. This also works with other mediums as well. I have photography, sculpture, and art on paper products as various collections. This also includes video editing, graphic design, music, and anything else you do that is creative. There are plenty of opportunities online to monetize your talent.

More Than One Business. I have a friend who runs a bakery with his wife and an art business. I have another artist friend who loves the idea of selling items that she has a passion for, from drop-shipping sites. I personally made money by visiting thrift shops and flipping things; I love visiting thrift stores and finding diamonds in the rough, like Indiana Jones. If there is anything you enjoy that you can make some extra money doing, don't exclude it as an option. Klee has a jingle business, along with her jewelry making business. I have several sides to my business that you'll see below.

Studio Visits And Open Studio. An excellent way to sell your art is to set up a studio visit by invitation or do an open studio. This works well for people that have a studio that can accommodate visitors. Although our studio is in our home, it is in the living room. Because of this, our guests walk right into the studio when they visit. Anything with our home is by invitation only. Years ago, we did an open studio to the public and had some random weird dude trying to sell steaks to our guests.

Local Markets And Festivals. I started my entire career from doing local festivals, farmers markets, and flea markets. Make sure you have everything you need. Remember to use every interaction as an opportunity to introduce yourself to the world.

Yart Sale (Yard And Art Sale). Any time Klee and I have put together a yard sale or garage sale, we've always had fun setting up a fine art section. Although we don't sell much art, it opens up a conversation with the local residents.

Organize An Exhibition Or Solo Show. I have put together several shows with varying degrees of success. For some, I did a pop-up method where I found an empty storefront to rent. Some I did in a friend's home by invitation, some were organized as a group exhibit 'art party' style. Some were set up outdoors. You don't have to follow the typical route, have fun coming up with creative ways to show your art.

Prints And Merch. You can either print and sell directly, or use one of the many online services. The easiest way to get your art printed on stuff is by using a print-on-demand with drop-shipping service. This type of service will take care of the printing, packaging, branding, and shipping of your custom products to your customers. I currently use Printful.

Social Media. Although I use social media primarily to share my work and life with the world, people often contact me to ask about some art. Make sure you make it easy for them to purchase the art. Either by instant message or you send them to the link to where they can buy it. I get a lot of sales and exposure, and a lot of artists I know do very well selling art on social media.

Create Impulse Art. Have small, easy to sell pieces that you can create into an impulse collection. I've done some of these as limited collection seasonal items such as wedding invitations, seasonal decorations, holiday decorations, greeting cards, diaries, journals, planners, calendars, small gifts, and more.

Have A Job. I know artists who have a full-time job, drive an Uber, deliver newspapers, or work part-time. A lot of artists ask me if they need to quit their job to pursue an art career, and my answer is no. Plenty of artists make it work, others like me started their career with nothing, so ultimately it is up to you to choose what is right for you.

There are many more opportunities that I will cover in my next book which will deal specifically with money and marketing. I just wanted to give you some examples. Ultimately you can create a stream of income from just about anything. As artists, we think that we just have to rely on one method. As creatives, you need to understand that there is no limit to your creativity or your possibilities.

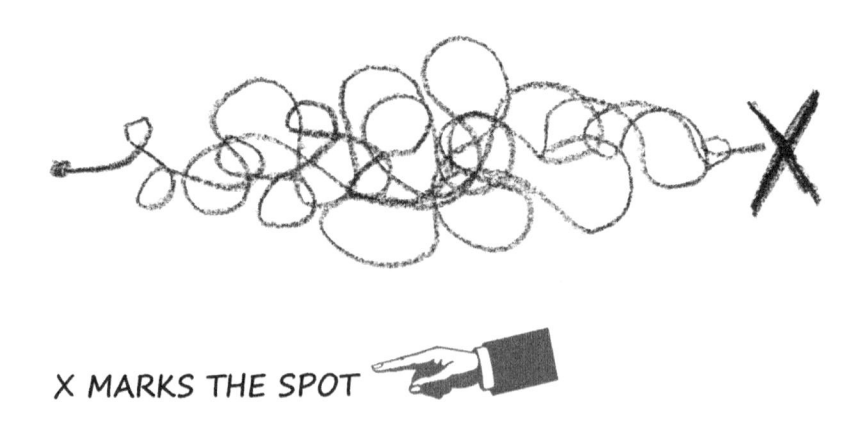

X MARKS THE SPOT

It seems like nowadays everyone wants a quick fix to all their problems. I get asked all the time, "So how do you become a full-time artist?" or "How do you grow your art career?" and although I enjoy being as helpful as I can, the truth is that I have no idea.

I don't know where you are in life, what you have done, or what you're afraid of.

- *What are your comfort zones?*
- *What do you believe is possible?*
- *What do you think it means to be successful?*
- *Where do you live?*
- *What opportunities are around you?*
- *What was your childhood like?*

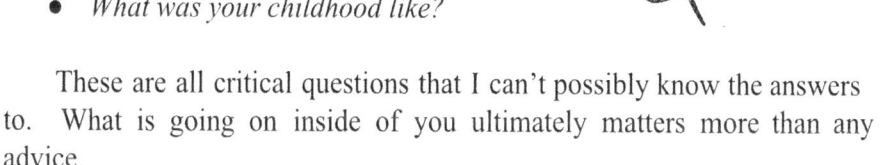

These are all critical questions that I can't possibly know the answers to. What is going on inside of you ultimately matters more than any advice.

There are basic rules to getting started, but the map that you end up with during your journey is entirely up to you. Even if I laid out exactly how I started my career in a straight line, it's still up to you to make it happen. Because everyone is unique, the X keeps moving all over the place and is hard to quantify. Ultimately, you already know for yourself what needs to be done, you just have your doubts.

Doubt and fear are the biggest obstacles you will run into in creating a career. When I say put your stuff out there, I get comments like this:

"I'm just afraid that if I put my stuff out there on Instagram and Facebook, someone will want to buy it or ask if there are prints available. What if I am not yet ready to really sell and produce stuff? Sure, money is the goal, but I don't even know how to sell stuff on the internet, what to consider when it comes to packaging and shipping, and writing a bill."

They continue, "I'm afraid should someone ask and I'm not ready, I'll lose their interest. It kind of gives me the feeling that I can only start going out there when I already know all this sales stuff. One worry is that because I'm not known that people can just steal my stuff and edit the signature out of the piece."

THE ROGUE

These are all legitimate fears, but ultimately really great excuses to not put your creations out in the world. First off, I don't agree that money should be the goal, it is just a bonus. Second, you can figure things out as you go. The first time someone wanted to order something online is when I figured out how to package and ship art. I also had to figure out how to accept money online the first time someone was interested.

The first time someone used my design without my permission, was the first time I looked into the copyright laws and learned what road to take. I've also had to learn how to deal with people losing interest in a commission. I learned about prints, I learned about producing art and timelines. I've had to learn everything as I went, and I am still learning.

Honestly, with all the information that is accessible at your fingertips, if you are saying you need to learn something before you put yourself out there, then you are making excuses.

There is A LOT to learn, and different circumstances require different approaches. If you are going to wait until you learn it all, you are always going to have questions, and you'll never get started.

There is no secret formula, no one has all the answers, and there are different solutions to every problem. Only by actually doing it will you gain the experience you need. You are going to find a lot of advice on the internet, from other artists, classes, and books, but remember that ultimately, the experience is what matters.

As Rogue Artists, we are skeptical of the information we get but are willing to see if we can tweak any formula and make it our own. Be prepared to take any information that you read in this book and tweak it to work for you, but take action.

JUST DO IT ALREADY!

A star does not compete with other stars around it... it just shines.

HOW TO GET NOTICED

I get approached by a lot of artists who are just starting out, who ask me how they can get noticed in a saturated art market. They think there is some trick or some magical formula that exists that causes millions of people to suddenly flock to their social media page, website, or art booth.

Usually I leave them very disappointed with my answer, because unless you are selling a gimmick, it is going to take time. It's all about building yourself up and putting yourself out there... a lot.

When an artist says, "I've been putting my stuff out there, and nothing is happening." I ask, "How long have you been doing it?"

"A month."

A month? Are you kidding me? It took me years to build up my career. Some people are under the misconception that overnight success happens overnight. Some artists look at me and say, "That's easy for you to say, you have 20K followers."

I didn't have 20K followers when I started, I had tumbleweeds... It took 10 years of consistently putting myself out there every day to get the little following I have.

So how do you get noticed?

Steve Martin was quoted as saying, "Be so good that they can't ignore you." I agree and disagree with this. I think you should be good, but I also think it doesn't end there.

First off, Steve Martin's brand of "good" humor is totally subjective. Some people like his humor, and other people find him irritating. I think Steve Martin's superpower is that he kept improving on HIS brand of fun for himself. I also think he put himself out there a whole lot.

If you want to learn anything about getting noticed, look at stand up comedians. Comedians are the holy grail of putting themselves out there and facing rejection. Stand up comedians will go to small comedy clubs and perform their skit and bomb as many times as they have to until they feel like they nailed it. Sometimes they get booed off stage, and they just adjust their skit for the next time they go up.

You have to love what you are doing to be able to keep going, and you have to be honest about the material that you are putting out there. Comedians go on stage with a seed of a comedy skit and fail miserably until they hit their stride.

Comedian Bill Burr said, " I can't do it at home, I have to go out there and just start throwing shit against the wall and see how to piece this stuff together."

That's why I would say, "Be good, love what you do, be real, keep improving, keep showing up and putting your stuff out there, even when everyone else says you should quit. Eventually, your people will find you."

Listen, no matter how good you get, some people are going to hate your work, some will love it. You just have to put your stuff out there and give your audience the chance to discover you.

The problem is that most newbie artists are under the impression that there is a secret spot where art collectors gather.

"Well, everyone that is interested in your art gathers under the east bridge at midnight. Show up with a bundle of art, the secret handshake, and a Snickers bar."

There is no perfect gathering, collector store, or secret sauce to finding art collectors, other than just sharing your work and being findable. You can target a market, but only if you create niche art.

You don't find art collectors or fans of your work, they find you. Just create what you love, share it, keep improving, and keep sharing it over and over.

I remember an artist once told me that my collectors weren't "real" collectors because they weren't purchasing my pieces at auction. I asked him how many pieces he had sold at auction, and he said none. He proceeded to say that art collectors were wealthy. I told him he was an idiot.

In my opinion, art collectors come in all shapes and sizes. I have wealthy collectors, middle class, poor, every race, gender, age group, or religion. I do not limit my possibilities by assuming that I have a target market. I am an equal opportunity art creator.

I have loyal collectors that own a vast collection of my work that never collected art before. You just never know. So don't limit yourself.

That being said, there are some things that I focus on when putting myself out there to keep things real.

Decide What You Want People To Know You For. Figure out your superpower, what sets you apart, and be that. Decide who you are and what you want to be known for. It could be your style of craft, it could be your mission in life, or it could be your personality. It could be anything.

What is crucial is that you share with the world. I share my paintings and art, but what I want to be known for is someone who spreads empowerment and happiness. That is the common theme of anything I share online or offline. It infuses into everything I create.

I think it is easy to look at someone else as a guide. The problem with that method is that you are playing someone else's role, and eventually that is going to become exhausting.

Be who you decide to be and show that to the world. Also, the most loyal collectors will be those who have gotten to know you… the real you.

Set Yourself Apart. This one is easier than you may think. Listen, you're already unique, weird in your own way, and have interests that are your own. Why fit in when you were born to stand out? Being a standout in your creative life really doesn't require any unique talents or skills. It just requires a sense of direction and a dedication to communicating growth in who you are and what you stand for.

Like-minded people will find you. Stand out by being yourself.

Make Friends, Not Buyers. It is time to take that scary step and stand in the limelight the way you would as a kid. It's all about making friends like you did when you were at the playground.

Your future followers and collectors are human beings and not just a gathering of statistics. Remember that.

Standing out is about building relationships. That starts with each and every encounter you have. Whether you are developing a relationship online or face to face, be human. It is that extra humanity and authenticity that will set you apart.

Be Genuinely Interested In People. People are what make up businesses, galleries, art studios, and everything else in the world. Create a real connection by actually being interested in them. Try not to focus on what you can get out of the relationship.

Most importantly, ask yourself: How can you add value to their lives after knowing what you know from meeting them.

A lot of typical marketing is mass targeted. With that approach, you might as well be throwing a dirty sock at the wall and seeing if it sticks (the imagery of both marketing and a dirty sock makes me gag a little).

When you are genuinely interested in the people you connect with, you reach out to them with specific content or creations that are relevant to them. Things that you know they are interested in because they are interested in you.

A lot of people in marketing will tell you to be unique so that you stand out when you market yourself. What they don't tell you is that you are already unique. There is no one out there quite like you, nor will there EVER be anyone out there like you.

THE ROGUE ARTIST SURVIVAL GUIDE

Put Yourself Out There. Take action, starting today, right now. Open your mouth, let your opinions be known, share your art, share your music, share your writing, share your videos, be remarkable, and go big or go home.

There are times when you just have to brag on yourself a little bit. Be proud of your accomplishments and successes. If you do something really great, talk about it. The right people will applaud your success. Also, share when you mess up, and what you learned. Share it all, the whole enchilada of the creative journey.

Putting yourself out there might mean stepping outside your comfort zone, doing something that you have never done before, and taking some risks. Push yourself beyond the walls that you have built around you. Stop telling yourself NO and start telling yourself YES. Go all the way.

At the end of the day, getting noticed is all about realizing that you are remarkable, and you have a voice. It's about growth and self-realization. It's not about forcing your opinions on someone, but merely speaking your views and sharing them creatively with the world. Share your creative way of seeing the world... we could all use a little more of that.

The world could use more of you. Whatever your next step is, whether it is starting your creative career or leveling up, get started now and share who you are.

Be the Rogue Artist of your own canvas of life, make your own rules, break them, and be awesome at being who you want to be.

Welcome To The club
Rogue Artist

12 Steps To Being AWESOME

1. IF IT "FEELS" WRONG <u>DON'T DO IT.</u>
2. SAY "EXACTLY" WHAT YOU MEAN.
3. DON'T BE A PEOPLE PLEASER.
4. TRUST YOUR GUT. YOU
5. DON'T SAY BAD THINGS ABOUT
6. DON'T GIVE UP ON DREAMS.
7. DON'T BE AFRAID TO SAY <u>NO.</u>
8. DON'T BE AFRAID TO SAY YES.
9. BE "KIND" TO YOU.
10. LET GO OF CONTROL OF THINGS YOU CAN'T CONTROL.
11. STAY AWAY FROM <u>DRAMA</u> & <u>NEGATIVITY.</u>
12. LOVE YOURSELF & OTHERS.

THE ROGUE ARTIST SURVIVAL GUIDE

MY NEXT ROGUE ARTIST BOOK

This book was focused on the mindset that allowed me to create an awesome career as an artist and creative. The next few books in the series will cover specific topics and be more in depth on those subjects. My plan is to expand on the concepts I discussed in this book with more specific detail.

The next book in the series will be *THE ROGUE ARTIST ON MARKETING AND MONEY*. The book will focus on money and marketing in a very non traditional way as a Rogue Artist.

Visit **www.TheRogueArtist.com** to find out more about myself and Klee. New book will be released towards the end of 2021.

268 The Rogue Artist Survival Guide

ABOUT RAFI PEREZ

Rafi Perez is an award winning contemporary artist who creates emotionally charged works. His art is meant to inspire empowerment, self awareness, and mindfulness. His diverse collection of work has been described as reminders of personal power and beauty. He is best known for his use of texture, bold color palettes, experimental techniques, and striking pieces that each have an emotional, and deep personal story to tell.

"My hope is that, in reading this book, you will understand how to grow your personal creative brand as an artist while still having fun. I hope to instill the same passion and excitement that I have for life and being a creative human in this modern world full of opportunities. Ultimately I want you to see this book as a tool or guide to help you understand how to grab the machete and cut your own trail through the dense forest that is the artist's life. I also want to secretly inspire you to blaze your own trail as brightly as any awesome human can."

Rafi also hosts a YouTube Channel, Podcasts, Live Streams, and speaking events where he talks about living the creative life. His primary focus is the Rogue Artist point of view, mindset, and being empowered to follow your dreams.

Made in the USA
Middletown, DE
29 July 2021